UNDERSTANDING

the
Business
of Library
Acquisitions

Karen A. Schmidt
editor

American Library Association
Chicago and London 1990

Text design by Interface Studio, Inc.
Cover design by Interface Studio, Inc.
Composed in Century Schoolbook and Univers Condensed
on a Compugraphic 9600 High Resolution Laser Imagesetter
by Interface Studio.

Printed on 50# Glatfelter B-16, a pH-neutral stock, and
bound in 10 pt. Carolina stock by McNaughton & Gunn.

The paper used in this publication meets the minimum
requirements of American National Standard for Information
Sciences—Permanence of Paper for Printed Library Materials,
ANSI Z39.48–1984.

Library of Congress Cataloging-in-Publication Data

Understanding the business of library acquisitions / by Karen A.
  Schmidt, editor.
        p.   cm.
     ISBN 0-8389-0536-6
     1. Acquisitions (Libraries) 2. Acquisitions (Libraries)—
  Accounting. 3. Libraries and booksellers. 4. Libraries and
  publishing. 5. Library materials—Prices. I. Schmidt, Karen A.
  Z689.U53   1990
  025.2—dc20
                                                    90-33772
                                                        CIP

Printed in the United States of America.

93 92 91 90 89   5 4 3 2 1

C O N T E N T S

Contents

F O R E W O R D

I am happy to write a preface to this excellent and much-needed work. It does not take very long to survey the monographic literature on acquisitions and not much longer to exhaust the serial literature on the topic. Even within this small compass, one finds that much of what has been written and published is very much concerned with the how of acquisitions and very little with the why, whence, or whither. The reader will find that all four are dealt with substantially and in detail in this work, which can lay legitimate claim to being a definitive work—a much over-used term that is, however, apt in this case. It is definitive figuratively because it treats all aspects of its subject and literally because the careful reader will come away with a clear understanding of the nature of acquisitions work and the reasons why this poor relation of technical services is of importance now and in the future.

I call acquisitions a poor relation because, though it has been practiced well in many libraries over many years, it has seldom attracted the interest of library educators, library theorists, and professional groups who, one would have thought, would have had acquisitions as a central concern. The definitive nature of this work is especially important because acquisitions has, for many years, been going through a complex identity crisis. Questions about the nature of acquisitions (Is it a professional activity?) mesh with questions of demarcation (Is acquisitions part of collection development or vice versa, or are they completely separate?) and with battles over turf (Should serial control be a part of acquisitions, or is "serialism" such a rarified branch of librarianship that it must be practiced separately?—the latter opinion having actually been advanced by librarians who appear, in all other respects, to be sane). Some questions have produced a lack of understanding of the nature of acquisitions that has even extended to its practitioners. The volume you are holding shows acquisitions plainly and simply as the important professional activity that it is and always has been.

One of the many unheralded and misunderstood aspects of acquisitions work is the pivotal role that it plays in relating the practice of librarianship to our colleagues in the knowledge and information business, that is, the publishers and sellers of library materials. The rest of us use those materials giving little or no thought to the ways in which they are created and disseminated. The acquisitions librarian is, from a somewhat fanciful point of view, the cook producing the meals upon which we feast while having little idea of the complex dealings the cook has had with the companies that produce and sell the food. Unlike the rest of us, a good acquisitions librarian has to keep up with all the latest trends in publishing and with all the moves in the Byzantine and sometimes positively Borgian world of the vendors of library materials. Publishers and vendors are big businesses, often owned by even bigger businesses. Michael Frayn once said that people were essentially either herbivores or carnivores. We bibliographic herbivores send some of our number—the acquisitions librarians—to deal with the carnivores of publishing and vending every day. It's hard and difficult work but someone has to do it. One of the considerable merits of this book is that it delineates the not-for-profit/for-profit interaction and provides sage advice to those who labor in that vineyard.

The reader of this book will come away with a due respect for and understanding of the work done in acquisitions. To take but one example, the intricacies of gathering plans (approval and blanket order) are seldom appreciated by the librarians whose work profits from a well-run plan. Such mechanisms have to be set up, appropriate vendors have to be found, acquisitions librarians have to monitor their functioning constantly, and adjustments need to be made on a continuing basis. In addition, the acquisitions librarian has to have a lively appreciation of the economics of the gathering plan and weigh its efficiency and convenience (I am writing here of successful plans) against the obvious costs (the cost of the service, for example) and the not so obvious (work that the plan causes the acquisitions staff as compared with the work demanded in "firm ordering"). Looking at this one example, we can see that the acquisitions librarian must possess knowledge of economics, knowledge of the publishing and bookselling worlds, high-level managerial skills, and the tenacity and adaptability required to keep a gathering plan operating efficiently and productively over a period of years. One could cite other instances (the labyrinthine complexity of tax laws that govern gifts of library materials comes to mind), but I think the fair-minded reader will concede both that acqui-

Foreword

sitions work requires professionalism and that effective acquisitions work is important to libraries and library service.

You have in your hand a text that will be of use to a wide audience: acquisitions and other technical services librarians, teachers and students, library administrators, and any other librarians who are interested in practical applications of our profession. The authors, editor, and publisher are to be commended on the production of a valuable and informative text.

Michael Gorman
Dean of Library Services
California State University, Fresno

ACKNOWLEDGMENTS

Numerous individuals must be recognized for their help in the long, and sometimes painful, gestation period this text has seen. Bettina MacAyeal, my editor at ALA Books, helped give the book focus and was consistently supportive and cheerful. Contributors provided much more than their chapters—they suggested new ideas, pointed out inconsistencies, suggested other contributors, and, perhaps most importantly, "hounded" the editor. It has been a pleasure indeed to work with these individuals.

Jytte Millan, from the UIUC Library, served as the typist of the final work and provided me—with patience and good humor—the innumerable versions of chapters that I required. Thanks are due as well to Michael Gorman for his guidance in editing.

Lastly, I want to acknowledge the encouragement and support I have received throughout my life and career from my late father, Jacob, and from the rest of my family. Their good wishes and gentle nagging have had the desired effect.

Karen A. Schmidt

INTRODUCTION

Karen A. Schmidt

Just a few years ago, acquisitions was characterized as a step-child of librarianship.[1] The analogy seemed apt then, and while it remains apt today, one finds the stepmother is becoming more understanding and supportive as acquisitions grows up. Nevertheless, acquisitions is often perceived as a rabbit warren of clerical tasks. It was not so many years ago that I subscribed to the "black box" theory of acquisitions: an order goes into acquisitions and gets transmogrified into the desired book, periodical, audiovisual set, and so on. I am sure that were I to poll my colleagues who are not connected with acquisitions work, a majority would admit to the belief in the acquisitions black box as well.

Much of the work in acquisitions is liaison in nature. Acquisitions is the bridge between the profit-making and not-for-profit worlds of publishing and librarianship. Many tasks that acquisitions performs *are* in fact clerical in nature. In the past several years, however, a new professional concept of acquisitions has developed. Once an adjunct task to collection development and the work of bibliographers, acquisitions is now a more defined field within librarianship. A strict definition of acquisitions includes the ordering, claiming, and receiving of materials, both monographic and serial. In fact, today's acquisitions departments may still include some of the tasks of collection development as well as bibliographic searching, accounting, and even copy cataloging. Given the relatively recent growth of acquisitions as its own subfield of our profession, as well as the vagaries of organizational structures that occur in different libraries, it is not surprising that the lines of definition are blurred. Neither is it surprising that many of the early writings on acquisitions concentrate on clerical tasks within the library rather than upon the external and communicative work that is at the heart of successful library acquisitions.

---

1. Karen A. Schmidt, " 'Buying Good Pennyworths?' ": A Review of the Literature of Acquisitions in the Eighties," *Library Resources & Technical Services* 30 (October–December 1986): 333.

Introduction

The body of literature on the work of acquisitions is of considerable size given the relatively short period of time which it has had to develop as a specialization within librarianship. In the first fifty years of the development of the profession, from roughly 1890 to 1940, acquisitions as we commonly refer to it today did not exist. From the beginning of this century, well into the late 1930s, students of librarianship studied "order work," which embraced some, but not all, of the work we now commonly associate with acquisitions, as well as some more dated concepts (including the art of accessioning). Training at that time paralleled the general organization of larger libraries, which had the order department as well as serial department and receipt division. The word *acquisitions* itself did not come into common usage until around 1940, a few years after Columbia University published its syllabus on the principles of library organization and administration.

Over the years, the books encompassing the work of acquisitions have been produced sporadically and reflect the growth of this area of expertise. The first was a text by F. F. Hopper[2], under the auspices of the ALA Committee on Library Training, which published, chapter by chapter, the *A.L.A. Manual of Library Economy*. Revised in 1930 by Carl Cannon,[3] this work, as well as a text by Francis Drury,[4] was for more than forty years the essential publication in acquisitions. In the early 1970s, two more books appeared. One was a series of essays by Daniel Melcher,[5] whose experience over the years at the R. R. Bowker Company convinced him of the need for librarians to have a better understanding of publishing and acquisition. The other was by Stephen Ford, who published *The Acquisition of Library Materials*,[6] a text that has remained since then as the handbook of acquisitions.

In addition to these books, two journals are devoted entirely to the topic: *Library Acquisitions: Practice and Theory* and *The Acquisitions Librarian,* which appeared in 1977 and 1989 respectively. In all of these books and journals, we learn many valu-

---

2. F. F. Hopper, *Order and Accession Department* (Chicago: American Library Association, 1915).

3. Carl Cannon, *Order and Accession Department, Manual of Library Economy, 17* (Chicago: American Library Association, 1930).

4. Francis K. W. Drury, *Order Work for Libraries* (Chicago: American Library Association, 1930).

5. Daniel Melcher, *Melcher on Acquisition* (Chicago: American Library Association, 1971).

6. Stephen Ford, *The Acquisition of Library Materials* (Chicago: American Library Association, 1973).

Introduction

able lessons. We do not, however, see the overall scheme of acquisitions in contemporary times; we do not see acquisitions as it operates in the library settings of the latter part of the twentieth century. It is hoped that this publication will help fill that void.

It is difficult to decide which aspects of acquisitions to include in an embracing description of this area of librarianship. Although acquisitions encompasses many aspects of librarianship, it also includes many areas that are not part of what is ordinarily perceived as the standard fare of the profession: personnel, in the form of department organization, staffing and training, and the sometimes capricious problems of managing large numbers of people; automation, which has only relatively recently addressed the issues unique to acquisitions; bibliographic searching and verification; budgeting, particularly as costs of library materials increase; business practices, especially between the not-for-profit library and the for-profit publishing and bookselling worlds; and the interplay among all layers of the library in the adventure of simply trying to get a book to a user.

The intention of this book is to answer some deceptively easy questions that an acquisitions librarian or a student of acquisitions would likely have in contemporary times. The questions concern publishing and the decisions that affect the cost and life of the book, the publication of serials and their cost and procurement, the world of vendors and how one decides if a vendor is performing well for the library, vendor-librarian ethics, handling gifts and exchanges, dealing with other parts of the bookselling world, approval plans, and basic information on accounting principles, audits, and business practices. The questions, and their answers, tend to be relevant for a long time and do not vary from library to library, as do questions about personnel or automation.

The contributors to this work all are noted experts in their areas. Each has been asked to amalgamate the important writings in his or her particular subject area and to present a consensus of how to address the question at hand. In some cases, as in Goehner's chapter, there is no body of literature—a situation that makes the contribution even more valuable for finally spelling out the problems. In other cases, such as the chapter by Reid, the body of literature is so large that the surest contribution is simply to point out the best works currently available.

It is hoped that this text will help define the components of acquisitions more clearly, not only for the acquisitions librarian or the library science student wishing to work as an acquisitions librarian, but also for the rest of the library world, which relies so heavily on the success of acquisitions for its own work. The chapters that follow can help dispel the black box theory of acquisitions once and for all.

the
Publishing
Industry,
Domestic and Foreign

The Business of Publishing

Kathy Flanagan

"Just to get a manuscript printed is not to publish it."
C. B. Grannis

One of the questions frequently asked by librarians is, "Why do some books cost so much?" The general answers involve the basic elements of the publishing process and the financial factors that make publishing a business (whether commercial or not-for-profit). For each particular book, specific answers rest with the type of book, the expected audience, and the consequent effects on producing and selling that title.

The basic elements of the publishing process are

1. decision to publish
2. producing the book
3. marketing and distributing the finished book.

In describing the publishing of several types of books (proceedings, professional reference, and textbooks), this chapter focuses on professional and scholarly books, particularly those in the sciences. The viewpoint is that of the commercial publisher. Among the topics covered are the editorial process, the physical process of producing a book, the means a company undertakes to get the book to the customer, and general factors that accompany the business of publishing. Less emphasis will be placed on describing the art of acquiring or developing books; however, it is understood that the quality of and perceived need for a particular title must be high.

Before reviewing the specific steps in the publishing process, a brief look at how publishing houses view their activities is in order.

3

THE FINANCIAL PICTURE

Table 1 lists costs and revenues for professional book publishers. These statistics are compiled annually by the Association of American Publishers and refer to overall expenses and revenues within a company.

The table shows that the largest single cost area in publishing a book is manufacturing (28.9 percent), followed by marketing (20.9 percent). The costs associated directly with producing books increases when editorial (book development—9.3 percent) and production (editing, design, and production—4.0 percent) costs are considered.

Table 1 cites publishing industry statistics for scientific and technical and business and medical publishers. The table layout, known as an income statement, is widely used in many industries. An income statement that compares revenues to expenses over a given period of time is one of several ways in which a company tracks and reports on its performance. Financial reporting is required of publicly held companies and is also used by companies to control costs and expenses. In Table 1, "sales" refers to revenue received for books sold and "expenses" refers to costs incurred to produce, sell, and distribute books,

**TABLE 1 Operating Data of Professional Book Publisher
(Including Scientific and Technical, Business and Medical)**

Costs as percentages of net sales	
Gross sales	117.2%
Returns and allowances	17.2
Net sales	100.0
Cost of sales	
Manufacturing	28.9
Royalties	10.7
Total cost of sales	39.9
Gross margin	60.1
Other income (book clubs, for example)	2.5
Operating expenses	
Editorial	9.3
Production	4.0
Marketing	20.9
Fulfillment	5.8
General and administrative	14.1
Total operating expense	54.2
Income from operations (pretax profit)	8.5

Source: AAP 1986 industry statistics

as well as to the costs associated with the day-to-day running of a business.

In order to have a standard for compiling and producing statistics, the Association of American Publishers uses sales revenues after returns and allowances have been deducted. "Costs as a percentage of net sales," then, allows for meaningful numbers, since returns can vary by type of book, by book, and by publisher. (Note: Gross sales then appear as a figure greater than 100 percent. "Gross sales" is defined as revenue received, that is, actual billings to customers after discounts have been allowed.)

"Cost of sales," or more aptly, cost of goods sold, includes "manufacturing," that is, costs of materials of books sold and "royalties" paid for books sold.

"Gross margin" is one of the ratios often used in financial analysis to track performance (others include operating margin and profit margin). The gross margin is a comparison (subtraction from, actually) of manufacturing costs of books sold to net sales.

"Operating expenses" refers to day-to-day costs such as personnel, book development, selling and marketing, order processing, and administration.

Figure 1 shows partial operating data of professional book publishers in graphic form.

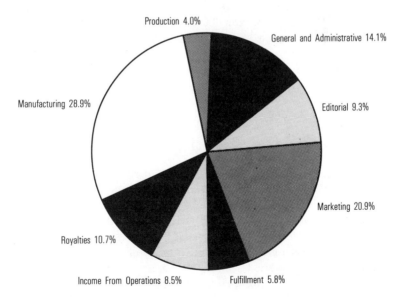

FIGURE 1 Partial Operating Data for Professional Book Publishers

"Income from operations," or operating income, is derived by subtracting operating expenses from the gross margin and adding in "other income". Income from operations is also known as pretax profit, because taxes have not yet been deducted. Corporate taxes vary, so pretax profits are recorded to make comparisons possible. (Corporate taxes can be as much as 50 percent).

As stated, income from operations is also called pretax profit. But note a comment that usually accompanies statistics:

> Operating expenses reported do not include certain corporate charges. Items that may not be reported are corporate staff compensation, legal and accounting fees, interest costs, and other charges not directly applicable to a particular business segment. Consequently, income from operations as expressed above does not reflect actual pre-tax operating margins.

TYPE OF BOOK

The various cost and revenue categories listed in Table 1 also apply generally to the way a publisher looks at an individual title. Specifically, however, different types of books have different costs, different revenue expectations, and, consequently, different prices. A discussion of three types of books—proceedings, professional reference, and textbooks—will illustrate the differences in how scientific books in general are planned, produced, and distributed. Comparisons and contrasts among them also will highlight the various facets of the publishing company's organization.

Proceedings

The strength of a good scientific proceeding is its rapid reporting of recent developments in a field. The publisher's editorial involvement in the manuscript is sometimes smaller because manuscripts are often camera ready, that is, authors or contributors submit cleanly typed material that is printed as is. The publisher's function is to judge the quality of the work, organize and produce the finished book quickly, market and distribute the finished book to the appropriate audience, and of course, assume the financial risk of publication. Proceedings in the sciences generally have a finite audience (sales of 500 to 1,000 copies) and short life spans of eighteen to twenty-four months, since the material becomes dated quickly.

Professional Reference

A professional reference work (defined differently from a traditional library reference work) requires more editorial involvement, that is, a closer working relationship between the publisher and the author. Generally, production takes about seven to ten months. The audience includes individuals and libraries and the life span is two to four years. Average lifetime sales for a professional reference work depend on the level of the material and usually are 2,000 to 5,000 copies for more specialized works and 10,000 to 15,000 copies for more general books.

Textbooks

The publisher's involvement is much greater in textbook publishing, because success depends so much on the relationship between content and presentation (concept, readability, study aids). Often there is significant early, up front investment by the publisher, and editing and production time takes commensurately longer (ten to twelve months or more). The audience is composed primarily of students and, to a lesser extent, those just entering or already working in a given field. Textbooks depend on course adoptions for the bulk of their sales. The average life span is three to five years and sales expectancy—not print run necessarily, as there usually are several printings—is 5,000 to 15,000 copies or more. Sales for a lower level (that is, introductory) text may run to ten times these figures.

Table 2 summarizes the features and editorial involvement in the three types of books.

PUBLISHING DECISIONS AND
THE PUBLISHING PROCESS

Editorial work generally means acquisitions, which is the art and science of bringing ideas (the authors' and editors') to print. The decision to publish, the first step in the publishing process, is initiated by acquisition editors, who are sometimes called sponsoring editors.

8

The Publishing Industry

TABLE 2 Types of Books and Editorial Involvement

Type	Features	Editorial Involvement
Proceedings	Camera-ready copy, multiauthor, average life span of 18–24 months	Modest editorial activity vis-à-vis writing of material
Professional reference	Generally typeset, average lifespan of 2–4 years, author(s) need 3–5 years to complete manuscript	Involvement of acquisition editor in presentation of subject. Project planned by acquisition editor and author(s). Editor reviews material and works with author(s). Average copyediting and design. Detailed index and tabular material
Textbook	Generally typeset, average life span of 3–5 years	Heavy acquisition involvement in concept, pedagogical approach, market need. Heavy editorial and design commitment. Detailed index and elaborate artwork

Several factors are crucial to success as an editor in scientific and technical fields:

1. understanding a field and where it is moving
2. contacts with people working in a particular field
3. awareness of the audience (those who will buy and read books in a particular subject area)
4. knowledge of publications currently serving a field

Editors acquire books according to their area of responsibility. Acquisition editors help to develop and subsequently follow the company's plan. For example, they may analyze and work in areas in which a company is strong (and would like to remain so) or in areas in which a company would like to grow. A company already well represented in the field of analytical chemistry, for example, usually will continue to acquire and publish important books in that area. The company stays in that subject area for two reasons: (1) contacts through editors, advisors, potential authors, and reviewers have been established and a certain level of editorial expertise has been reached, and (2) once a program has been established, a degree of credibility and recognition will have been achieved for the company, making it attractive to potential authors and readers.

Once a subject area has been targeted, an editor talks with experts in the field who are knowledgeable about current research, teaching, and applications. Some projects develop because an editor knows someone who is already writing a manuscript. At other times, the editor will see a need for a book in a certain area or for a particular kind of subject treatment. The editor then contacts key people and enlists them to write such a book.

When a book is in the proposal stage, the editor submits the idea for formal review within the publishing company. Typically, the proposal is reviewed by representatives from the editorial group(s), the marketing department, and perhaps the finance department. A proposal includes the following:

1. outline of the projected work (scope and content): at this point, the author will have submitted at least one chapter, or, at minimum, a detailed table of contents
2. audience: level of the expected book; number of potential buyers; in the case of a textbook, applicability for certain courses
3. purpose of the book: why does it need to be written; uniqueness
4. anticipated time schedule for completion of manuscript
5. credentials of authors
6. reviewers' comments: book proposals normally are sent to outside experts for comments on quality, contribution to the field, scope, and ability of authors

In addition, the editor will present an estimated financial picture (see Table 3).

Each facet of the publishing process adds to the cost of producing a book. Manufacturing costs are major factors affecting the price of a new title. The relationships among cost, list price, and eventual profitability are examined at the early stage in the decision-to-publish process. Costs and revenues are reviewed over the projected lifetime of the proposed book; of course, regular overhead costs must be factored in at some point.

Each of the different types of books described will have a different financial picture. Whereas a proceedings generally would realize most of its costs and sales in its first year, a textbook would have high costs booked in its first year but no significant revenues until its second or third year. Naturally, one of the most important questions to be answered when deciding to publish a book is how much the book costs to produce in relation to the price for which the editor expects it to sell. One important benchmark is the break-even point, that is, the point at which costs expended equal sales revenue received.

Once the decision to publish has been made, the acquisition editor is responsible for negotiating an agreement between the

TABLE 3 Editorial Estimate for New Book Proposal

	Year 1	Year 2	Year 3	Year 4
Net sales—units	5,000	3,500	2,000	1,000
Net sales—dollar	60,000	50,000	30,000	15,000
Total sales	70,000	60,000	35,000	17,500
Plant	4,000	0	0	0
PP&B	18,000	0	0	3,000
Grants/advances	2,000	0	0	0
Royalties	6,000	5,000	3,000	1,500
Editorial development	2,000	0	0	0
EDP development	2,500	0	0	0
Interest	2,000	1,200	0	0
Total direct costs	36,500	6,200	3,000	4,500
Gross margin	23,500	43,800	27,000	10,500
Marketing	9,000	7,500	500	500
Overhead	7,200	6,000	3,600	1,800
Warehousing/shipping	3,600	3,000	1,800	900
Total indirect costs	19,800	16,500	5,900	3,200
Total costs	56,300	22,700	8,900	10,400
Other income	0	0	0	0
Pretax profit	3,700	27,300	21,100	7,300
Return on sales	6%	55%	70%	49%

PP&B = paper, printing, binding. EDP = editorial, design, production.

author and the publishing company. The contract protects the interests of both parties and outlines the responsibilities and expectations of each. It covers everything from amount and payment of royalties to guidelines for granting translation rights.

EDITORIAL, DESIGN, PRODUCTION

When the publisher has a completed manuscript in house, the production process begins (Table 4). At this stage, the manuscript is reviewed by the editorial, design, and production departments for evaluation of work and initial cost estimates. Note that with advent of microcomputers and word processors, some authors submit manuscripts on disk or tape. In such cases the following traditional formula changes.

The manuscript is copyedited and sent back to the author for review. Copyediting includes everything from corrections of grammar and syntax to, in a few cases, major rewrite. Once copyedited and reviewed, the completed manuscript goes to the design

Kathy Flanagan

TABLE 4 Steps and Timetable for Publishing a Book of 500 Pages

Initial review of manuscript by editorial design, and production and editorial	2 weeks
Copyediting and return to author for review	2 months
Design	
Cover design	2-3 weeks
Text design	4 weeks
Typesetting (compositor)	4-6 weeks
Galleys read by proofreader and author	2 months
Pages	2 weeks
Corrections to compositor	2 weeks
Prepares Prep/Review of Blues	2 weeks
Printing and binding	4-6 weeks

department, which formulates cover design concepts and interior design specifications such as type size, margins, indentations, arrangement of illustrations, and so forth. The manuscript then goes to the typesetter, or compositor, who sets the typewritten words into type.

Galleys (continuous columns of typeset manuscript) are read by the publisher's proofreader and by the author. Galleys are then sent back to the typesetter for corrections and for assembly into pages. In some cases the design department produces a dummy—the physical layout of pages of type, illustrations, front matter—from which the compositor can produce the final layout of pages. In major textbooks or other special situations the author also reviews pages. In many cases, the typeset material will go directly to pages without the galleys stage.

Typesetting and Design

Typesetting is an important factor in the cost and appearance of the final book. The choice of a typesetter is based on the size and complexity of a project, time and scheduling considerations, and, naturally, budget limitations. Typesetters offer a variety of options, and many specialize according to the needs of a subject (such as physics, chemistry, music, or straight text).

Camera-Ready or Typewritten The simplest form of publication is a ready-for-printing manuscript supplied by an author. Whether it is typewritten or produced on a word processor or computer, the implication is that the manuscript is ready to print as is (that is, it is camera ready). Publication is therefore speedy because the intermediate design and editing steps are eliminated. Negative aspects of camera-ready copy (CRC) can be uneven appearance and style in the finished book because the publisher was unable to edit or design in an intermediate stage.

Photocomposition Photocomposition is the most common form of typesetting today. As the term suggests, photocomposition involves a photographic process in which film or light-sensitive paper is exposed to images of letters. The "film" is developed and a positive image is produced (black letters on white background).

The format of the composition has a great bearing on the cost of publication. A book with relatively straightforward composition will have a lower per-page typesetting cost (fewer keystrokes) than will one with a more complex format such as chemistry or built-up math. And since the composition charge is the same whether the print run is 1,000 or 10,000 copies, the composition charge for a limited-audience book will cost significantly more per unit than will a book with a wider audience.

Single-Column Composition Single-column typesetting format is typically seen in monographs in all subject areas. The level of complexity (and therefore cost) often depends on the subject matter. A single-column page that consists of unbroken paragraphs is easier to produce than a high-level science monograph in mathematics, physics, or chemistry, for example, which involves allowing frequent breaks for complex formulas and equations.

Double-Column Composition Double-column composition is frequently used for textbooks, manuals, and handbooks. The complexity depends on the subject and level of material presented. A double-column page also holds more typeset material than a single-column page, thus increasing the labor cost per page. Double columns normally are used to save paper.

Desktop Publishing A revolution on the horizon for many scientific and technical publishers is desktop publishing, defined as a system or workstation that can produce high-quality typeset manuscripts ready for printing. As already noted, some authors now use and some publishers now supply word processors or microcomputers. Although these devices certainly have aided the writing process, their use in the industry has not yet significantly affected the overall time or cost of producing books in the sciences. Compatibility has sometimes presented problems, as has redesigning the traditional sequence of production and

Kathy Flanagan

editing steps. The promise of desktop publishing is that it advances technological possibilities. The reality for scientific publishers now is that it is still more cost effective to have specialists at a typesetter handle complicated typesetting and page makeup.

There are several general components of a desktop publishing system:

1. A microcomputer is configured and equipped to prepare manuscript text. In some models these manuscripts can be coded (marked up) in the machine in a fashion consistent with traditional copyediting. The Association of American Publishers has adopted the Standard Generalized Markup Language (SGML) as the industry standard for electronic manuscript preparation and mark-up. The mark-up code can then be used to drive outside or in-house typesetting devices.
2. The system is designed so that it can be expanded to include a number of users.
3. The system is a WYSIWYG (what you see is what you get) operation. This step involves the actual design or makeup of pages. With this feature, the production department actually sees design and page makeup on a computer screen.
4. A laser printer or computerized typesetting equipment produces the text in page form.

The promises of desktop publishing for the future are reduced manufacturing costs and reduced production time and costs.

Paper

The choice of paper has a major impact on the cost of producing a book. For example, the larger the book or the more copies printed, the more paper used, and, consequently, the more money spent.

A variety of factors influence paper selection: type of book, size of final printed book, nature and quality of illustrations, readability, number of printed colors (black vs. four-color process), type of printing press, and permanence and durability. Qualities of paper that affect these factors include weight and caliper (pages per inch), color, opacity, finish, and acidity.

A medical atlas, for example, will have a number of critical halftones (photographs) in which it is necessary to maintain a high degree of contrast. For this type of book, a designer would select a white (rather than off-white—to maintain the contrast), high-gloss paper, so that the ink will be on top of the paper and sharper images will result.

Printing and Binding

The most common method for printing books is photo-offset lithography, called offset. The printer creates a negative film and produces a blueprint (called blues) for final review or quality control.

The many different kinds of offset plates made can be roughly divided into three categories. The first, and most commonly used, are surface plates, so-called because the printing is on the surface. These are often used with shorter-print-run titles and are disposed of after the initial run.

The second type of offset plate, used for longer runs and able to produce a higher quality of printing, is called deep-etch. In these plates, the greasy printing areas are very slightly below the nonprinting areas. The third kind of plate, called bimetal, is based on the principle of a light-sensitive protective coating on a metal, ink-receptive base. Deep-etch and bimetal plates can be stored for use in subsequent printings. However, the general need to provide for updates or corrections to the text make the use of surface plates more economical.

From the plates, the ink impression is made on press. For sheet-fed printing (smaller runs) the press prints onto sheets of paper which are folded and gathered ("F and G") and sent to the publisher for review. The rest of the "F and G's" are sent to a bindery where the finished books are bound and covers are added (binding can be glued or sewn). For larger runs, a web press is employed (paper is on a roll, rather than in sheets).

Pricing and Print Run

When the book is well along in the production cycle, actual costs are reported and remaining costs are estimated. At this point, the final list price for the book is determined along with the number of copies to be printed. The original book proposal is compared with the work in hand, sales expectations are discussed, and final costs are introduced. An initial print run is set based on sales expectations.

Table 5 shows a book production estimate for a typical book

Kathy Flanagan

TABLE 5 Book Production Estimate
(500 pages, single column, simple art program)

	Quantity		
	1,000	**2,000**	**3,000**
Plant costs			
Editing	2,000		
Design	2,500		
Typesetting (composition)	10,000		
Illustrations	2,500		
and plates	2,000		
Total plant	19,000		
Unit	$19.00	$9.50	$6.33
Paper, printing, & binding costs	5,200 sheets	9,600 sheets	13,200 sheets
(PP&B)			
Paper	1,150	2,100	3,000
Printing	1,500	2,000	2,500
Binding	1,500	2,500	3,500
Cover printing	400	450	500
PP&B	4.550	7,050	9,500
PP&B unit	4.55	3.53	3.17
Total unit cost	$23.55	$13.03	$9.50

(500 pages, single-column typesetting, simple art program). It illustrates how print run (number of copies printed) can affect the cost to produce and print a single copy (unit) of a single title. Plant costs (editing, design, typesetting, illustrations) are *fixed* costs; that is, the costs do not vary regardless of the number of copies printed. Paper, printing, and binding costs are considered to be *variable* costs; that is, the costs change with the number of copies printed.

One method for determining the total unit cost—the cost of producing one copy of a book—is to add total plant costs per copy to the paper, printing, and binding (PP & B) costs per unit. The resulting total unit cost is then used as one of the factors to compute list price. Different publishers have varying methods of amortizing plant costs (over one year, five years, and so on), and the one used can affect the book's price considerably.

If the book copy is camera ready, as might be found with a volume of conference proceedings, total plant costs might be lower. However, the plant cost per unit will be relatively high because of the low number of copies printed. The situation is similar with paper, printing, and binding. If there are no illustrations, paper costs might be lower because of the type of paper that can be used, but the printing charge per unit will be higher because of the low print run. Start-up costs—what the printer charges for preparation, set up, and starting the machines—are expensive, and the cost per book decreases as the number of copies printed increases. Printing costs are high for runs of under 1,000 copies.

At the other end of the scale from the proceedings title is a typical textbook, for which plant costs and paper, printing, and binding costs are much higher, but because of larger print runs, the cost per unit is lower.

MARKETING AND DISTRIBUTION

What is marketing and why does it constitute a cost factor in the publishing process? Table 1 shows that except for manufacturing costs, marketing is the largest cost segment in the publishing business.

Webster's Ninth New Collegiate Dictionary defines marketing as "an aggregate of functions involved in moving goods from producer to consumer." This definition is fairly straight forward if the audience is a single group or if there is a single product involved. In fact, publishers have a large number of products (books) that are sold to diverse groups of customers. In some cases, different groups of customers are approached by different marketing methods.

Table 6 highlights major customer groups for professional books (scientific and technical and business and medical). As can be seen, sales break easily into three groups: through bookstores, to libraries (the majority of wholesalers' sales being to libraries), and directly to individuals. Because of the mix of customers, a variety of marketing techniques is employed.

Factors that affect marketing decisions include audience (professional, researcher, student, or library—each of which may

TABLE 6 1986 Sales of Professional Books by Type of Customer

Retail Stores	27.4%
Wholesalers	23.0
Libraries and institutions	7.6
Government	0.9
Industry	5.9
Special sales	1.8
Individuals	33.5
	100.0%

Source: 1986 AAP statistics

be approached in a different way), type of book, and distribution (a book that will be sold widely through bookstores will be promoted differently from a book with a small, specialized audience).

Throughout the chapter, the emphasis has been on *a* book. Naturally, a publishing company has many books in print at any given time, both new and backlist. One of the challenges for any marketing operation is to promote all titles while managing expenses. Marketing is often a juggling act of balancing the aim of promoting titles with efficient use of the money available.

A brief review of the methods of marketing and promotion activities (listed alphabetically) illustrates the responsibility of a typical marketing department.

1. Advertisements: Announcements or descriptions are placed in appropriate periodicals. CPM (cost per thousand—the amount of money it takes to reach 1,000 readers) and the type and size of the audience are crucial factors.

2. Author relations: The marketing department generally works with the author in positioning the book in the marketplace.

3. Book reviews: To promote coverage in standard periodicals and professional publications, bound proofs (for prepublication review) or actual books are sent to designated journals or magazines for review.

4. Catalogs: Catalogs include prepublication announcements (what is forthcoming), annual listings of in-print titles, subject listings, and listings of titles no longer available.

5. Conventions and exhibits: National or regional meetings, which often are sponsored by professional associations, afford publishers the opportunity to meet with current and potential authors and to display books.

6. College textbook representation: Brochures and sales letters, direct representation, and telephone contacts play a part in reaching the college market. Depending on the textbook list—the number of titles involved and the subject areas covered—a publisher of college texts uses one or all of these methods to reach faculty who make the decisions on textbooks to be used by students. Publishers of texts for large introductory college courses generally have a large, regionally based staff of sales representatives who regularly visit professors. A publisher of books for upper division undergraduate or graduate level courses with small

enrollments generally tries to reach the desired faculty by mail and telephone. It is too expensive to employ representatives to promote texts for courses with small enrollments.

7. Customer service: The customer service department handles correspondence and telephone calls relating to the purchase and receipt of books. It handles written requests for price quotations, inquiries on price and availability, and claims on nonreceipt of orders.

8. Direct mail and direct response: Direct mail involves flyers and brochures to potential book buyers. Direct response refers to an expected action; that is, the individual decides to buy and returns the order form to the publisher. These activities are particularly important in the sale of books to individuals or in sales of a very specific subject area to a very specific audience. Libraries will often be included in the mailing of these pieces, although it is recognized that libraries do not order through the order forms. Direct response also has a spillover effect (sometimes called the echo effect) since it sends individuals into bookstores or libraries.

9. Distribution or distributor relations: Distribution commonly falls under the sales group of the marketing department. Depending on the type of books published, a publishing company will rely more or less on the services of various distributors nationwide. Regular and consistent terms are designated by each company for its different classes of customers.

10. International sales: Terms, techniques, and traditions for selling books outside of North America vary. Depending on the volume of business, a publishing company may have an entire division devoted to international sales.

Why are all these marketing functions necessary? Publishing involves many products and many buyers; different types of books are promoted by different marketing techniques.

Costs associated with catalogs, new book announcements, and exhibits are spread over all the titles that are included; therefore, it does not cost significantly more to include more titles. The "cost" associated with book reviews is the cost of the books themselves; however, book reviews can take over a year to appear in print. If the expected audience is small or the life span of the material limited, there will be a more effective way to reach potential buyers. Ads and brochures generally are more expensive, and costs will vary with the magazine in which an ad is placed or with the number of brochures produced and mailed. Since a response of 2 to 3 percent is desirable in direct response, it can be seen that many brochures must be mailed to produce the desired effect.

Related Departments

Departments that are related to but not necessarily part of the marketing department are fulfillment, inventory control, returns and accounts receivable. Fulfillment is the department that eventually gets the book to the customer. It includes order processing (called order entry), invoicing, warehousing, and shipping. Inventory control is a department devoted to receiving new titles, maintaining stock levels of current titles, providing accurate and accessible information on available titles, disposing of out-of-print material, releasing new and reprinted titles, maintaining price information, and providing management with information on stock forecasting. In some cases, inventory control is responsible for print runs and ordering reprints. Carrying inventory of each title is an ongoing challenge. If a company does not have enough copies of a book in the warehouse, it can mean lost sales. The practice of accepting returns is unusual in many industries, but it is a normal occurrence in publishing. The policy is justified by the nature of the publishers' products, that is, many discrete products. For professional publishers, the returns rate as a percentage of gross sales is 17.2 percent (Table 1). The accounts receivable department handles the billing and collection of payment from purchases. The average collection period in 1985 for professional and scholarly books was 97 days. The range reported was 58 to 138 days. The rate at which revenue is received has an impact on the functioning of any business.

SUMMARY

This brief introduction to the business of publishing does not attempt to describe in detail all of the processes that are involved in the publishing of a single book or in the successful management of an entire publishing operation. It is important to identify the *main* elements of publishing—deciding to publish,

The Publishing Industry

producing, and marketing and distributing the finished books—
and to recognize that different types of books will be handled
differently throughout the publishing process.

What is much more difficult to describe is the excitement
inherent in publishing good books: knowing books sell, getting
good reviews, and seeing the books used by readers. At least one
element in this excitement is risk: the uncertainty about whether
or not books will succeed and the financial risk of betting that
they will. When "all's right with the world," the reward for that
financial risk is profit.

Publishers, Vendors, Libraries: Troublesome Issues in the Triangle

Audrey Melkin

How do publishers look at the library market? How do they distinguish it from the bookstore market or the direct mail market? Publishers often feel that it is an invisible market. Are they right in this perception? And in what ways are they wrong? How does the publisher regard the bookseller-vendor-wholesaler, the oft-chosen conduit for the distribution of the publishers' products to the library?

These are some of the questions that librarians ask about publishers and that publishers wonder about themselves. Although the library market has been estimated to generate from $1 to $3 billion,[1] with a predicted growth of 7 to 9 percent,[2] there still remains an enormous gulf between the various players in this market and their understanding of each other's modes of operation. Understanding the reasons why this gulf exists provides the basis for appreciating the difficulties the major players in this market have in interpreting each other's roles.

1. Among other sources, these figures were presented by Jane Dietzel, Cahners Publishing Company, at a seminar entitled "Selling a Billion Dollar Market: Libraries," sponsored by *Library Journal*, December 4, 1987 and by Karen Muller at a presentation made at the Oklahoma Library Association Public Library Division program, Tulsa, March 10, 1988. Muller referred there to "the 3.7 billion dollars libraries spend on books annually."

2. Jane Dietzel, "Book Spending at U.S. Libraries Tops $1 Billion in 1987," *Publishing Markets* 3 (January-February 1988): 2.

It is as difficult to speak about how *all* publishers view the library market as it is to speak about all types of libraries. Although some remarks may apply to all publishers selling to all libraries, the type of publisher being considered here most closely approximates a commercial scholarly and professional publisher. Naturally, therefore, marketing to academic libraries, larger public libraries, and special libraries will be emphasized.

QUANTIFYING SALES
TO LIBRARIES

In publishing as in other businesses, what one can measure or quantify as the effect of one's efforts gets high visibility, prominence, and attention. When advertising can be directly related to an increase in sales at bookstores, when sales significantly exceed production costs, or when a direct mail brochure has a favorable cost to net sales ratio, a publisher can point to the effectiveness of his or her marketing techniques.

For many reasons, this quantifiable factor has been missing from the library market. Librarians respond to many different stimuli to purchase—from favorable reviews, to inclusion on a vendor's approval plan, to publishers' advertising, to faculty requests. Librarians also are likely to order materials through many different channels: direct from the publisher; through a varied number of booksellers, both wholesalers and retailers; and from subscription agents. Most publishing houses cannot easily determine which part of the business of these various channels actually represents library sales. This occurs because the method of sales reporting in publishing houses is more accurate in reflecting the sales of particular titles. Sales to libraries are often reflected in several channels including wholesalers (which may include trade as well as library wholesalers); direct mail response orders, and institutional, industrial, and government categories.

Since publishers are aware that they cannot easily or authoritatively determine their sales to libraries they are more likely to give their attention to other more quantifiable channels. Not too long ago, particularly in the 1960s and early 1970s, publishers had become accustomed to a boom market for library sales. There was a routine sales expectation that certain titles, mainly cloth-bound books would *automatically* sell to libraries. These sales usually took place without any additional efforts on the part of the publishers, other than the usual advertising and

Audrey Melkin

marketing to their more identifiable channels and, of course, the usual advertising in the library media.

The economics of the educational market has changed in the last ten years or so. College textbook publishers have slowly but surely been waking up to that fact. To a great extent educational budget changes have been imposed upon the library market through decreased funding for school, public, and academic libraries. More recently, special and corporate libraries, which are so sensitive to the state of the nation's business health, have also felt the pinch.

The dynamics of the library world have changed as well. Librarians more readily question the assumptions that they suspect publishers hold about the library market, including the notions that the library market is invisible, that it is not price sensitive, and that it does not need to be specially targeted, unlike other markets. Publishers gradually are beginning to see the necessity of clarifying to themselves, and to the vendors and libraries with which they are inextricably connected, their perceptions of the library market. On the publishing side, many sales and marketing people are waking up to the fact that times have changed and that the library market is definitely inelastic and has more special needs and requirements, for example, acid-free paper, full bibliographic information in all promotions, and the courtesy to be recognized and treated as a major sales market. A growing number of programs, surveys, and forums for communication are taking place between the three critical players (publisher, vendor, library). While there may often be an element of acrimonious interchange between librarians and publishers, an increase in meaningful dialogue is occurring as well.

STRATEGIES FOR SELLING TO LIBRARIES

Although the library market has seemed invisible to many publishers for the reasons indicated, sales and marketing strategies have evolved over the years. Publishers are using distribution channels and promotions to achieve their sales targets and expectations in the library market.

Not all publishers have a library or educational sales force in place. The decision to go directly to the library market through a specialized sales force usually is based on the historical circumstances of a publisher, the types of titles published, and the size of the publishing house. With a large list or products from many divisions to sell, the economic justification for having a library sales force becomes more feasible. With this decision, of course, come other economic realities. To support such a sales force, a publisher will need to attract a larger amount of direct orders from libraries, and the discount to libraries will need to be competitive with that offered by the library wholesaler. Likewise, some publishers will try to get a high percentage of library sales as direct business by mounting extensive and attractive direct mail or telemarketing operations. While many academic, public, and special libraries will buy only through vendors, a publisher's sales force can be effective in the many elementary-high school libraries and in smaller public and special libraries. When a publisher's sales representative develops a special and close relationship with the librarians in his or her territory, this technique of selling can prove highly productive. When a direct mail piece or telephone sales call comes just at the right moment, that is, when the product offered and the price quoted are agreeable to the librarian, a sale can be made as well. Of course in other cases these sales initiatives will find themselves in the wastebasket or will be met with silence at the other end of the receiver.

Librarians as well as wholesalers have become concerned in recent years at the tendency of some publishers to sell "direct only" to the library market, thereby eliminating an element of choice otherwise available to librarians. For the vendors, of course, this is a loss of business, and their ability to provide service to the library community is diminished. Likewise, as Eaglen writes,[3] librarians often are incensed to find that they are forced to purchase books directly from the publisher. Eaglen also points out, "there are a growing number of major trade publishers who are severely restricting libraries' options to buy their books directly from them." The main issue appears to be one of denying choice to the consumer—in this instance the librarian. Such a situation is not often encountered in our consumer-oriented society. It is the assertion that publishers *know* the best way for libraries to receive their material that really irks librarians. In the case of bestsellers, for example, it is imperative that libraries be permitted to order directly from publishers if they are to be able to satisfy their patrons in a timely fashion. Additionally, if one regional distributor is given the responsibility to provide

---

3. Audrey Eaglen, "Publishers' Sales Strategies: A Questionable Business," *School Library Journal* 34 (February 1988): 19–21.

a publisher's book to a large market, there may be some abuse of service without any real method of checking or redress on the part of the library.

There is a middle ground between publishers who only sell directly to libraries (known as sole source publishers) and publishers who sell only through wholesalers. These are the publishers who for sound economic reasons prefer that their sales to the library market be primarily through the wholesalers, yet who routinely accept direct orders from libraries, although they do not encourage them. The discounts to libraries from these publishers will usually be small or nonexistent in order to avoid competition with the publishers' primary customer, the wholesaler. Such publishers may continue to spend their advertising dollars to inform the library market of their particular products, but with the expectation that those products will be bought from the vendor. For these publishers the vendor often becomes an ally, a partner in reaching an ultimate end customer, the library patron. It may be that this middle-ground scenario is most conducive to the mutual benefit of all three players in the library market, the publisher, the vendor, and the librarian. Certainly the opportunity for communication and open dialogue among all three is greatest with this arrangement.

Two channels of distribution and the incentive strategies that are likely to accompany each approach have been discussed: direct library sales and sales through the wholesaler. Direct library promotion is a constant in almost all publishing houses that aim to sell to libraries, however the sale is made. Although a wholesaler may be the prime channel of distribution, it is the publisher who is uniquely qualified and expected to publicize and promote the house's list. What varies from publishing house to publishing house is the specificity of this promotion. Is there a regular catalog of new titles mailed to libraries? Is there a mailing piece designed specifically for librarians? Are institutional ads (ads in the library media specifically designed to reach librarians) placed regularly? Attendance at major library meetings both as exhibitor and as participant in the committees and activities of library associations is another arm of library promotion. Although publishers often hear complaints about the surplus of mailing pieces librarians receive and how many are simply thrown away unread, hope springs eternal in the publisher's heart and library promotion managers continue to produce promotion pieces with no quantifiable way of knowing which piece will "clinch the sale." Since a recent survey[4] has shown that second to reviews, librarians rely on the publishers' own promotional material in making their acquisition decisions, the in-house library mailing list will continue to be greatly prized and utilized.

DISTRIBUTION ALTERNATIVES

In contrasting libraries to bookstores as channels of distribution, librarians are often concerned that the publisher favors the bookstore. Public librarians, in particular, need to be treated and seen as a bookstore when it comes to marketing the books to the ultimate consumer, the retail customer or library patron. Both the bookstore and the library share a goal of making materials as attractive as possible to their customers. Although the library has no sales target or budget to attain, it does have to improve circulation figures in order to attract more revenues for library support. But the bookstore is perceived as receiving higher discounts and better terms even though the return rate of unsold items is considerably higher. From the publisher's point of view the bookstore, even though it is a retailer, bears a great similarity to that other bookseller, the library wholesaler. Both are set up with a resale number for tax purposes, and both are in business to buy books and other materials and then resell them. The library, however, is the final place of sale. The materials have been bought to be presented to a third party, the library patron, but this is different from a buying and selling relationship. In this area it may be that the publisher can be educated by the library community to acknowledge that libraries and bookstores are more similar than dissimilar. A publisher can provide libraries with additional book jackets and promotional materials, and can keep the library community informed about promotion and publicity, just as the publisher always does vis-à-vis the bookstore.

Bookstores and wholesalers are resellers while libraries are not; thus a higher discount is justified for the bookstore and wholesaler. In addition to the resale issue, a bookstore qualifies as another class of customer for the publisher. While the

---

4. Hendrik Edelman and Karen Muller, "A New Look at the Library Market," *Publishers Weekly* 231 (May 29, 1987): 30–35.

Audrey Melkin

Robinson-Patman Act[5] specifically prohibits publishers from offering different discounts for the same product to the same class of customers, they are permitted to set a discount schedule that is based on the type of customer. What goes into determining the cost of doing business with a given type of customer? Certainly purely economic factors such as the order quantities, the volume of sales, and turnover will affect the cost of doing business with a certain type of customer. In the case of many scholarly publications, for example, the number of copies that can be sold may be small. If a sizable discount were offered to the library (which may represent the primary customer for the title but will only buy one copy), the book would probably be very expensive or so unprofitable that it would not be feasible to publish at all. Publishers also feel that in order to attract well-known and prestigious authors it is necessary for the books published by that house to have high visibility and, by definition, bookstore distribution. For university and smaller presses, especially, this may mean offering advantageous terms to bookstores in order to get shelf space.

Although the purchase of a publisher's title by a library may ultimately ensure a much greater distribution of that title to the general public, the bookstore buy is more visible, more easily tracked, and therefore receives a higher priority. Of course, if a book really sells well, there will be greater chance for multiple sales through bookstore distribution than through the libraries. For university presses, just as the offering of more advantageous discounts to bookstores is a relatively recent phenomenon, it may be that the next evolution will be the realization of the benefits of extending a similarly favorable discount to that other group of booksellers, the library wholesaler. Since university press titles are so heavily purchased by academic libraries and these libraries buy primarily through vendors, it may be that the university presses will see a similar advantage in supporting the services that the vendors do provide to their ultimate customer.

That university presses may have even closer ties to libraries, particularly academic libraries, was pointed out by Herbert S. Bailey, Jr., director emeritus of Princeton University Press in a paper given at the fiftieth anniversary meeting of the American Association of University Presses in Tucson, Arizona, in June

---

5. 49 Stat. 1526 (1936), 15 U.S.C.A. 13.

1987.[6] He suggests that as the system of scholarly communication develops, the differences between a university library and a university publisher will become much less visible. For example, if network publishing among libraries becomes common practice, there will be serious repercussions for university press publishing. Perhaps university presses can be instrumental in the effort to save brittle books by selective reprinting or by doing on-demand editions on acid-free paper. As parts of the same university system and as providers of services in a large degree to the same market—students and scholars—the university library and press have a natural affinity that can become the basis for greater cooperation in the future. There are, however, issues that have to be worked out.

For the present, it is clear that certain practices of the university presses contribute to conflict between the two rather than harmony. Joyce Knauer, the owner-manager of the Tattered Cover Book Store in Denver, Colorado, reports that bookstores are finding that the university presses are undermining the market for the trade store through direct mail discounting.[7] While this policy represents a clear loss of sales for these bookstores that stock books for the academic community, it may also be an irritant for the librarian who is unable to take advantage of the discount since the library wholesaler has often not been offered the same or equivalent discount.

In fact, many of the larger commercial scholarly and professional publishers run large direct mail programs, but generally *without* offering a discount, thereby driving business into bookstores as well as to wholesalers. Even though increasingly it is the librarian who chooses and buys the scholarly book in academic libraries, the mailing of brochures to faculty by the publisher can serve to promote the use of the scholarly books already acquired by the library.

In a recently published paper, John Secor, president of Yankee Book Peddler, expressed the concerns of the library vendor on these matters.[8] Secor believes that without appropriate

---

6. Herbert S. Bailey, Jr., "The Future of University Press Publishing," *Scholarly Publishing* 19 (January 1988): 63–69.

7. Joyce Knauer, "Scholarly Books in General Bookstores," *Scholarly Publishing* 19 (January 1988): 79–85.

8. John Secor, "A Growing Crisis of Business Ethics: The Gathering Storm Clouds," *Serials Librarian* 13 (October-November 1987): 67–90.

Audrey Melkin

recognition of the vendor's services to the academic library community on the part of both publishers and librarians alike, this important link in the distribution network may be in serious trouble and could thereby jeopardize the orderly and efficient flow of information from scholar to practitioner. He also thinks that an increase in communication and dialogue in the publisher/vendor/library community, if constructive, can lead to creative solutions to problems faced by all three players.

The area of net pricing provides an interesting example of the importance of dialogue. The practice of setting a net price in lieu of discount for retailers and wholesalers primarily originated in some publishing houses as a response to challenges in the college textbook market. College bookstore managers wanted greater flexibility in setting prices, and publishers, hurt badly by the increasingly well-organized used book business, were ready to cooperate. The implications for the library market were often not fully considered within the publishing house and also not carefully explained to the wholesaler or librarian. Typically, a publisher charges the wholesaler and bookstore the net price and charges the library customer who buys directly from the publisher a higher-than-net suggested list price for the title. The publisher's library promotion department also must decide at what price to list the title in advertising and promotion materials. The publisher may feel that it is problematic to advertise the title at the publisher's suggested list price since there may be a vendor who has set a higher price. The vendor's customers might be incensed to see that the title could be bought for less directly from the publisher, which they can in any case easily find out by calling the publisher and asking for the price that the publisher would charge the library. The option of advertising without a price remains, but that seems undesirable since the library community needs price information even when it is only an approximation.

The better informed the librarian is about the net pricing structure—why it's been instituted, what it means for the vendor, and so on—the less likely it is for misunderstandings to arise. Studies such as the one presented by Marsh and Lockman can go a long way toward illuminating the issues involved.[9] In their study, they present the background and explanation of net prices

---

9. Corrie V. Marsh and Edward J. Lockman, "Net Book Pricing," *Library Acquisitions: Practice and Theory* 12 (1988): 169–176.

and illustrate several net-priced titles as supplied by the publisher and by three separate vendors. They point out that librarians should be aware that it is a legitimate practice for wholesalers to mark up the margin on net books in order to cover their costs. They conclude that "there are no grounds for accusations of unfair practice if the dealer marks up the margin on these net-priced items."

Another factor in the eternal triangle of publisher, vendor, and librarian is the assumption that underlies the relationship between the publisher and the vendor, namely, that the vendor's role is only to fulfill demand and not to create it. In a sense, vendors and publishers agree on this issue, since vendors often articulate it as part of their business credo. In fact, given all the competing publishers' whose materials they stock, it might prove unwise to attempt otherwise. Yet, understandable as the vendor's position may be, publishers may feel some resentment. They ask, "Why should I, the publisher, extend to you, the wholesaler, a discount to sell my product when you don't really attempt to aggressively sell it?" The argument follows that many publishers feel that they can do better by continuing their direct relationship with librarians by offering some added discount to them, but not as high as that given to the wholesaler. The difficulty here is that the vendor may be providing something in addition to direct selling, namely, service in the form of consolidated ordering, bibliographic information, and time savings in payment and in claiming. The publisher cannot provide such service. Only when all three parts of the publisher, library, vendor triangle are taken together can solutions to problems be found.

CHANGING RELATIONSHIPS AND CHANGING TIMES

Library schools have not generally included curriculum in the acquisitions process, therefore, little has been presented to student librarians about the publishing process and its dynamics. Similarly, the publishing industry has been slow to create special departments or marketing and sales people specifically designed to focus on the library market. Where there should be a natural affinity there often seems to be none. Several publishers have for a long time recognized the importance of the library market to their publishing programs and have active library advisory boards as well as librarians on their staff. But in general,

Audrey Melkin

publishers have hesitated to create such departments or specialties because they have not felt sufficiently knowledgeable about
the discipline. And since library sales in many publishing houses
are somewhat invisible, these publishers have not felt a great
need to learn more about the library market.

Natural bonds exist between publisher and librarian: they are
both interested in encouraging reading, fighting illiteracy, and
opposing censorship. The issue of acid free paper may be another
potential rallying point, especially as more publishers discover
that the costs of using such paper are not substantially greater.
With the establishment of the Copyright Clearance Center, the
historical disagreement over photocopying may be handled more
harmoniously.

Likewise, there has been a historically close relationship
between the publisher and the retail bookseller. There are often
job exchanges between these two industries, and the fact that
neither industry requires any formal specialized education may
be a link. Both also have perceived themselves as businesses
involved in marketing and selling as well as publishing. Perhaps
with the growing emphasis on marketing library services and
a growing sophistication as librarians are increasingly seen as
business managers, more dialogue among the players will occur.
However, more conscious efforts will have to be made since these
historical groupings are so well entrenched.

Similarly, vendors seem to have evolved closer relationships
with librarians than publishers have with vendors. Perhaps, there
is more understanding of the role of the librarian in the vendor's
business which regularly has librarians on staff. Since the publisher may be trying to sell to the library directly as well as
through the wholesaler, there may be a built-in competition
between the publisher and the wholesaler which is not so prevalent in the publisher-bookstore relationship.

The future seems to portend a closer relationship among the
players, if only for purely business reasons. As publishers have
realized the necessity to become market driven rather than product driven, all of the publisher's many markets are being
scrutinized anew. Publishing executives are now beginning to
ask themselves what their customers want, rather than to whom
they can sell a given title. Librarians are particularly well
equipped to tell publishers which subject areas and formats are
most in demand. The recent proliferation of surveys on library
acquisition procedures is a clear indication of how much more
publishers now want to know about this market.

The library has become a different institution from what it was years ago. With the advent of the information manager, the position of librarian has achieved a greater prestige, whatever one's personal opinion of this trend may be. All types of libraries, including public, academic, and special, are being run by more sophisticated, quantifiable, business-oriented methods. The librarian's role and voice has changed. Librarians are asking more questions of both wholesalers and publishers. Wholesalers and publishers are being challenged to demystify the process of which they are a part. After the initial panicked reaction on the part of publishers and vendors passes, this request leads to a much richer exchange among all three.

An all day program, "Deja-Vu or the Library Market Revisited," given at the ALA summer meeting in San Francisco, 1987, was attended by nearly 500 vocal librarians, vendors, and publishers[10]. All were eager to hear panel presentations and to engage in discussions on the recently completed library acquisitions survey and to talk about recurring problems in their relationship. Two major areas of concern emerged in that meeting. First mentioned was the problem of books going out of print too soon. For librarians this represents a lost opportunity to develop their collections as they would like; for publishers, it is a lost opportunity to sell books. Vendors, too, suffer loss of sales. The second problem occurs in the area of review media where too few books are reviewed and often well after publication. This is a critical issue, since reviews are frequently listed as the librarian's number one acquisition tool. The joint Resources and Technical Services Division, American Library Association, and AAP committee that put on the "Deja-Vu" program has committed itself to addressing these concerns in subsequent programs.

Although there may be no utopian solutions to these problems, through varied efforts some workable partial solutions can be found. If the educating process continues among the players, and if each comes to better appreciate the business requirements of the other, some insights can will likely result to the benefit of everyone involved. If greater understanding can be fostered among the publisher, the librarian, and the wholesaler, the real winner will be the end customer of them all, the reading public.

---

10. Edelman and Muller, "A New Look at the Library Market," pp. 30–35.

The Business of Scholarly Journal Publishing

Gary J. Brown

The escalating costs of serials continue to erode acquisitions budgets and threaten to cut into even more of the monies budgeted for the acquisition of monographs. In many academic libraries it is not uncommon to witness at least 60 to 70 percent of the acquisition budget allocated for the purchase of periodicals, journals, and other serials. The average price for a U.S. hardcover monograph in 1987 was $35.34—9 percent over the 1986 average of $32.43. In comparison, U.S. periodicals averaged $71.41 per title in 1987—a 9.9 percent increase over the average price of $65.00 in 1986. When the output of European-based journal publishers is added, an even larger increase is evident for all serials: $105.00 for a serial in 1987—a 13.4 percent increase over the 1986 average of $93.32.[1]

The questions that immediately come to mind are: Why do serials cost more than monographs? Is the editorial and publishing process more expensive for serials than for monographs? Or is it, as some suggest, that publishers simply charge what the market will bear?[2]

1. Leslie C. Knapp and Rebecca T. Lenzini, "Price Index for 1987: U.S. Periodicals," *Library Journal* 112 (April 1987): 39–44; Rebecca T. Lenzini, "Periodical Prices 1985–1987 Update," *Serials Librarian* 13 (September 1987): 49–57; Chandler B. Grannis, "Title Output and Average Prices," *Publishers Weekly* 233 (March 1988): 30–33.
2. The concern and frustration with journal publishers has been argued with different intensity and focus. For part of the background and related bibliography see the following articles: Deana Astle and Charles Hamaker, "Recent Pricing Patterns in British Journal Publishing," *Library Acquisitions: Practice and Theory*

The Publishing Industry

THE JOURNAL IN SCHOLARLY AND SCIENTIFIC COMMUNICATION

This chapter focuses on the nature and economics of scholarly and scientific journal publishing.[3] To understand this process it is helpful to look at the role of the journal in communicating scholarly and scientific information. In some disciplines such as physics and the pure sciences, the journal is the primary publishing mode for communication. The journal is preferred over the monograph not only because of the need for immediacy but also because of the nature of the research itself (for example, the limited scope of a particular topic, problem, report, or letter of information). Indeed, as studies at the end of the 1970s have indicated, the fields of science and technology devote much more of their financial resources, time, and publication efforts to the journal than to the monograph.[4] There are a number of reasons for

8 (1984): 225–232 and "Pricing by Geography: British Journal Pricing 1986, Including Developments in Other Countries," *Library Acquisitions: Practice and Theory* 10 (1986): 165–181; Siegfried Ruschin, "Why Are Foreign Subscription Rates Higher for American Libraries than they are for Subscribers Elsewhere?" *Serials Librarian* 9 (1985): 7–18. The articles of Robert L. Houbeck, Jr. address similar concerns for the pricing practices by publishers: "British Journal Pricing: Enigma, Variations, or What *Will* the U.S. Market Bear?" *Library Acquisitions: Practice and Theory* 10 (1986): 183–189 and "If Present Trends Continue: Responding to Journal Price Increases," Journal of Academic Librarianship 13 (1987). Nigel Cross criticizes the proliferation and pricing of the journal in "The Economics of Learned Journals," *Times Literary Supplement* (November 23, 1984): 1348.

3. Our use of the term *journal* refers to scholarly, refereed periodicals and thus excludes popular trade journals, newsletters, and bulletins.

4. In the studies by Donald W. King and his colleagues, data were collected back to 1960 and projected with time series models into 1985. "Much more activity is associated with journals than with the other forms of published literature. . . . The resources expended in journal publishing are much greater than for other forms of the published literature. The total amount of resources expended on the scientific and technical literature was $12 billion in 1977 . . . an estimated $4.7 billion worth of resources were expended on scientific and technical journals, 61 percent of the total communication expenditures." Donald W. King, Dennis D. McDonald, and Nancy K. Roderer, *Scientific Journals in the United States: Their Production, Use, and Economics* (Stoudsburg, Penn.: Hutchinson Ross Publishing Co., 1981), pp. 25–26. The National Science Foundation and The National Endowment for the Humanities among other agencies helped fund the analysis of scholarly journal publishing in the United States in the late 1970s. See also, *Scholarly Communication: The Report of the National Enquiry* (Baltimore: Johns Hopkins University Press, 1979); Bernard M. Fry and Herbert S. White, *Publishers and Libraries: A Study of Scholarly and Research Journals* (Boston: Lexington Books, 1976); F. Machlup and K. W. Leeson, *Information Through the Printed Word: The Dissemination of Scholarly, Scientific and Intellectual Knowledge,* Vol. 1: *Book Publishing;* Vol. 2: *Journals;* Vol. 3: *Libraries;* Vol. 4: *Books, Journals, and Bibliographic Services (New York: Praeger, 1978–80).* For an analysis of British journal publishing see chapters 9–11 by Alan Singleton in Peter J. Curwen, *The UK Publishing Industry* (Oxford: Pergamon, 1981).

this condition, not all of which can merely be summarized by the needs of researchers to "publish or perish" or by the needs of publishers to increase profits by increasing the number of journals.

Given an academic structure that rewards and grants tenure to faculty largely on the basis of published contributions to scholarship, and given the need for an established scholarly reputation to attract grants and research monies to an institution, the mandate to publish one's research is widely understood. The preferred medium in some disciplines is the scholarly journal because of the rapid dissemination of information. In a sense, there is a circular process that instigates research and publication: one publishes to further a field of knowledge, which brings recognition and promotion; this in turn makes one highly eligible for research grants, which also in turn bring monies to the parent institution and foster both the progress of research and the researcher's career. The reverse side of these pressures upon both researchers and publishers is the proliferation of journals and serial publications with their overwhelming number of articles, fragmented reports, letters, and reviews—a phenomena descriptively referred to as the process of "twigging."[5]

THE JOURNAL PUBLISHING PROCESS

Traditionally the publishing process has organized itself around the sequence of planning, producing, and disseminating. These activities are assigned to editorial, production, and marketing, whether represented by entire divisions within large publishing houses or by one person in a small operation. Publishers of both monographs and journals generally fall into the categories of university presses, commercial publishers, and learned societies or professional associations.

In book publishing, an editor (acquisitions, developmental, or copy editor) deals with the process of acquiring, preparing, and editing the manuscript for publication.[6] Levels of editorial

---

5. See the study by Deana Astle and Charles Hamaker which discusses in some detail this changing aspect of journal publishing. "Journal Publishing: Pricing and Structural Issues in the 1930's and the 1980's," in *Advances in Serials Management,* Vol. 2 (Greenwich, Conn.: JAI Press, 1988), pp 1–36.

6. For discussions of monographic and journal editorial procedures see Elizabeth A. Geiser, ed., *The Business of Book Publishing: Papers by Practitioners* (Boulder, Colo.: Westview Press, 1985) and Lewis I. Gidez, "Editorial Operations," in *Economics of Scientific Journals,* edited by Ad Hoc Committee on Economics of Publication (Bethesda, Md.: Council of Biology Editors, Inc., 1982).

involvement and responsibility vary depending upon the nature and perceived market for the book—whether mass-market paperback, trade, scholarly, professional reference, medical, or textbook. Editorial responsibilities in journal publishing differ markedly since the editors and the editorial board of a journal often are not members of the publishers' staff but instead are affiliated with an academic, corporate, or governmental institution where they conduct research, teach, or do both, and publish within their discipline. The relationship between author and editor is often a relationship between colleagues. Large publishers, however, maintain an editorial staff to manage the editorial and production procedures. Thus the process of acquiring manuscripts for publication and the decision to publish rest not with the publisher but with academic or professional peers who anonymously referee submitted or requested material. Of course, this process varies when the item being considered for inclusion in the journal is a report, letter, or note of information. As a result, many journal publishers traditionally do not incur the major costs of a salaried editorial staff to the extent that book publishers do, nor do journal publishers provide royalty payments to authors as is the practice with commercial publishers of monographs. In the case of many learned societies in the United States, page charges which are paid by the authors are assessed in order to help defray journal publication costs.

The production process for a book or a journal essentially follows the same procedures: (1) Design decisions are made about what typeface and size to use and whether illustrations or halftone reproductions will be employed. (2) Specifications involving page size, paper quality, and weight are established. (3) Composition vendors are selected (if composition is not handled in-house). (4) Printing and binding are scheduled or assigned to vendors if not part of a publisher's operation.

The journal like the monograph has fixed and variable production costs. Fixed costs such as composition, author corrections, plates, illustrations, and press make-ready procedures, remain constant regardless of the number of copies printed. Variable costs such as paper, printing, binding, and postage increase with the number of pages and copies printed.

The important difference between books and journals, however, involves the journal's serial nature. Because of its frequency pattern and the successive repetition of the production procedures, both fixed and variable manufacturing costs are higher. Special issues and larger page counts to accommodate the

Gary J. Brown

increasing number of accepted articles contribute to the rise of costs and subscription prices.

Marketing efforts to publicize, promote, and distribute a book vary widely according to the nature of the book in question (for example, mass-market paperback versus a university press scholarly title). Author tours, television appearances, and radio talk show interviews to promote a popular title obviously would not be used for a specialized monograph such as *Introduction to Interactive Computer Graphics* (Addison-Wesley, 1983) or for a scholarly or scientific journal such as *Brain Research* (Elsevier). The scholarly or scientific journal has to develop a much more conservative marketing plan that targets research libraries, academics, and specialists and that relies principally upon traditional means of advertising: brochures, catalogs, and direct mail. In addition, a prestigious editorial board composed of widely recognized researchers and academics is a valuable advertising asset that will help a new journal on its way to success and insure continued subscription by libraries and individuals.

JOURNAL COSTS AND REVENUE

Like any organization, in order to continue operations journal publishers need to insure that income exceeds expenses. Commercial publishers cannot survive without profit, and where profit is lacking for society publishers and university presses, some form of subsidies are sought.

By way of summary, the cost side of the balance sheet for a journal lists expenses such as editing (copyediting, proofreading, layout), production and manufacturing (typesetting, illustrations, paper, printing, binding, reprints), marketing (advertising, direct mail), and distribution (postage, delivery, subscription fulfillment). On the income side of the balance sheet journal publishers rely on the following sources of revenue: subscriptions (member or institutional), page charges, advertising, sale of back issues, reprints, microform sales, and permission rights.[7]

---

7. An example of a balance sheet for the *Journal of Mathematical Physics* (1978) is provided by Robert H. Marks who describes the cost factors involved in publishing eighteen primary journals, three member society bulletins, and nineteen Soviet translations for the American Institute of Physics. See "'Not for Profit' Doesn't Mean 'For Loss,'" in *Proceedings of the Third Annual Meeting of the Society for Scholarly Publishing* (1981), p. 184.

Since the journal has production and manufacturing costs that cannot be lowered readily by the economies of scale normally associated with monographic publishing, it must look at other areas on the balance sheet to recoup expenses. The principal source of revenue for a journal is its subscription base, which publishers try to keep as broad as possible through different member and institutional rates. Nonprofit association and learned society publishers in the United States can rely upon page charges to authors to help defray the fixed and variable costs of publishing but university presses and commercial publishers traditionally have not used this procedure.[8] Added sources of revenue such as advertising, reprints, and so on contribute less significantly to overall profitability. Since the frequency of a journal and number of pages directly affect costs, publishers rely upon an important analytic tool referred to as the break-even analysis. It allows the calculation of the number of journal subscriptions needed to offset basic costs and the number beyond that point to insure profitability. Cost per page can thus be determined and average price per page set (and thus the overall price of the journal) in order to insure needed revenues and projected profits.[9]

Annual cost and revenue statistics for journal publishing are not available readily because traditional publishing industry sources such as the annual *Industry Statistics Report* of the Association of American Publishers do not break out cost figures for periodical or journal publishing. Nevertheless, extensive studies of U.S. scientific and scholarly journal publishing by Machlup and King provide a point of reference for understanding the economics of journal publishing. As an example, one of Machlup's surveys of 137 journals (72 from learned societies, 25 from university presses, and 40 from commercial publishers) revealed that nearly 65 percent of publisher revenue was derived from subscription sales. University presses relied upon subscriptions for a full 79 percent of their revenue. The second largest source of revenue, 13.7 percent, came from advertising. Page charges levied by 22 society publications and two university journals provided 8.3 percent of total revenue. In actuality, these 22 society pub-

8. For a discussion of the practice and history of assessing page charges see Marjorie Scal, "The Page Charge," *Scholarly Publishing* 3 (1971): 62–69 and A. F. Spilhaus, Jr. "Page Charges," *Economics of Scientific Journals*, pp. 21–27.

9. See Ben Russak "The Economics of Journal Publishing," *Proceedings of the Third Annual Meeting of the Society for Scholarly Publishing* (1981), pp. 174–177, for a discussion and application of break-even analysis for a new journal.

Gary J. Brown

lishers alone derived a full 13.2 percent of their revenue from page charges. The sale of back issues, reprints, microforms, permission fees, and miscellaneous sources provided cumulatively 13.5 percent of revenue.[10]

A more recent look at six journals from the American Institute of Physics (AIP), a nonprofit society publisher, provides both cost and income statistics from 1982. On the revenue side they coincide in many respects with Machlup's findings for journals studied in 1974.[11] For the six AIP journals, subscriptions account for 61 percent of revenue as opposed to 65 percent in the Machlup sample. Voluntary page charges, however, contribute almost three times more—33 percent compared to 13.2 percent in Machlup's study. Table 1 shows expenses and income for *Applied Physics Letters, Journal of Applied Physics, Journal of Chemical Physics, Journal of Mathematical Physics, Physics of Fluids,* and *Review of Scientific Instruments.* Publication expenses for the six AIP journals amounted to $5,026,000, leaving earnings of $1,174,000 from the total income of $6,200,000. The overall margin of profitability for these journals is thus calculated at 23 percent

These examples make clear that the subscriber plays a critical role in the economic viability of a journal. A vicious circle ensues

TABLE 1 Summary of Expenses and Income for Six Physics Journals

1982 Journal Expenses			1982 Journal Income		
	Amount	Percent		Amount	Percent
Editorial	1,360,000	27%	Page Charges	2,039,000	33%
Composition	1,378,000	28%	Subscriptions	3,835,000	61%
Illustrations	50,000	10%	Advertising	57,000	1%
Paper	525,000	10%	Microfilm Sales	67,000	1%
Printing & Binding	506,000	10%	Back Number Sales	29,000	1%
Mailing	468,000	9%	Reprint Sales	141,000	2%
Subsc. Fulfillment	142,000	3%	Royalties	32,000	1%
Reprints	362,000	7%			
Misc.	235,000	5%			
Total expenses	5,026,000		Total income	6,200,000	

10. Machlup, *Information,* Vol. 2, p. 137, Table 3.4.13. For a more complete discussion consult Vol. 4, Part 8, "Journal Publishing: Costs and Gross Margins." In King, McDonald, and Roderer, *Scientific Journals,* see Chapter 4, "Publishing Scientific and Technical Journals" and Chapter 8, "Economics of the Scientific and Technical Journal System."

11. Rita Lerner, "The Professional Society in a Changing World," *Library Quarterly* 54 (1984): 36–47 (1984).

when publishers increase prices to compensate for low subscription revenue and subscribers then cancel because of higher prices.

JOURNAL PRICING TRENDS

The question presented at the outset—why do journals cost more than monographs?—can be answered partially by the fact that lower margins are derived from the manufacturing and publishing procedures for the journal because of higher production costs for smaller and more frequent print runs. The efficiencies provided by new editorial and production applications (word processing, software for universal page mark-up language, new typesetting systems, desktop publishing) can help contain expenditures, but the smaller operations and quantities implied in journal production coupled with a decreasing subscription base result in higher costs and pricing.

In the view of many librarians, part of the answer for increased prices also rests with some publishers who charge what the market will bear. These librarians feel that some commercial European publishers, for example, charge exorbitant prices at higher differential rates for U.S. libraries. This seems to be borne out for scientific and technical journals which historically have been more expensive than humanities journals and monographs.

In the usually heavily funded areas of research and development, premium prices are paid for related materials and information. The explosion of the size and number of journals is also a response to this reality. Journal prices for the sciences over the past decade, like the trend for all periodicals, display a steady curve upward over the inflation rate. Figure 1 demonstrates the extent of that upward movement by comparing data from the Consumer Price Index (CPI), U.S. Periodicals Index, and the Faxon Periodical Prices Updates.[12] Statistics for this

---

12. The U.S. Periodicals Index indicated in Figure 1 refers to the "Price Indexes for (year): U.S. Periodicals and Services," published annually in the *Library Journal.* The Faxon comprehensive database provides information reported in "Periodical Prices: (Years) Update" which has been published in the *Library Journal* and since 1981 in the *Serials Librarian.* All data from these sources represent the years 1975 to 1987. For a discussion of these and other indexes as well as periodical pricing concerns see, Ann Okerson, "Periodical Prices: A History and Discussion" in *Advances in Serials Management,* Vol. I edited by Jean Cook and Marcia Tuttle (Greenwich, Conn.: JAI Press, 1986), pp. 101–134. Also consult the useful study by Michael R. Kronenfeld and James A. Thompson, "The Impact of Inflation on Journal Costs," *Library Journal* 106(1981): 714–717 which emphasizes that "the key point is not how much the prices have increased, but how this increase compares to the overall price increase (inflation rate) for the same time period." (p. 714).

Gary J. Brown

CPI COMPARISON

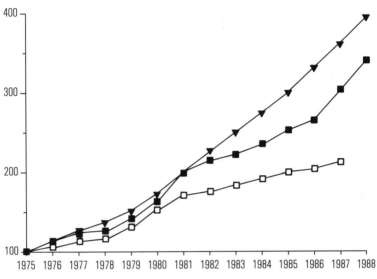

Year	CPI	U.S. Periodical	Faxon
1975	100.0	100.0	100.0
1976	105.7	112.9	112.7
1977	112.6	123.3	121.1
1978	121.2	138.3	130.7
1979	135.1	152.3	145.0
1980	153.2	173.2	165.6
1981	168.9	196.2	196.3
1982	179.0	224.7	213.9
1983	184.5	251.9	225.9
1984	193.0	275.7	238.7
1985	199.9	299.4	251.2
1986	203.7	326.0	267.2
1987	211.2	358.2	303.1
1988	n/a	390.9	340.9

CONSUMER PRICE INDEX

FIGURE 1 Upward Movement of Journal Prices as Evident from the Consumer Price Index, U.S. Periodicals Index, and Faxon Periodical Prices Updates

The Publishing Industry

figure include a broader base than scientific and scholarly journals.

Isolating the humanities and scientific journals indicates the extent to which they have outstripped the CPI. Nine periodical abstract and index services, three for the humanities and six for the sciences, offer a fifteen-year perspective (1973–1987).[13] Figures 2–4 reveal that even in the area of the humanities, journals have surpassed the CPI by as much as 218 percent. Titles in the *Social Science Citation Index* increased four and a half times more than the CPI; titles in *Biological Abstracts* were 388 percent above and titles in *Index Chemicus* were 420 percent above. These are disturbing figures, exacerbated in the last few years by the weakness of the dollar in the foreign exchange markets.

Explanations for the increases in prices depend upon the perspectives involved. From the publisher's side, the reduced number of subscriptions, photocopying, telefacsimile and interlibrary loan consortia, the increase in materials costs, new journals, and the expanded number of pages all have necessitated higher prices. Holden's article in *Science* summarizes publishers' perspectives: Michael Bowen of the American Chemical Society attributes growth in journal size and "shrinkage of the subscription base, which has been going down between 0.5 and 1% a year as factors for price increases"; A. F. Spilhaus, Jr., of the American Geophysical Union "says price increases of AGU journals have been necessitated by increased paper and postage costs...as well as increased pages"; Don Swanson of Academic Press points out that the CPI is "irrelevant, because the price index does not take into account rising costs of such factors as paper, typesetting, and postage"; Robert Hiranda of Pergamon Journals "says

---

13. The data for these tables were taken from the Faxon Periodical Price Updates using Table 1. The actual CPI numbers (1967=100) were converted to a base year of 1973=100 by multiplying each index number by 100 and then dividing by the CPI for 1973 (133.1). The actual CPI numbers are included in parenthesis. Percentage increases over inflation are indicated to provide a basis for judging the significance of price increases for journals in these disciplines. Of course, the statistics do not address such cost factors as increases in the number of pages or words, which provide a more accurate analysis of price increases and value per subscription dollar. In this respect see the discussions about cost per thousand words/characters (kiloword pages) in King, McDonald, and Roderer, *Scientific Journals,* pp. 115–118, Henry H. Barschall, "The Cost of Physics Journals," *Physics Today* (December 1986), and Astle and Hamaker, "Journal Publishing" in *Advances in Serials Management,* Vol. 2.

Gary J. Brown

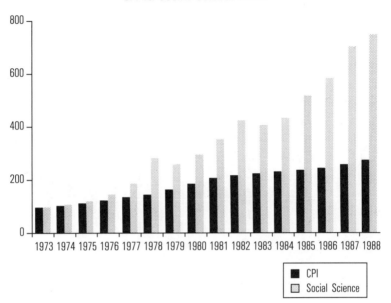

CPI vs. SOCIAL SCIENCE INDEX

| | CPI |
| | Social Science |

SOCIAL SCIENCE CITATION INDEX

Year		CPI b.1973	# of Titles	Avg. Price	Percent Change	Index
1973	(133.1)	100.0	943	$16.48		100.0
1974	(147.7)	111.0	913	19.03	15.5%	115.5
1975	(161.2)	121.1	889	21.72	14.1%	131.8
1976	(170.5)	128.1	878	24.57	13.1%	149.1
1977	(181.5)	136.4	2,278	29.71	20.9%	180.3
1978	(195.4)	146.8	2,186	47.96	61.4%	291.0
1979	(217.4)	163.3	1,858	41.50	-13.5%	251.8
1980	(246.8)	185.4	1,763	48.94	17.9%	297.0
1981	(272.4)	204.7	1,768	57.36	17.2%	348.1
1982	(289.1)	217.2	1,866	70.78	23.4%	429.5
1983	(298.4)	224.2	1,817	67.59	-4.5%	410.1
1984	(311.1)	233.7	1,692	72.76	7.6%	441.5
1985	(322.2)	242.1	1,694	87.97	20.9%	533.8
1986	(328.4)	246.7	1,701	97.21	10.5%	589.9
1987	(340.4)	255.7	1,695	116.55	19.9%	707.2
1988	(360.1)	270.5	1,703	123.28	5.8%	748.1
					Total % incr.	648.1
					% incr. over CPI	477.6

FIGURE 2   Comparison of Increase in Social Science Journals' Prices and Consumer Price Index.

The Publishing Industry

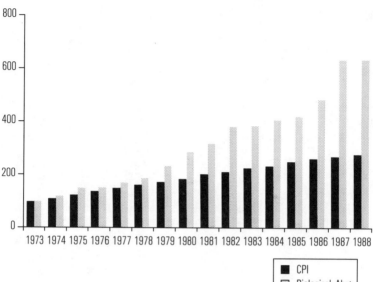

CPI vs. BIOLOGICAL ABSTRACTS

BIOLOGICAL ABSTRACTS

Year		CPI b.1973	# of Titles	Avg. Price	Percent Change	Index
1973	(133.1)	100.0	2,852	$30.86		100.0
1974	(147.7)	111.0	2,756	36.61	18.6%	118.6
1975	(161.2)	121.1	2,663	47.61	30.0%	154.3
1976	(170.5)	128.1	2,620	48.23	1.3%	156.3
1977	(181.5)	136.4	2,534	51.14	6.0%	165.7
1978	(195.4)	146.8	2,430	58.00	13.4%	187.9
1979	(217.4)	163.3	5,075	71.45	23.2%	231.5
1980	(246.8)	185.4	4,224	86.15	20.6%	279.2
1981	(272.4)	204.7	4,179	98.85	14.7%	320.3
1982	(289.1)	217.2	4,406	115.17	16.5%	373.2
1983	(298.4)	224.2	4,363	117.46	2.0%	380.6
1984	(311.1)	233.7	3,846	124.44	5.9%	403.2
1985	(322.2)	242.1	3,860	132.07	6.1%	428.0
1986	(328.4)	246.7	3,727	149.94	13.5%	485.9
1987	(340.4)	255.7	3,728	198.71	32.5%	643.9
1988	(360.1)	270.5	4,524	198.92	0.1%	644.6
					Total % incr.	544.6
					% incr. over CPI	374.1

FIGURE 3 Comparison of Increase in Biological Journals' Prices and Consumer Price Index.

Gary J. Brown

CPI vs. INDEX CHEMICUS

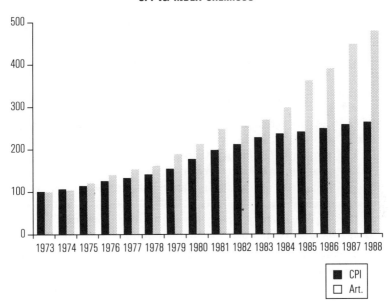

	CPI
	Art.

INDEX CHEMICUS					
Year	CPI b.1973	# of Titles	Avg. Price	Percent Change	Index
1973 (133.1)	100.0	103	$81.70		100.0
1974 (147.7)	111.0	97	100.96	23.6%	123.6
1975 (161.2)	121.1	95	116.85	15.7%	143.0
1976 (170.5)	128.1	95	130.15	11.4%	159.3
1977 (181.5)	136.4	96	139.37	7.1%	170.6
1978 (195.4)	146.8	101	158.01	13.4%	193.4
1979 (217.4)	163.3	151	193.92	22.7%	237.4
1980 (246.8)	185.4	144	223.22	15.1%	273.2
1981 (272.4)	204.7	155	232.07	4.0%	284.1
1982 (289.1)	217.2	165	276.78	19.3%	338.8
1983 (298.4)	224.2	172	283.53	2.4%	347.0
1984 (311.1)	233.7	162	290.48	2.5%	355.5
1985 (322.2)	242.1	156	305.80	5.3%	374.3
1986 (328.4)	246.7	152	358.80	17.3%	439.2
1987 (340.4)	255.7	158	552.09	53.9%	675.8
1988 (360.1)	270.5	160	493.28	−10.7%	603.8
				Total % incr.	503.8
				% incr. over CPI	333.3

FIGURE 4 Comparison of Increase in Chemical Journals' Prices and Consumer Price Index.

that labor costs have been the largest factor (aside from the decline in the dollar) in pushing up prices."[14]

Librarians feel that journal publishers constantly raise prices knowing that their captive market does not like to break a serial run. According to Herbert S. White "Libraries are charged higher prices because experience has shown that they will pay higher prices, and that the cancellation rate in response to price increases is much greater for individuals than for libraries."[15] Librarians also express concern about the growth of large international commercial publishers who, having taken over publishing responsibilities from a number of scientific societies and associations, are creating near-monopolies in certain disciplines.[16] In a recent survey of 471 libraries conducted by Faxon, 54 percent of the respondents agreed with this statement: "Publishers are making outrageous amounts of profit through their increases."[17] The Faxon *Library Profile* also revealed the following points:

- The most popular option for dealing with high prices is canceling subscriptions to low-use journals.
- Fifty-five percent of all libraries are likely to cut back on high-priced technical periodicals.
- Nearly 80 percent of librarians agreed to some extent that they should organize and pressure publishers to reduce costs.
- While interest in new technologies and services is high, there is little expectation that electronic storage of periodicals will permit libraries to discard paper volumes.
- Predictive as well as retrospective price studies are viewed as valuable both for budget planning and internal lobbying.

---

14. Constance Holden "Libraries Stunned by Journal Price Increases," *Science* 22 (1987): 909. For more studied publisher views that go beyond the issue of price, consult the papers of Morris Philipson (University of Chicago Press), Frederick A. Praeger (Westview Press), and Peter F. Urbach (Pergamon) in *Publishers and Librarians: A Foundation for Dialogue, Library Quarterly* 54 (1984).

15. Herbert S. White "Differential Pricing," *Library Journal* 111 (1986): 170. For comments from ARL libraries see "Paying the Piper: ARL Libraries Respond to Skyrocketing Journal Subscription Prices" by the editor of *Journal of Academic Librarianship* 14 (1988): 4–9.

16. In this respect see the report of Stuart F. Grinnel, "The 6 Percent Effect" in *Library Issues: Briefings for Faculty and Administrators* (Ann Arbor, Mich.: Mountainside Publishing Co., 1988).

17. *Library Profiles* No. 1, Faxon Collection Development Series (Westwood, Mass.: Faxon Press, 1988).

Gary J. Brown

CONCLUSION

To some extent the predicament in which we find ourselves is the result of an evolving, radical transformation of the information chain—the process through which we create, acquire, and use information. High costs, the fragmentation and twigging of knowledge and traditional disciplines, the digitalization of information and its consequent alteration of the ways in which we access, acquire, store, and utilize this information are all contributing factors that are altering the communication of scholarly information. This process of transition needs to be understood as the context from which a reevaluation of the scientific journal is urged by Deana Astle and Charles Hamaker: "It is important that librarians recognize the scientific journal for what it has become—the scientific archive, the record of research, the teaching tool—rather than the front line of information for major researchers in a discipline. Ongoing reevaluation of journal collections and decisions for purchase should be made with this information in mind."[18]

Recommendations such as organized cancellation projects among consortia and the compilation and maintenance of indexes to monitor the pricing policies of selected publishers, while useful, necessarily lead us to the larger issue—the information process itself. Richard M. Dougherty believes that "the time has come for everyone to rethink the current system. The issue is so important that it deserves the attention of all groups involved—government agencies, private foundations, societies, and organizations such as the AAU, the ARL, and the ACLS. Librarians have become the bearers of bad tidings with their gloomy forecasts of impending cancellations. Instead, they can and should be participants in developing a new system."[19]

More than a decade ago there was equal concern about the scholarly information system. The report of the National Inquiry on Scholarly Information, the National Science Foundation, and the National Endowment for the Humanities-funded studies of Fry, White, Machlup and King are all prologue to our present concerns. The major issues they dealt with are still with us today: the dissemination of scholarly information, access to it, the use

18. Astle and Hamaker, "Journal Publishing...," in *Advances in Serials Management,* Vol. 2, pp. 1−36.
19. "Serials Prices: Outrageous or Just the Cost of Doing Business?" *Journal of Academic Librarianship* 14 (1988): 3.

of it, and what it costs. Instead of the library-publisher dialogue these reports encouraged and anticipated, what we now witness is a disenchanted reexamination of relationships between libraries and publishers. How we resolve these issues in the future and what role libraries, publishers, and the other links of the chain take must not be left to the exclusive interests of any one sector.

Taking the Mystery Out of European Book Pricing

Jana K. Stevens

In the past few years almost every U.S. library has had to face up to the unpleasant necessity of cutting its budget. With less money available to serve library users' growing needs, acquisitions librarians might have justifiably contemplated sacrificing foreign book purchases to the budgetary ax. Foreign books, after all, are expensive, have fewer readers, and are generally less accessible to the bulk of library users, especially those published in languages other than English.

Statistics, however, do not reflect a sagging book import market. For example, in 1986 U.S. book imports exceeded exports, while in 1987 book imports and exports were about equal.[1] Seven European countries—Belgium, France, Italy, the Netherlands, Switzerland, the United Kingdom, and West Germany—account for nearly half of all foreign book purchases by U.S. libraries. In a world grown increasingly interdependent in important areas of scholarly research, library users and librarians have decided that even in financially lean times, building their foreign book collections is an important priority that has to be preserved. Clearly, American acquisitions librarians are going to have increasing contact with foreign publishers and vendors. And with so many dollars flowing abroad, it won't be surprising to discover more U.S. vendors expanding their ties outside of the United States to satisfy the American libraries' seemingly insatiable appetite for foreign books.

---

1. Chandler B. Grannis, "Balancing the Books: U.S. Exports, Imports Almost Equal in 1987," *Publishing Weekly* 234 (September 9, 1988): 105–106.

Despite the trend toward more business between the European book trade and American libraries, the literature on European selling practices is scant. Accustomed to dealing in a common language across a single, large national market, American acquisitions librarians tend to assume that European publishers and vendors follow the same business conventions prevalent in the United States. When they cast their gaze across the Atlantic, U.S. acquisitions librarians expect to see a European book trade that resembles its American counterpart. This is not always the case.

MERGING AND SPECIALIZING

Like their American counterparts, West European book publishers and vendors operate by the rules of the market and are profit driven. To help lower their operating costs and boost profit margins, many smaller West European booksellers have formed cooperative distribution networks which allow them to be more efficient and to compete effectively with the larger publishing and distribution houses. In the Netherlands and Sweden, for instance, smaller publishers use common warehouselike depositories which reduce inventories and handle distribution. As in the United States, some academic societies and research institutions support loss-making publishing activities as a means to promote their scholarly purpose. In Eastern Europe, international book publication and sales are an important source of hard currency, and state-run trading companies act to maximize foreign earnings. Rapid political changes which can lead to the privatization of some publishing activities will alter this situation.

The scale of operation required to serve worldwide markets has tended to encourage the emergence of larger, full-service publishers and vendors. Competitive forces have reshaped European publishing and bookselling. Even so, many U.S. acquisitions librarians approach Europe's book markets as though they were independent fragmented fiefdoms, and often they select a single vendor to serve their needs in each. In fact, the book trade in western Europe, as in the United States, is becoming internationalized and normalized, and the borders between sellers' markets, if not wholly obscured, are less formidable barriers than they once were.

As in the United States, the past two decades have seen a wave of major mergers and acquisitions that have changed the look and size of many European companies involved in the book trade. The result of this trend has been very straightforward: fewer publishers produce most books and increasingly publishers have become specialists in select disciplines. They have also become more internationally oriented and appear to have adopted many of the same practices of their U.S. counterparts.

The example of the Netherlands illustrates this development well. From a country whose rich bookselling tradition supported a score of small- and medium-sized book firms, most of which published in all subjects and disciplines, two international powerhouses—Elsevier and Kluwer—dominate the Dutch book trade today. The two now produce more books in English than the rest of the publishing industry in the entire country does in Dutch. With a small demand from their domestic market, their orientation is overwhelmingly international in scope, and they search for specialized market niches—such as Elsevier's renown in the sciences—where they perceive a competitive advantage. The location of their Dutch home base is almost a quaint historical artifact. The United States, where both houses maintain a large presence, is the biggest market for both. For the U.S. librarian, acquiring their publications is no more difficult than getting them from any large U.S. publisher.

FIXED RETAIL PRICING

In the broadest sense, the organization of the European book trade is based on historical models that found their origins in developments in Germany and England dating back to the beginning of book printing and the guild traditions of each land. Both traditions take the view that reading material should be available to all buyers at the same price wherever books are sold. In both systems, the bookshop occupies a central role. The American concept of the specialized institutional vendor serving as an intermediary between the publisher and librarian is unknown in European tradition. Libraries acquired books through the bookshop which combined the retail and wholesale selling function. Institutional sales to libraries, therefore, emerged as a sideline to the booksellers' role as retail shop, and many of Europe's most important institutional vendors—England's Blackwell's is a prominent example—still function both as bookshop and institutional intermediary.

Both the German and British book trade models, therefore, reinforce a common basic principle of fixed retail pricing. Unlike the prevailing practice in most other industries where manufacturer's suggested prices are not binding, prices in the European book trade are fixed by publishers, and vendors are legally bound

The Publishing Industry

to sell at a uniform fixed price to all buyers, with few exceptions. Price setting in the book trade in Italy and Spain is not bound by legal arrangements but by the manufacturers' suggested price, which allows discounts to be passed on to nonprofit institutions such as libraries.

Because fixed pricing eliminates competition between the publisher and the bookseller, their relationship is amiable. Conveniently, many booksellers also have become publishers and many publishers also are booksellers. To make the "marriage" work, in some countries publishers are not allowed to sell directly to the public, making the bookseller the only point where books can be obtained. In the West German model, for instance, this relationship has been formalized by a convention between publishers and booksellers. If a librarian orders directly from the publisher, the publisher will simply refer the library order to the distributor; the library receiving clerk may not even know that the order has traveled this route. In some countries of course, publishing houses will supply books directly, but the smaller publishing houses shy away from this practice.

Generalizations about European book trade can only be carried so far. While it may not be entirely misleading to view the most prominent international publishers and vendors as representing the European book trade, local rules and regulations that govern competition within each national market remain important. Anyone who has ever spent any time in Europe knows that Europeans do not shed traditions easily. Despite all of these homogenizing trends, parochial practices still abound, and it is useful to review some of the country-specific business practices of the European book trade before turning again to the consequences of the internationalization of publishing and bookselling on the buying practices of U.S. acquisitions librarians. Table 1 is a country-by-country listing of the basic features of the national book trades.

As the brief survey in Table 1 shows, there are significant small differences between European markets. But, except in the case of the state-controlled East European book trade where the librarian often has no choice with whom he or she deals, these differences are not so significant that they should govern the librarian's selection of a vendor. The librarian new to the field of foreign acquisitions should consult *The Book Trade of the World*,[2] an

---

2. Siegfred Taubert, ed., *The Book Trade of the World*. Vol. 1, Europe and International Section (Hamburg: Verlag für Buchmarkt-Forsung; London: André Deutsch, New York: Bowker, 1972).

Jana K. Stevens

TABLE 1 Pricing and Publishing Practices of East and West Europe

Country	Pricing and publishing practices
Austria	Prices fixed by law; exports are taxfree
Belgium	Prices fixed by law; direct orders to publishers discouraged
Bulgaria	Prices are fixed, with occasional fluctuations permitted; purchases made through government-designated agencies only; publishing is nationalized
Czechoslovakia	Price set by size and type of book, not actual production costs; purchases made through government agencies only
Denmark	Net price is same as retail price; steep VAT, except on exports
Finland	No fixed prices on books
France	Prices fixed since 1981; VAT, except on exports
West Germany	Prices fixed by publishers; small discounts for library sales; geographically-designated wholesalers handle book distribution
Greece	Prices fixed by publisher, with discounts to wholesalers and libraries
Hungary	Prices set by size and type of book, not actual production costs; prices are fixed
Italy	Prices fixed by publishers; discounts available to wholesalers and booksellers
Netherlands	Prices fixed, with discounts available to wholesalers, booksellers, schools, and libraries
Norway	Prices fixed, with limited discounts available to libraries; books are not taxed
Poland	Prices fixed by state; most publishing is state owned
Portugal	Prices guided by publisher recommendations; discounts generally are not available
Romania	Prices set by size and type of book, not by actual production costs; publishing handled by state
Spain	Prices fixed by publishers, with generous discounts available, particularly for older books; exported titles are not taxed
Sweden	Prices recommended by publisher, with generous discounts to libraries available
Switzerland	Prices fixed by publishers; books are not taxed; small discounts available to libraries
Turkey	Prices recommended by publishers; book trade somewhat unorganized, making purchase by U.S. libraries difficult; exchange programs recommended
U.S.S.R.	Prices fixed by government; exported books handled by a government agency, Mezhdunarodnaia Kniga; short print runs for most titles; exchange programs recommended
United Kingdom	Prices fixed at net price; no VAT on exported books
Yugoslavia	Prices fixed by publishers, with discounts available in practice

encyclopedic guide to the world book trade. Volume one of this three volume set is devoted to Europe and provides an international overview containing invaluable data. Though this work needs updating, it is still the best source available. The most complete directory of booksellers and publishers is *The International Literary Market Place*.[3] It is a helpful starting place for identifying publishing houses and specialist vendors, which are listed by country. For the major European book markets—Britain, France and Germany—the national trade association of each produces a booklet containing relevant information on the country's book trade.[4] All are available free of charge.

INTERNATIONALIZATION

A close relationship between the bookseller and publisher on the one hand and the American library on the other, based on years of doing business together, has been the traditional way that business has been conducted in the past. Maintaining that direct personal link has merits that are worth preserving in the absence of a compelling reason to change suppliers. Well-established clients can usually count on receiving preferential treatment. Ideally, the choice of vendor should be based on the quality of services that the vendor offers and the vendor's reliability confirmed by the librarian's experience. The local rules of publishing will take care of themselves. What is more important is how well the vendor takes care of his or her customer.

Fortunately, the services that vendors offer are becoming more comprehensive than at any time in the past. The competitive and economic forces that have reshaped the trade practices of Europe's giant publishers and vendors have also transformed life for their surviving smaller European rivals. The recent strategy of the traditional smaller-scale book dealers has been to imitate the behavior of the large firms. Many publishers are carving out a new role for themselves by acquiring translation rights to the works of foreign authors. Some have become narrow subject spe-

3. *The International Literary Marketplace* (New York: Bowker, Annual).
4. *How to Obtain German Books and Periodicals* (Frankfurt am Main: Boersenverein des Deutschen Buchhandels, 1982); *How to Obtain French Books* (Paris: Syndicat National de l'edition, Bureau d'information et de liasion pour l'exportation, 1985); *How to Obtain British Books* (London: Publishers Association, 1982).

Jana K. Stevens

cialists concentrating on serving specific market needs. And they
are often broadening their business base by reaching across
Europe's national boundaries to embrace markets where a common language is spoken and read.

Obviously, language remains one of the biggest areas that
differentiates European book trade, but even this traditionally
divisive barrier to internationalization of the book industry is
melting away. English has become the common language of business convenience for the world book trade, but linguistic borders
remain important determinants of how the European publishing and bookselling industry is organized. Language boundaries
may still narrow the outlook and market reach of many of
Europe's book dealers, but the strongest publishers and vendors
are moving beyond the limitations of a small home language base.

In some countries, the challenge of competing for a small home
market has driven book dealers to find new ways to be competitive in a larger international arena. Publishers in the Netherlands serve a very small Dutch readership, and the great
publishing houses could not have survived had they not merged
and aggressively sought markets outside of their home language
base. West German publishing, on the other hand, serves a large
German language population outside of West Germany's borders
in Switzerland, East Germany, and Austria. Similarly, relatively
small Austrian publishers and book dealers can sell to the same
relatively wide German language market. France may be the
home of French language publishing, but the economic vitality
of France's book trade gets a big boost from its close ties to the
Francophone countries of Belgium, French Canada, and French-
speaking Africa. Because languages cross national borders, it
should not surprise anyone to learn that business practices look
broadly similar across the continent.

Tradition and local practice is further complicated by the fact
that in some European countries there is not one but several official languages. The best example illustrating how complex multi-
language publishing in one country can be is in Switzerland. The
organization of the Swiss book trade reflects the fact that three
distinct language cultures coexist within a small geographic
area. The Schweizerische Buchhandler und Verleger Verband
(SBVV) is responsible for the organization of Switzerland's German speaking publishers, the Association Suisse des Editeurs
de la Langue Francaise (ASELF) organizes the country's French
publishing, and the Societa degli Editori della Svizzera Italiana
(SeSI) is the controlling agency for the Swiss Italian language

publishing industry. These trade associations extend the reach and clout of the Swiss book industry beyond the small home language base.[5]

In recent years, there have even been signs of a movement away from language-specific publishers and vendors, each specializing in the language of a principal market. Now the trend is toward cross-national alliances between publishers and vendors based on the vendor's ability to provide a broader range of service to librarians in the market where the vendor sells. The German book jobber Harrasowitz, for example, has taken over the job as the intermediary between North America and publishers in France, a cross-national link that would have been hard to imagine a decade ago.

The case of Harrasowitz is instructive because it illustrates well the trend toward a more service-oriented relationship between libraries and vendors that overrides parochial national considerations. Harrasowitz is a century-old, family-owned firm that has long been the biggest book dealer handling German orders from North America. It expanded into the French market in the early 1980s when France's government-supported Syndicat Cercle de la Librarie lost its funding and cut its services. One of the areas cut was the advanced processing of bibliographic information on forthcoming books in print, a service that American librarians had come to expect. No private French bookseller foresaw the consequence of this action, and none was either interested or had the resources to provide this service independently. As a result, U.S. libraries that relied on this service for their selection purposes were only too happy to discover that their German supplier who had always professed the ability to obtain French materials aggressively took up this challenge. Since then, Harrasowitz has become the biggest exporter of French books to North America.[6]

RELATIONS BETWEEN EUROPEAN SELLERS AND AMERICAN LIBRARIANS

Unfortunately, many European booksellers still perceive their role as order-takers rather than as a dynamic one of active part-

---

5. Peter Oprech, Schweizerischer Buchhaendler- und Verlager Verband, correspondence with J. Stevens, November 25, 1985.
6. Marie Chantal-Pridun, Syndicat National de l'edition, Paris, correspondence with J. Stevens, May 5, 1986.

nership. With the exception of the British for whom the U.S. market has always been extremely important, it appears that tradition has kept many European booksellers from being familiar with the American librarian's procedures. Too few European vendors have the resources to maintain direct ties with American libraries through regular visits to the United States where they can learn firsthand the requirements of their American clients. The profession needs to create more regular occasions that bring vendors and customers together to cultivate a more cooperative relationship based on closer personal contact. One mechanism to improve contact could be to establish forums at professional library conferences. The presence of large groups of librarians congregated in a single place would render it simpler and more economical for smaller European specialized publishers and vendors to meet their clients and discuss their libraries' requirements. Sponsored visits coordinated by the European trade groups is another way of bringing buyers and sellers together.

Until a mechanism is developed to improve contact, it will be up to individual libraries to negotiate the special requirements of their library, and librarians must make their needs clear to the vendors with whom they do business. Major European vendors are as fully capable as their American counterparts to provide approval and blanket order plans based on a subject or country, and to develop invoicing procedures that fit individual library needs. Since they often cannot give discounts, savings can be made elsewhere. For instance, many booksellers are willing to cover or split postage costs, which can be considerable.

Because discounts from European booksellers do not play the role they do in the United States, it will become more important for European vendors to compete on the quality of their services as the book trade continues to move toward a larger scale. Undeniably, one of the biggest changes in the European book trade has been that publishers and booksellers are now beginning to provide services to librarians that librarians formerly had to provide for themselves (for example, prepublication notification, approval plans, blanket order plans, and selection slips that eliminate much paperwork). Librarians with these services at their disposal from the vendor need only determine that the book exists and is not already a part of their library's collection. Where European vendors have made these services a part of their repertoire, order verification and processing have been made simpler, and library acquisition costs that would otherwise have gone to library personnel overhead can be devoted to new purchases.

European book trade has been complacent in the past, but new practices are emerging on this side of the Atlantic. Many in the European book trade still believe that when it comes to dealing with European markets, North American librarians have little option but to place their orders through a European firm familiar with the local market. To order European publications through an American intermediary, according to the industry rule of thumb, normally adds 10 to 25 percent to the final cost and causes inordinate delay in getting delivery.[7] But this last area of resistance to cross-border standardization of procedures may be in the process of breaking down. The major U.S. book supplier Baker & Taylor announced a joint venture with a Spanish vendor earlier this year. The company promises to deliver material from this traditionally difficult country, to do business quickly and efficiently, and to eliminate the cost penalty that has often come with placing an order through an American firm. Baker & Taylor and its Spanish partner may be able to offer the North American buyer the advantages of native access to the Spanish market along with the standard discounts and level of service that the U.S. market now expects. This move appears to be a promising one for the industry because it reinforces the trend that has been observed in the relationship between European sellers and North American buyers—a shift from the passive seller operating in a narrow market to the active seller serving the needs of more sophisticated institutional buyers. It will be interesting to watch this experiment which presages the arrival of a uniform book trade between North America and Europe.

---

7. Margaret F. Johnson, "Foreign Bookdealers and Collection Development," *Library Acquisitions: Practice and Theory* 1 (1977): 181–185.

Publishing and Export Bookselling in Western Europe

James Campbell[1]

Western Europe has traditionally been the second most important acquisitions area for North American libraries, and for scholarly libraries it was probably even more important than the
United States until well into this century. In the last few decades
there has been a seeming decline in European acquisitions, even
those from the English-speaking areas. The European share of
world publishing has also declined somewhat, but in absolute
numbers publishing in Western Europe has continued to expand,
following a trend for the largest publishing centers to grow
rapidly while the others stay steady or decline. European countries continue to produce books at a rate far greater than that
of other regions with much larger populations. Of the nine countries in the world reported in 1985 or 1986 as producing more
than 30,000 titles, four (West Germany, Great Britain, Spain, and
France) are in Europe, as are ten of the seventeen countries that
produced over 10,000 titles. In 1986, Spain, Britain, West Germany, and several smaller countries published four times as

1. The author is indebted to his colleagues C. Jared Loewenstein and George
Crafts for providing a Mediterranean perspective; to Theodore H. Campbell III
for his work on British prices; to Jane Maddox and Charles Fineman for their
help when printed works failed; and to members of ACRL's Western European Specialists Section, to many book dealers and publishers, and to Cornelia Kelley and
Alderman Library's Acquisitions Section for continuing his education over the years.

many books per capita as the United States, and Denmark published eight times as many.[2]

High levels of literacy and income support literary and other cultural publishing. The prosperous economies of the European countries allow them to invest large sums of money in scholarship and research, most of which is then published in Europe. Europe's prominent position in the world's book trade is also due to diversification and specialization. Publishers concentrating on particular subjects, whether nuclear physics, do-it-yourself manuals, or experimental poetry, exist in most countries. In addition to this type of specialization, Western Europe also has a complete parallel book trade—publishers and booksellers whose readers are not confined to one nation or even to one language area. Just as there have long been publishers and booksellers specializing in music who cross national boundaries through the universal language of musical notation, so these new specialists rely on the general use of English in scholarship, technology, and business and the specialized use of some other languages to produce books that are sold in many countries.

Often the reader is not even conscious of the origin of the book. The chairman of British Macmillan has noted, "It would not be untypical for a book of ours to be written in America, printed in Hong Kong on Japanese paper, and bound in German boards,"[3] and that same book might bear any of several imprints, depending on the market in which it was bought. European publishers have used their national bases to expand their operations and their sales territories; for example, they publish in English and buy companies and set up distribution arrangements in North America and elsewhere. Titles from these international companies and from European publishers who sell part of an edition to an American publisher make up a hidden European component of our acquisitions. Europe's importance for the English-

2. UNESCO, *Statistical Yearbook (Annuaire statistique)* (Paris: UNESCO, 1988), Tables 1.7 (population) and 6.1 (book production); Chandler B. Grannis, "Balancing the Books," *Publishers Weekly* 235 (June 2, 1989): 42–45. Variations in coverage of countries (for example, the UENSCO figures cover only UNESCO members, so Chinese data appear only after 1980, U.S. figures are not currently included, and the Middle East is underrepresented) and in the way data are reported make the historical trends somewhat difficult to compare, and the various national book trade sources often record figures quite different from those of UNESCO. Some of my conclusions about the world book trade were suggested by the analyses of UENSCO data in Stefano Mauri, *Ol libro in Italia: Geografia, produzione, consumo* (Milan: Hoepli, 1987), 1–12.
3. The Earl of Stockton, "Publishers' Pricing II," *Bookseller* (June 9, 1989): 1940.

James Campbell

language book market, the importance of Europe generally in world trade, and the fact that French, German, and Spanish are, at least for the time being, the most taught and read languages in North America mean that Western Europe will continue for a while as the most important foreign supplier to North American libraries.

The rush by so many publishers to get a share of the world English language market is exerting an upward pressure on prices for academic and business publications. A 1989 British study suggests that the market for such publications is overcrowded, that too many titles are being produced, and that sales and print runs of individual books are down and costs are consequently up.[4] So even more international mergers will probably occur.

Other changes are also taking place in European publishing. The scholarly book trade will be affected in as yet undetermined ways by electronic publishing and other technological advances, and possibly also by the library reaction to current methods of journal pricing. Trade publishing and some forms of specialized publishing will continue to consolidate as a few big firms with a strong financial base come to dominate the national markets and seek new expansion possibilities beyond their traditional areas. This internationalization of the world book trade is evening out some of the historical differences among the countries. The European Community (EC), an economic and political association whose members include Ireland, Britain, Denmark, West Germany, Belgium, the Netherlands, Luxembourg, France, Spain, Portugal, Italy, and Greece, seems likely to increase the pace. The community's intention is to remove all barriers to the movement of goods between members by 1992, and to that end it is making efforts to "harmonize" such things as industrial standards, tax laws, and pricing policies. These efforts are giving an added impetus to publishing mergers across national and linguistic lines, and there are signs that the retail book trade will also begin to cross borders, probably helped by the speed and ease of the various electronic ordering and billing systems now in use in Europe, some of which already cross national boundaries.[5]

4. "Markets and Prices," *Bookseller* (May 15, 1989): 1622.

5. European Communities Commission, *Completing the Internal Market: White Paper from the Commission to the European Council* (Luxembourg: European Communities, 1985) provides an overview of the planning for 1992. Recent summaries of developments and attempts at prediction include W. Gordon Graham, "The Shadow of 1992," *Publishers Weekly,* 234 (December 23, 1988): 24–26; "1992 and All That: A PW Round Table," *Publishers Weekly,* 235 (February 3, 1989): 21–28 (2/3/1989); "The Book Trade in 1988," *Bookseller,* (December 23 and 30, 1988): 2344–2346; and "1992 and a Free Market Europe," *British Book News*

Library suppliers, too, are merging and expanding their traditional bases of operation. As they offer ever more varied services in their competition for customers, the larger vendors with a better capital position are developing an advantage through computerization, better communication with customers, and the ability to provide management data and information services for new publications. What follows is an overview of the current state of publishing and library bookselling for exports; the ways in which the European circumstances differ from those in North America are emphasized.

PUBLISHING

Only seldom will American libraries find it useful to send orders directly to a European commercial publisher. Many microfilmers and reprinters will sell to libraries, and some even prefer not to go through vendors, and of course there are a few publishers who specialize in direct sales. Most scholarly and virtually all trade publishers, however, prefer not to deal with individual or institutional customers. In many cases orders and even inquiries sent to a publisher will be passed on to a bookstore for fulfillment. Even if a publisher does provide the item, several problems may occur: retail price agreements often prevent any discount to libraries, outside of Britain and Ireland, correspondence and invoices are unlikely to be in English; and prepayment may be required or additional charges for shipping or check conversion may be imposed. Although most library orders will go to a vendor, we cannot understand or negotiate with our suppliers without some knowledge of their suppliers, the publishers.

Vendors can differ greatly in their services and in their personalities, but a certain similarity is forced on them by the need to present a face to the customer. Publishers operate in much more varied circumstances and have much more varied goals. They are more affected, although less so every day, by being a part of historical traditions that vary from one region to another. Thus it is difficult to generalize about European publishing, and it is impossible in this space to give a detailed

(December 1988): 874. Derek Greenwood, "Books and Electronic Data Transmission," *British Book News* (January 1989): 16–17, compares the development of electronic transmission of commercial transactions for the book trade to the electronic exchange of bibliographic data among libraries.

introduction to the publishing activities of each country.[6]

The types of publishing that we know in North America are generally also present in Western Europe—big trade houses, ambitious younger publishers, old and new scholarly houses, small presses publishing literary and regional titles, scholars putting out their own specialized books, official publishing, reprinters, microfilmers. Even the smallest countries are likely to have examples of all these kinds of publishers, although there are fewer of them with smaller lists. European trade publishers have some problems that are not common in North America: value-added tax rates, fees for library use, and competition from cheaper English language originals. For some countries and publishers, exports are a much larger issue than they are in North America. Still, a reader of *Publishers Weekly* who looks at *Boekblad*, *Livres hebdo*, *DeLibros*, or any of the other European book trade journals will find much that is familiar; the same concern with blockbuster bestsellers; the same kinds of self-help books, cookbooks, and children's books; the same problems with computers, television tie-ins, individual stores, chains, and book clubs; and the same concern for the future of the business.

Mergers and Acquisitions

Mergers and acquisitions are a fact of life in Western Europe just as they are in North America. Some of them take place within one country, some of them cross national boundaries, and some cross the ocean. They affect specialized publishers as well as large trade publishers. Acquiring or increasing a share in the very large English language market concentrates takeover activity on Britain and North America, but Spain, with its rapidly growing internal market and potential for Latin American sales, has also attracted attention. For example, Italy's Mondadori and Fabbri, France's Hachette, and Britain's Longman have acquired interests in major Spanish publishers, and the Dutch Wolters Kluwer group has acquired several Spanish legal publishers. The name Wolters Kluwer demonstrates another common phenomenon. The big takeovers, particularly those involving Rupert Murdoch or Robert Maxwell, get the most publicity, but there

6. Peter Curwen, *The World Book Industry* (London: Euromonitor, 1986), discusses the larger Western European countries in detail. An outdated but still useful introduction to the individual countries can be found in Siegried Taubert, ed., *The Book Trade of the World*. Vol. 1 (Hamburg: Verlag für Buchmarket-Forschung; Paris: André Deutsch; New York: R. R. Bowker, 1972).

are also many companies that join together more or less amicably to gain the advantages of scale or to dominate a market. Wolters and Kluwer were, with Elsevier, the largest firms in the Dutch market and had substantial interests elsewhere. They joined and immediately used the new capital base to increase their rate of expansion. Incidentally, Elsevier was not altogether left out. It owns a sizable percentage of the stock in the new company and will profit from any success of its rivals. This type of interlocking ownership is common among the larger companies and has caused speculation about a decline of competition in specialized areas of publishing. Any such effect, however, is more likely to show up in serials publishing, where each new journal requires a substantial outlay of capital before it starts to make a profit. Still, as companies are bought or merge, doing away with some of the separate imprints and closing some less profitable book areas, it sometimes seems as though there will soon be only one enormous publisher left. So far though, each year brings new publishers. Often they begin their lists by taking on one of the specialized areas rejected by the big firms. Indeed, a recent study found that one third of the books published in France during 1988 and one quarter of the French books in print that year came from firms established within the last fifteen years.[7]

The trend to mergers and the integration efforts of the EC will only accelerate a process that is already well under way in European trade publishing, that of spreading out the risk of publishing a book by arranging in advance for editions in various countries and languages. Art books, illustrated children's books, and other works such as popular encyclopedias on nature, gardening or cooking are frequent candidates for this treatment. Such books have a transnational appeal, often require expensive color printing, and can be translated fairly cheaply and quickly. There are differences in marketing from one country to another, but language and the problem of translation are the major barriers to greater cooperation among trade publishers,[8] and, in general,

---

7. "Les petits éditeurs ferment de l'édition," *Livres hebdo,* 9 (May 22, 1989): 31–32 reporting on Jean-Marie Bouvaist and Jean-Guy Boin, *Du printemps des éditeurs à l'âge de raison, les nouveaux éditeurs en France (1974–1988)* (Paris: La Documentation française/La Decouverte, 1989).

8. See the comments by British, French, and German publishers in Craig R. Whitney, "No Common Market in Book Publishing," *New York Times* (March 28, 1989): C15, C19. As his title suggests, Whitney is dubious about a European market for books but he focuses on bestseller lists and ignores both the numbers of children's books, exercise books, and so on that are translated and also the market for scholarly and business books.

James Campbell

language differences represent the biggest obstacle to internationalization. Certainly English is important for specialized publishing, but it is much less so for the market in general and popular books. *Publishers Weekly,* which had been considering putting out a European edition, announced early in 1989 the decision that an English language trade journal for all of Europe would not be viable.

Although language problems prevent many joint development projects, there is a lively traffic in rights to publish national editions among European countries and across the Atlantic. Generally, but by no means always, the works originate in the larger language areas.

Academic Publishing

In European academic publishing there are also similarities with what we know in North America. There are commercial publishers specializing in the sciences or social sciences and there are noncommercial publishers in research institutes, university departments, and the basements of scholars. In some countries, there are also large state-sponsored publishers, such as C.N.R.S. in France, and there are national peculiarities such as the Italian banks that issue quite substantial and usually beautifully produced monographs. Learned societies and academies, also often with some relationship to the state, are still common in most of Western Europe, though they do not have quite the importance that they do in contemporary Eastern Europe. University presses do not exist in some countries and nowhere do they dominate scholarly publishing to the degree that their North American counterparts do. Outside of Britain their activity often concentrates on the work of professors at that university and the dissertations of students, perhaps with a few specialized series started by professors. A similar role is often played by commercial publishers that have a close tie to the university in the same town. The publisher may have had its origin in a bookstore or may have been involved in printing dissertations, and today still it publishes lectures and scholarly series originating at that university. Many of these publishers have also developed one or two academic areas in which they specialize. These and other specialized publishers still account for most of the scholarly output in the social sciences and humanities and a sizable share of science publishing. The large number of publishers with two or three specialties makes it difficult to have a publisher-based approval plan for a European country.

The scholarly monographic series is a type of publication that is more common on the European continent, especially in the German-speaking countries, in the Netherlands, and in Scandinavia, than it is in the English-speaking world. When library budgets were fatter, many academic libraries used the monographic series as a gathering mechanism. Publishers took that into account, and many series came into being that had no real focus or that lacked adequate quality control. With the budgetary constraints of the eighties, particularly with the inflation in serials budgets, many libraries have reviewed and canceled these marginal series in favor of individual selection or an approval plan with the possibility of returns. This was a necessary and probably even an overdue correction, but a clearly defined series from a good publisher is still a good way to acquire books. European scholarly publishers do specialize and will often put all their works on a given subject into one or two series, so that subscriptions to series can offer the advantages of the publisher-based approval plan: predictability of what will be received, general quality, and ease of handling.[9] Returns are not possible, but if the series are carefully selected, that should not be a problem.

Government Publishing

Government publishing is perhaps the aspect of European publishing that is most different from its counterpart in the United States, principally because each Western European country has a distinctive pattern of official publication. Most countries (West Germany is an exception) have an official publisher, like the United States' Government Printing Office, but the degree of centralization and the control exercised by that agency vary greatly from country to country. The proportion of centrally issued titles ranges from a few titles to almost 100 percent of Swedish national publications. Other publications are often issued directly by the agencies concerned.

Increasingly common is a publisher or distributor of govern-

---

9. For a more extended discussion of the advantages of the publisher-based approval plan, see Karen A. Schmidt, "Capturing the Mainstream: Publisher-based and Subject-based Approval Plans in Academic Libraries," *College & Research Libraries,* 47 (July 1986): 365–369.

ment publications that is a public corporation. The Belgians have had such a system since 1962 and the Portuguese since 1969, and the Dutch and Austrians have more recently adopted variations of it. Such institutions usually have a degree of autonomy and contract with various agencies to distribute their titles. In West Germany for many years and more recently in other countries and in the EC, privatization has been a factor in official publishing. Titles with commercial possibilities, such as editions of laws, are contracted out to publishers, as are titles intended to reach a broad audience (the latter sometimes receive a subsidy from the originating agency to keep the price down). These titles are of course readily available from booksellers, and frequently titles published by a central government printer will also be available through the book trade. Publications issued by a specific agency are usually best acquired from that agency.[10]

Availability of European Books

Many people have heard about one major difference between North American and European publishers, namely that the specialized publishers in Europe are less likely to remainder or pulp their unsold copies and that books therefore stay in print much longer. Unfortunately, this is an area in which the two continents have drawn much closer in recent years. There are still a very few publishers, mostly nonprofit groups or specialists in religion, that have some less popular titles from the first half of this century or even from the last century available. World War II, however, destroyed a lot of older stock all over Europe, and the rebuilding of destroyed libraries, the expansion of research libraries, and the opening of new universities claimed many of the books that survived. In some countries, tax policies now do not favor holding large stocks. Everywhere the inability of small firms to tie up too much capital in unsold titles has limited edition sizes, although not yet to the extent true in Eastern Europe where length of time and in print is measured in

---

10. *Official Publications of Western Europe*, edited by Eve Johansson, Vols. 1–2 (London: Mansell, 1984–1988), is primarily concerned with the publications themselves, but W. David Rozkuszka's "The Art and Acquisition of Foreign Official Publications" in volume 1 (pp. 1–11) contains much practical advice, and each of the essays on a country has a brief section called either official publishing or manner of publication.

weeks or months. It is still true that there is less remaindering of scholarly titles in Europe than in North America, so European books tend to stay in print a little longer, but for both sides of the Atlantic the best practice is to buy the book when it comes out.

Finding out whether or not a European book has been published or is in print can be a challenge. Good and fairly current national bibliographies exist in most countries (although the Irish bibliography is annual, the Italian is normally late and has occasionally been suspended, and the Spanish is also slow). In many countries supplementary tools serve the book trade, such as the list of books received in *Books Ireland* or the new publications list in *Giornale della Libreria*. Still, many libraries do not get these publications or do not have the time to use them; instead, they rely on lists from vendors. OCLC and other bibliographic utilities are also a help in verification of new titles, especially with the availability of UKMARC and the possibility that other European versions of MARC may also be added to databases. Many titles, however, including some from Britain, are out of print long before they appear in our bibliographic utilities, and libraries should not insist on finding cataloging copy before ordering.

Verification of a book's current availability can be especially difficult. The larger countries (Britain, Italy, Spain, and the French- and German-speaking regions) have reference works that list titles in-print, but they all have the problem of any large annual work: by the time the data are gathered and the book is printed and distributed, the information is out of date. CD-ROM and microfiche editions now provide greater currency in some cases, but are far too expensive for most American libraries. Various of the smaller countries have tried to publish regular lists of in-print titles (for example, currently there is a Norwegian books in print), but their smaller markets and today's short store life for books generally have kept these undertakings from being successful. Curiously, there are in-print lists for some of the very smallest book trades, those of such minority languages as Scottish Gaelic, Rumantsch, Faroese, and Frisian. In these cases the small number of titles and of publishers makes the lists relatively easy to compile, and compilation and publication are usually supported by some sort of cultural organization. Publishers' catalogs used to provide a good supplement to the national lists, but increasingly publishers issue only brochures for their new titles.

James Campbell

The backlist is less important to them, and the cost of preparing and mailing a list of all their titles is prohibitive. For the newest titles and for all titles in the countries that do not have a list of books in print, most libraries can only send off an order and see if it is successful. As a general rule, this is worth trying on trade books for one to two years after publication and for scholarly books for at least three or four years, unless the topic is one in which information is quickly dated. In either case the vendor should be told that a later edition or a quality paperback will also be acceptable. Societies and academies may well have material available for longer periods of time, but university departments and research institutes often do fairly small printings that will be available only for a short time. For these and for official publications librarians should be willing to accept a lower standard of order information. In particular, price will often be missing from the bibliographic citation. It can either be estimated based on experience with similar titles, or the vendor might be asked not to supply if the item costs over a certain amount. A letter to confirm information about a $5.00 research report will cost more to prepare than an order form and may well not be answered before the report is out of print.

International Perspective of European Publishers

Both tradition and economic forces give European publishers a more international perspective than is common in the United States, and both the worldwide market for English language books and its largest component in North America have attracted much attention from Europeans. Some have chosen to enter that market by expanding their existing operations (Germany's Springer-Verlag now has offices in five countries outside the German-speaking area and 60 percent of its list is in English), and, as we have seen, others have expanded by acquisition.

But the transnational, transatlantic giants are not the only publishers to be concerned with the international book trade. The export of books, particularly scholarly books, is a major element in European publishing. British publishers, admittedly an extreme case, derive over 30 percent of their total profits from exports, and it has been estimated that for scholarly imprints the figure is well over 50 percent.[11] The British figures are so high not only because of the traditional emphasis in British publishing on exports to the Commonwealth countries and to the United States, but also because the British have natural access to the large English language market. Thus Oxford University Press estimates that 40 percent of the 10,000 copies of the *Oxford English Dictionary's* second edition will be sold in the United States, followed by 30 percent in Japan, only 20 percent in Britain and all the rest of Europe, and 10 percent in the rest of the world, for a total of 85 to 90 percent of sales outside of Britain and 40 to 45 percent of sales outside the English-speaking countries.[12] The other large Western European publishing countries come well behind the British export volume, but Spain exports to Latin America; France exports to Belgium, Switzerland, Canada, and the former French colonies; and West Germany exports trade books to Austria and Switzerland and scholarly works in German, English, and other languages all over the developed world.[13]

Portugal has a market in its former colonies, but the other smaller countries lack an outlet for materials in their languages. The Netherlands and the Scandinavian countries have met this problem by publishing in other languages. This is not a new solution for the Netherlands, where many of the Humanists published their research in Latin, where seventeenth century

11. Curwen, *The World Book Industry,* p. 78; Christopher Hurst, "Publishing: the View from King Street," in *The Eternal Triangle: Proceedings of the Second Annual Conference of the National Acquisitions Group 1987* (Loughborough: National Acquisitions Group, 1988), p. 12. Hurst's essay is an excellent introduction to the situation of an independent scholarly publisher.

12. Israel Shenker, "Annals of Lexicography (O.E.D.)," *The New Yorker* (April 3, 1989): 99. The dictionary's production is also an interesting example of transatlantic effort: the editorial and administrative work was done in Oxford, but with equipment provided by a grant from IBM's wholly owned British subsidiary and with programming help from the Canadian University of Waterloo; the keying into machine-readable form was done in Pennsylvania by a company owned by the British Reed publishing group; and the actual printing was done in Massachusetts by Rand McNally.

13. It is possible to identify general levels of export, but it is very difficult to identify trends or to be too specific because the statistics are so variable. Figures for monetary value of exports are skewed by exchange rate fluctuations. Figures for numbers of books are skewed by the internationalization of the printing industry. Books with title pages saying they were published in one country may be shipped by their printer in a second country directly to a third country for sale. All figures are confused by reexports, for example, an American book imported into Britain and then resold to Ireland or Sweden. See Curwen, *The World Book Industry,* pp. 63−65 and Marie-Pierre Dillenseger, "Quelques reflexions sur le livre francais a l'etranger," *Bulletin des bibliogheques de France* 30, no. 2 (1985): 146.

James Campbell

refugees from Britain and Germany (including the Pilgrims) were able to continue publishing their tracts, and where many works of the French Enlightenment appeared in order to avoid censorship.[14] Publication in other languages became even more common in the smaller countries during the nineteenth century, when their scholars were concerned to reach an audience outside their national boundaries. They wrote in the international scholarly languages, mostly German, French, or English, but they published locally. Publishers like Brill and Nijhoff acquired a reputation for quality and were sought out by scholars from other countries as well. These international publishers and other publishers like the Norwegian University Press or Almqvist and Wiksell, who distribute mostly the research of their country but not necessarily in the language of the country, and many academies, research institutes, university departments, and even government agencies, all continue to publish significant scholarly works.

Ordering European Books

To gain a greater share of the international market, publishers attempt to make their books known and have them distributed in as many countries as possible. A librarian could easily receive information about the same new title directly from a European publisher, from an American distributor, from a vendor in the original country of publication, and from a specialized vendor in yet another country. Where then should the library order the book? This question is especially hard to answer for British publishers because of the many different types of books they sell in North America and the many different types of distribution and pricing arrangements. British companies with offices in North

---

14. Exile and refugee publishing is still an interesting component of European publishing. The original Russian edition of Solzhenitsyn's *Gulag Archipelago* was published by the YMCA Press in Paris. There are publishers in Western Europe specializing in almost all the languages of Eastern Europe: Poles in England, Ukrainians in West Germany, Czechs in Switzerland, Lithuanians in Sweden, and many others. These European exiles have been joined by Iranians, by Afghans in Germany, Surinamese in the Netherlands, Algerians in France, and representatives from many other countries where poltiical opponents are made to feel uncomfortable. Now a certain amount of publishing is conducted by those who are economic exiles from their countries. Diana Chlebek and Michael W. Albin presented papers on exile and refugee publishing at the 1988 ACRL Western European Specialists Section Conference. Albin's article has been published ("Refugee and Exile Publishing in Western Europe," *College & Research Libraries News* 50 (May 1989): 381–385) and Chlebek's will appear in an upcoming issue of *Collection Management.*

America and the North American publishers and distributors who buy rights to sell certain books would argue that the library should buy from them. They provide a service to American libraries, bookstores, and readers by maintaining a stock and distribution system here and by providing information to American readers and libraries through advertising and review copies. The distributors rightly feel entitled to charge for those services, although librarians may sometimes disagree about how much they should charge, and they rightly argue that they are cheated when a library finds out about a book from their catalogs or listings in *Weekly Record* and then buys it from overseas.

However, there are many reasons why libraries, on occasion or systematically, buy the British rather than the American edition of a book. Perhaps the most obvious is that the library found out about a new publication from a British source, such as the *British National Bibliography* or a review in the *Times Literary Supplement*. Frequently, several months elapse between the publication of a title on one side of the Atlantic and its distribution on the other (Rushdie's *Satanic Verses* was in its fifth British printing before the first American edition appeared), so even if a check of OCLC or *Forthcoming Books* is made, it may not turn up an alternative edition. Speed is then the second reason for buying overseas, particularly now that most larger British vendors ship via airfreight. Anthony W. Ferguson's 1985 study of approval plans from British and American vendors found that the British book would have been received earlier 94.4 percent of the time and that in 84 percent of the cases the difference was over 30 days and could be as much as 144 days.[15] However, as this and other studies have pointed out, the library may have the book in hand but still not be able to find readily usable cataloging copy for the foreign edition. This situation has improved in the last few years as UKMARC has become widely available here, but even now many libraries, especially if they use LC classification, prefer to wait and buy the American edition. Alternatively, they may hold the British book until cataloging copy is available for the American edition and then modify the classification and subject tracings accordingly, but such a procedure nullifies the speed advantage in some cases and adds to processing costs.

Still, if there is no indication, such as a CIP record on one of the bibliographic networks or a listing in *Forthcoming Books,* that

15. "British Approval Plan Books: American or British Vendor?," *Collection Building,* 8, no. 4 (1987): 20.

there will be an American edition, it is not advisable to wait and assume there will be one sometime. Ferguson found that 19.8 percent of the titles supplied by a British approval plan vendor in 1985 would not have been supplied by the library's United States vendor.[16] Even allowing for some differences in selection policy between the two vendors, this and my own less systematic observations suggest that there are a number of British scholarly books that do not find American distributors. Ferguson believes these are works of less interest to North American libraries, and subject matter undoubtedly does play a role in many decisions to take on a book, but American distributors generally require a large discount before they will import part of an edition, so that good, but moderately priced scholarly books may also not find their way across the Atlantic.

The third and most controversial reason for sometimes preferring the foreign edition its price. Publishers determine whether they can afford to publish a book and what its price or prices will be by complicated formulas, different ones for each type of book they sell.[17] Basic ingredients in each formula include the publisher's editorial and general business costs, the cost of manufacturing and of advertising and distribution, the desired profit level for publisher, bookseller, and author, and finally the price each intended market will pay for the item. If a publisher anticipates that a book will sell to a very limited market—for example, to specialized libraries and a very few individuals in Britain—then the typesetting and printing costs plus overhead will have to be covered by sales of a small number of relatively highly priced copies. If sales can be increased, either by more advertising or by selling the book in other markets, then the publisher is more likely to decide to bring the book out and occasionally may even be able to reduce the price.

What more typically happens is that the publisher retains a relatively high price for hardback copies to be sold to domestic libraries, then sells part of the edition overseas at a discount, and possibly brings out a paperback edition aimed at individual

---

16. Ibid., p. 21.

17. Christopher Hurst, "Publishing: the View from King Street," in *The Eternal Triangle: Proceedings of the Second Annual Conference of the National Acquisitions Group 1987* (Loughborough: National Acquisitions Group, 1988), p. 16 the Earl of Stockton, op. cit., pp. 1939–1942, are good introductions to pricing practice. Hurst's discussion of discounting to overseas distributors is especially interesting.

buyers. Paperback editions of scholarly books and increasingly of some other titles are frequently published in Britain at the same time as the hardback edition. So that type does not have to be reset, they are commonly printed at the same time as the hardback, and, because it would add expense to change paper in the middle of a print run, these editions are normally printed on the same paper and have the same method of leaf attachment as the hardbound version. Only the cover and the price are different. The difference in manufacturing costs between hardbound and paperback books is fairly small, and developmental and sales costs are usually loaded onto the hardbound copies, so the paperback editions are priced at production and distribution cost plus profit. Paperback sales cut into hardcover sales, so the fixed costs are divided among an even smaller number of even higher priced hardbound copies. Price differences of $20.00 between paperback and hardcover are common and $30 to $35 differences are not unheard of. Of course, any library that purchases the paperback has to consider not only binding costs, including staff costs, but also the loss of use of the new book while it is at the bindery.

Sales outside the United Kingdom, whether in the industrialized nations of Europe and Asia or in the Commonwealth and the United States, have long been an important way for British publishers to increase edition size. Sometimes a special cheap edition is done for sale in Asia and Africa. For a bestseller, where British and Commonwealth sales alone are enough to make for economical print runs, the rights for North American publication will be sold and a separate edition done, but most books do not sell enough copies to justify this extra expense. Instead the book may get a new title page and possibly a new jacket design; then the physical item is exported according to one of several possible arrangements.

The simplest form of export is for the book to be distributed by the North American office of the British publisher. At one time, only a few companies did this, but recently the trend to mergers and internationalization has made it the most common method of distribution. The two branches may or may not have the same name. For example, Macmillan Publishers UK Ltd. no longer has any connection to the American Macmillan Company and distributes in the United States through their subsidiary St. Martin's Press, which also acts under contract as a North American distributor for two other smaller British scholarly publishers, Manchester University Press and Berg Publishers. In some cases several British imprints that have been acquired by a larger firm

James Campbell

will be combined for American sales under what the owner feels is the best known name. They will be priced in one of two ways. Some prestigious scholarly publishers feel they can command a higher price in North America and charge as much as 25 to 30 percent over their British prices, though they may also offer library discounts and hold occasional sales. Other publishers with lower name recognition choose to set their prices more in line with similar American books. Their markup over the British price will reflect the additional cost of exporting, advertising, and distribution, and, especially when the dollar is falling, will include some factor to cover possible changes in exchange rates. Especially when the dollar is low, some publishers may absorb some of the costs to stay competitive and keep sales volume up, but a British book distributed in North America by the same publisher will usually cost more than it does in Britain.

Publishers that do not have an American branch or partner and still want to increase edition size by exporting will try to sell part of the print run and the rights to the North American market— either to an American publisher or to a company that specializes in import editions. Since the distributors' profits depend entirely on American sales, they have to price competitively and demand a substantial discount from the British publisher before they will take the book on. Since this discounting practice tends to drive up the British price of the book, the American edition will usually sell at a price well below the British, sometimes as much as $30 below.

For some titles they have not sold abroad, some British publishers will contract with companies that specialize in distributing foreign imprints in North America. The book retains its original title page, but a part of the edition is shipped to North America and the distributor mails out catalogs of titles available in America, arranges a listing in *Books in Print,* and from stock fills orders from American libraries and jobbers. American pricing will usually be above the British list price, but not much more than will cover the import and publicity costs. A vendor's discount can cancel the additional cost in some cases. Now that so many British companies have entered the American market or have become part of a transatlantic publishing operation, this type of distribution is becoming less common.

Unfortunately, the pricing situation changes,[18] and a library

---

18. Ferguson (p. 20) found that for Brigham Young's approval plans in 1983 it would have been cheaper to acquire the dual imprints from their American vendor and in 1985, from their British vendor.

that uses price as a factor in determining its acquisitions strategy will have to keep an eye on the relative value of the dollar and the pound. When the dollar is strong, the British edition will generally cost less to libraries. When the dollar is weak, the situation is much more complicated. Getting the American version will more often be cost-effective, but the type of distribution arrangement will determine the price. Books bought by an independent American distributor will almost always be cheaper than the original edition; books distributed by the American office of the original British publisher will tend to be more expensive. All of these pricing factors apply only to newly published books. Whether the dollar was weak or strong when a book was first priced will usually determine if a backlist title is less expensive here or in Britain, no matter what the distribution arrangement. Any discount from the library's American vendor should be figured in comparing prices. British vendors are required by the Net Book Agreement to charge full retail price. It is difficult to control the importing of single copies of a book because European publishers who have sold distribution rights to another company have no financial incentive to prevent sales to library suppliers for export, and since single copy purchases directly from Europe are not widespread enough to be a major factor in the sales of most importers. Thus little or no effort has been made to discourage libraries from ordering dual imprints from Britain. Libraries should be aware that in a changed economic situation attempts could be made to enforce book distribution agreements, just as publishers have exerted pressure on vendors and libraries to enforce their serials prices.

Continental publishers, both scholarly and business publishers with a substantial part of their lists in English, also have American operations, and some of the Dutch publishers have begun to originate a part of their lists in the United States. As a general rule, they import part of an edition as soon as it's printed, so their titles are available fairly quickly on this side of the Atlantic. The amount of stock held here varies somewhat from publisher to publisher, and it is possible to experience delays when backlist titles have to be restocked from Europe.

It is difficult to generalize about pricing policy for the continental publishers, although most of them follow one of two courses. A few price their stock in the original currency and then convert that price to dollars when they invoice the order. Their dollar prices in catalogs, in the *Weekly Record,* or in *Books in Print* are approximations only. The library that orders from these publishers gets the European price, but it may have to pay shipping costs, something most larger European vendors absorb. Many of the more recently established American offices set a price when they import the edition or issue a catalog. Like any other publisher, they raise prices as needed, but the dollar price is fixed for a period of time. Most of these companies have set up their American branches to attract customers who do not wish to place foreign orders. Their interest is in increasing sales volume, so their markup over the European price is often fairly small, and, because they are usually specialized and largely interested in the library market, they will often sell directly to libraries, sometimes at a discount.

Finally, every year there are a few companies in *Books in Print* with an office number or a post office box listing titles from various European publishers; these companies hope to make a market for some titles that the original publisher could not sell or did not try to sell to a North American distributor. These companies usually do not have exclusive North American sales rights to their titles; they have simply bought a few copies at the bookstore discount in the hope of selling them. As a general rule, their prices will be a bit higher than the price when ordered from Europe. Their listed prices in *Books in Print* may be based on prepublication information or an old exchange rate. A library ordering from them may want to confirm the price first.

BOOKSELLING

There are four types of book dealers that a North American library might consider. Each has advantages and disadvantages, and none should be excluded out of hand for any type of library in a particular situation. The first is the North American vendor, who usually specializes in one or two of the larger language areas. These vendors maintain an international stock on this side of the Atlantic, and issue catalogs that can be used for selection. They correspond in English, invoice in dollars, can easily be phoned for rush orders and problems, and, if the book needed is in stock, may provide fast service. Their stocks typically consist of current bestsellers; a large selection of basic works on language and literature, including many paperbacks; and a basic selection of works in other subjects, more or less reflecting the typical demand for imports from that language area. For example, an Italian dealer may have more art books and a German dealer more theology. If a library has some special subject interest, the vendor may have relatively few of the needed titles in stock, and, since stocks are often fairly small, the vendor may no longer have all the items listed in the latest catalog. Of course, titles not held will be ordered, but with some dealers, perhaps because they do fewer special orders, this can take longer than ordering the title from a European vendor. Holding a large stock of foreign books requires a substantial investment, and, not unreasonably, that cost is usually passed along to customers; so domestic vendors will typically be a bit more expensive than vendors in Europe. Prices may also be affected, for better or for worse, by the exchange rate at which the stock was originally acquired.

The second common type of vendor is the export specialist in the country or language area where the book was published. Except in some of the smaller countries, where the exporter may work out of a bookstore, most of these dealers do not maintain a stock. Almost all export specialists in Western Europe can correspond in English, although until the library has some idea of a vendor's capabilities, letters should be simple and avoid unusual idiomatic expressions. Many exporters offer lists or slips with information on new books, and their situation makes them the most likely to provide accurate, up-to-date information and to deal well with problem books, such as small press items, publications of foundations, and university department publications. Often they will also search for out of print books. Most will invoice in dollars, usually noting the original price and stating the exchange rate. A few of the larger vendors now have permanent representatives in North America who visit libraries and handle customer relations. Shipment is normally by sea mail or, from some countries, by airfreight, and airmail is available for rush orders.

Few libraries deal solely with vendors in the country of a book's origin. Unless they have a special interest in some of the smaller countries, even the largest libraries will often use one dealer for each language area rather than have a separate vendor for Ireland, for French books from Belgium, or for German books from Switzerland. This is the third type of vendor. For a long time, some of the larger dealers have been willing to go beyond their own geographic or language area if a customer so requested. A library that needed a book from Norway or from Finland once every five years might ask one of its regular vendors to supply these items. In recent years, large vendors such as Nijhoff, Harrassowitz, and Blackwell have begun to offer this service on a

James Campbell

regular basis. Although they cannot offer the same level of expertise for all of Europe that they offer for their own specialties, such vendors are attractive to libraries that want to consolidate orders for many countries with one or two dealers who know the library's order and invoice requirements.[19]

The fourth type of dealer is the international vendor who specializes in particular subjects. For some subjects, such as music, there exists almost a parallel book trade. For many scholarly areas, the most important literature is produced by a relatively small group of publishers. The special library or the library with a few specialized needs may be served best by this type of dealer.

Even the small library may choose more than one type of vendor. In choosing among types or among vendors and in evaluating service, the acquisitions librarian will use many of the same criteria that apply to domestic vendors. There are, however, some issues that are more important for foreign vendors and some considerations that apply particularly to Europe. Fairness should be a concern in making a choice. If a vendor's information service is used, that vendor should get those orders. If a domestic dealer is used for rush orders or a geographic or subject specialist is used for hard-to-find items, that vendor should get a share of more normal orders. Otherwise they may not be able to stay in business to serve special needs.

INFORMATION

Bibliographic coverage varies a good deal in Western Europe. It is increasingly common for dealers to provide or supplement coverage with lists of new publications or slips that can also be used as order forms. Some are also experimenting with making information available electronically. Usually it is possible to get multiple copies of lists to distribute among library selectors or teaching faculty. Whether this information is important or not will depend on the country in question and on the library. For example, there are good national bibliographies for the Scandinavian countries and libraries with a serious interest in Scandinavian material will probably use them for selection. Libraries interested primarily in English language publications from Scan-

19. The work of Blackwell and Harrassowitz is described by members of their staffs in Theodore Samore, ed., *Acquisition of Foreign Materials for U.S. Libraries*, 2nd ed. (Metuchen, N.J.: Scarecrow Press, 1982), 42–85.

The Publishing Industry

dinavia (from 7 to 12 percent of total Scandinavian output)[20] may well prefer to use only the highly selective lists of such vendors as Almqvist and Wiksell, Munksgaard, and Akateeminen Kirjakauppa. For some countries, the national bibliographies may be slow or occasionally nonexistent; vendor lists will provide the only consistently reliable and comprehensive coverage of new materials. Lists from specialized vendors or slips matching a subject profile from international vendors can also save a great deal of time in selection. Vendors can also often obtain publishers' catalogs, an important service at a time when many publishers are reluctant to mail overseas, but they should be discouraged from including unrequested catalogs in book parcels if the library pays for postage. Libraries interested in audiovisual materials or other special formats should inquire if the vendor can also provide lists for them.

Timely and accurate information is an important factor for the acquisitions process. If a book is not ordered until it appears in one of the scholarly reviewing journals, it may already be out of print. If the information is not accurate and complete, the order may duplicate another order or it may not be understood by the publisher, causing delay or an erroneous report on the status of the publication.

Judging the quality of vendor-supplied information requires cooperation among the acquisitions librarian, the selectors, and the supervisor of preorder searching. Data should be in a format comprehensible to selectors and searchers. It is desirable that punctuation and forms of entry follow international standards, but North American librarians should remember that AACR2 is not spoken worldwide. Subject areas or brief classifications from the Library of Congress or Universal Decimal Classification systems are useful for ambiguous titles and for those who may have to sort slips by subject. Prices should be in the vendor's currency and no more than the publisher's suggested list prices, with any additional charges over the publisher's list price (for example, a service charge on titles not discounted by the publisher or a special shipping charge for a bulky item) clearly stated. If dollar equivalents are also supplied, it should be clear whether they are fixed prices or whether the exchange rate will be recalculated at the time of invoicing.

It is particularly important that information about each title

---

20. UNESCO, *Statistical Yearbook* (1988), Table 7.7.

be as complete as possible. Since choice of entry may differ from country to country and librarian to librarian, as many options as possible should be provided. Information on reprints and the extent of revision in new editions will be very helpful to the selector. Information on series is often lacking when the vendor's service relies on advance word from publishers, and a missing series statement can cause duplication. Some vendors who have encountered this problem will ask for order confirmation if an order does not include the series. In any case, they should accept the return of any duplicates that result because of their information.

Information from vendors should be monitored and evaluated for a few months. Information not received, that is, titles published but not cited by the vendor, can take much longer to be recognized as a problem. Any vendor will be happy to advertise expensive items with a high profit margin that are likely to be bought by many libraries. Inexpensive items, those produced by nonprofit agencies, and highly specialized materials may not be worth the cost of preparing and mailing information. Many large vendors will still cover these sorts of titles and make up the cost from sales of more expensive items. A library that is unhappy with the coverage of an information service might try a bookseller with a higher volume or one who specializes in the less well-covered subjects. If this is not a possibility or it does not work, the library will have to investigate other sources of information.

COMMUNICATION

A few large European vendors try to improve communication with their North American customers by having a representative available on this side of the Atlantic. These people visit customers to develop a sense of library problems and will telephone, cable, or fax their home offices with urgent inquiries. In some cases, local representatives function only as a conduit for messages, but in the better situations the representative has a good knowledge of both American libraries and the European firm, can advise on problems without having to check with Europe, and in many instances can commit the parent firm to a course of action. Such service can be a great convenience, but the mere existence of an American representative, even of the better kind, should not by itself be a reason to choose a dealer. Many vendors establish good contacts with libraries by touring regularly on this side of the Atlantic, and there are vendors who do not have a representative and have never left their own countries, but still understand the needs of libraries, respond promptly to inquiries, and provide the needed material.

When dealing with an importer in North America, communications take the same pattern that they do with any domestic vendor. When dealing with an exporter in Europe, any orders or letters not sent airmail may take three to six weeks to arrive at the vendor's office. Regular use of airmail can add considerably to postage costs. Holding orders to a particular vendor for a few days and batching them may save on postage, but holding them for a long time will reduce the advantage gained from airmail. Libraries that use a bulky, multipart order form should reconsider just how much of it is strictly necessary. Both in sending mail and in evaluating order fulfillment, remember that postal strikes are not uncommon in Europe. If they go on for more than a few days, other postal services will usually refuse to accept mail for the country experiencing the strike. Library mail rooms should always let acquisitions know when mail is sent back to be held during a strike, so that fax or cable can be used for rush orders and so that staff time can be reallocated. Many European countries now have computerized ordering systems linking bookstores and wholesalers. The Teleordering system is linked across the Atlantic to Baker & Taylor in the United States, and European booksellers using it estimate that it cuts delivery time by two weeks. Some such system may eventually be extended to libraries.

There are several options for sending urgent messages to your European vendor. It's natural to pick up the telephone, and transatlantic telephone service is both quite good and much less expensive than it once was, especially when used to take advantage of reduced rates (a long distance telephone company can provide a schedule). However, it is still significantly more expensive than domestic long distance service, and the time difference (Western Europe is six hours later than Eastern Standard Time) may mean that there will be little or no overlap between the library's and the vendor's office hours. Remember that around the Mediterranean, offices are often closed in the early afternoon and then open again in the early evening. In countries where English is not the language of the office, there may be a delay while someone with good spoken English is found, and there may be no such person available at that moment.

The cable, a transatlantic telegram, is the traditional alternative to the telephone, especially for communicating with antiquarian dealers to reserve items from catalogs. The inter-library loan telex made sending cables easy in many libraries. Now cables are more commonly sent on a personal computer, using a modem to reach Western Union, but telex is still a good option. A night letter is reasonably priced and will reach the vendor at the start of the next business day. An increasingly popular alternative to the cable is the fax, popularized by its presence in the library's interlibrary loan office. A fax machine allows an actual copy of the order or invoice in question to be sent, with comments. Fax costs a bit more than airmail, but, if there are no problems with the telephone lines, it is more sure and, if the vendor's machine is left on after office hours, it is not subject to the time constraints of a regular telephone call.

ORDER FULFILLMENT

Two basic issues are relevant to order fulfillment: getting the material in a timely fashion and getting the material at all. They are not unrelated. Short print runs in some countries and from some publishers can mean that a delayed order will never be filled.

Judging vendor performance on delivery time and setting claim cycles is difficult. Obviously, it is inappropriate to hold foreign vendors to the same standards applied to domestic vendors. Shipment by sea mail can take anywhere from three to eight weeks (the shorter times are more common on the heavily traveled North Atlantic routes, the longer times from the Mediterranean). Airfreight is increasingly common and fast (shipments go by airfreight to an American airport and are then sent on by domestic mail or a parcel service), but there may be an additional charge for the service and it is still not available from some areas. Airmail is expensive and appropriate only for urgently needed items. One Dutch dealer's 1989 shipping charges show airfreight costs at 2.8 times the surface rate and airmail at 6.6 times. Mail strikes can be a problem, even for vendors who use airfreight, since they are usually dependent on domestic mail to get books from publishers, and the Christmas season can bring considerable delays. United Parcel Service (UPS) has recently begun an international parcel delivery service, which may be a useful alternative for book shipments.

Distribution systems vary greatly from country to country. On the continent, West Germany and some of the smaller countries have efficient wholesalers linked electronically to the retail trade. More typical is a mix of wholesalers, publishers who distribute their own and possibly some other publishers' books, and publishers who warehouse and distribute out of a back room; all of them do not have electronic links. Since only the last of these operations can afford storage space in large cities, warehousing and distribution are usually at some site removed from the editorial and business offices (the place in the book's imprint). As in North America, delivery time is often more dependent on the publisher's or wholesaler's response time for single volume orders than on the method of shipping. No response from a publisher, orders kept open for a promised new printing that doesn't happen, or titles delayed in publication for six to eight months can distort average delivery time significantly. Similarly, outstanding orders for one or two volumes in multivolume sets can be confusing. Mean delivery time may well be a better indicator of vendor performance than the average. Useful data for setting claim cycles can be obtained by simply comparing order date and arrival date at intervals over a period of time, being careful not to take samples during mail strikes or the Christmas mail crunch. For vendor evaluation, comparisons can be made among vendors from the same part of the world who use similar shipping methods.

If a fair amount of material is ordered from prepublication information, this must take that into account in evaluating performance and especially in setting claim cycles. If selectors work from national bibliographies that contain CIP information, they should use it instead of waiting for final cataloging copy. The final information may appear as much as a year after publication, and an order then will result in a book that is late or one that is not received at all. For East Germany, as for the other Communist economies, it is essential that the order be placed in advance of publication because print runs are based on advance orders.[21] Claiming too early on these announced titles causes unnecessary work for vendors and publishers. Unfortunately, some libraries do not take these and other individual factors into account in setting claim times and hold all vendors to a similar standard. As a result, some vendors have become a bit cynical

---

21. East German books for which distribution rights have not been sold to West German publishers now are listed in the German in-print bibliography, the *Verzeichnis lieferbarer Bücher,* and supposedly are to remain in print somewhat longer, but print runs are likely to remain comparatively small. The proposed German reunification plans may change this situation.

about claims, especially about the rush that comes when a library first gets a computerized acquisitions system.

On the other hand, the library does have a right to know something about the status of an order. If six months or so have gone by, and the library has claimed and waited a reasonable time for a response to the claim, it is useful to check if the book has been published. A simple way to do this, more effective for English books than for foreign language titles, is to look at a bibliographic utility and see if any other library has received and cataloged the title; be careful to distinguish libraries that actually hold the book from CIP cataloging by a national library. This is not a futile exercise. In regular reviews of orders over one year old, trade books with dozens of holding libraries recorded on OCLC have been easily identified. Large vendors, whose overall performance is otherwise excellent, had reported these books as not yet published or had supplied no report at all. Their reports were based on what the publishers had told them; additionally, stock clerks can mislay orders or misread ISBNs, titles and ISBNs can change between announcement and publication, and books can change publisher.

Part of the problem can be blamed on computers. It is easy to misread an ISBN, but it's also easy to assume the computer is taking care of the claiming. At some point there has to be a human review. If there has been no report, a letter should ask why. If there have been several reports indicating not yet published or temporarily out of stock, then a decision needs to be made to keep the order open or cancel it; for British books and books from other publishers with North American offices, the decision may be to get the book from an American copublisher or distributor.

Can the vendor provide the materials needed? If one is able to meet a prospective vendor, it may be possible to answer the question by noting how much of what is said is understood. A vendor who speaks knowledgeably about scientific serials but has never thought about libraries wanting government documents or small press books is probably inappropriate for an institution whose European buying is largely in the social sciences and humanities. A vendor whose focus is solely on scholarly books may not be the best choice for a public library.

If vendors seem to have difficulty supplying the books needed, the library can work with them to identify the problem areas. These may be related to subjects, to type of publisher, to format, or to geographic area. A vendor who provides very good service in one subject area will probably try to get other types of books, but may not have the same expertise. Government documents, small press books, or publications from research institutes may be a problem, as may be microfilms or audiovisual material. In their own neighborhoods, all good vendors will have had experience with problem publications and know when prepayment or a follow-up phone call may be needed to pry an item loose from a shy publisher. Outside their territory the level of knowledge declines, and the library may find that, if it does a lot of business in other areas, it will have to add additional vendors. Despite all that has been said about European economic unification, vendors can have problems even within their own language areas. British dealers may not do well in Ireland, German dealers may not have good connections in Austria, or French or Dutch dealers may fail with material from Belgium. One Parisian bookseller reported having trouble with publishers in southern France.

It is also possible that the fault lies not with the vendor but with information and orders. If there is a relatively high percentage of unfilled orders, or if there are a large number of outstanding orders, the library should examine a sample of its orders and discuss the results with the vendor. Check the orders against a national bibliography, in-print tool, or the bibliographic utilities to make sure that accurate information has been supplied. If there are a lot of out-of-print reports, the library may be relying too heavily upon reviews in journals and not ordering soon enough. If there are a lot of not-yet-published reports, the library may be working from CIP data in national bibliographies or from prepublication information supplied by publishers or a vendor and may want to try verifying publication or adjusting the claim cycle.

PRICING

In Western Europe it is generally not possible to negotiate a discount from a vendor. Vendor selection must be made on the basis of service, such extras as management data or information about new publications, and delivery method and cost. Absorbing all or part of shipping charges is in fact an important form of discount. For example, a flyer from an art specialist proclaimed a 5 percent discount to libraries, but then quoted a 7 percent shipping charge plus a fixed per-shipment fee of $6.

James Campbell

Fixed Prices

In some countries—currently in the United Kingdom, the Netherlands, France, Germany, Austria, most of Switzerland, Denmark, and Norway—there exists some form of retail price maintenance, that is, an agreement that retail booksellers will not sell books below the publisher's list price, or, in some countries, that they will not sell below a certain percentage of the list price. In Britain, libraries can apply for a discount and in some of the Scandinavian countries they can obtain a discount through a central library purchasing agency, but these discounts are not available to foreign libraries.[22] Many of these countries have laws prohibiting restraint of trade, that is, price fixing, but have decided, in the words of an often quoted British judge, that "books are different," and that some sort of price agreement is necessary in order to have a healthy, independent retail book trade.

There is by no means unanimous agreement on the wisdom of fixed prices. Pressure to end retail price agreements usually comes from bookstore chains, which expect that their volume will allow them to negotiate a larger discount from publishers. Sentiment in favor of fixed prices comes from the independent booksellers, who fear being undercut by the chains, and from the publishers who anticipate pressure to increase discounts. Italy had price maintenance but abandoned it when intense competition made it impossible to keep up. France did not have price maintenance, although publishers did set a recommended list price; then in 1979 a law to encourage competition forbade publishers from suggesting a retail price, from putting a price on the book, or from listing a retail price in their catalogs or advertising. The law created chaos and actually led to a rise in book prices, especially outside the major urban areas. In 1982 a new law required the publisher to put a fixed price on all books and forbade bookstores from discounting more than 5 percent in the first two years after publication. This is the only retail price agreement in Europe that is actually prescribed by law, and it

---

22. For a general discussion of retail price maintenance, see Curwen, *The World Book Industry,* pp. 210–216. Dana Alessi, "Books Across the Waters: An Examination of United Kingdom Monographic Pricing," in *Pricing and Costs of Monographs and Serials: National and International Issues* (New York: Haworth Press, 1987), pp. 38–39, gives a history of the British Net Book Agreement; Charles Willett and Peter Phelan, "The Willett-Phelan Letters," *Library Acquisitions: Practice and Theory,* 9 (1985): 169–176, discuss the British Net Book Agreement and debate the exclusion of foreign libraries from discount licensing.

was generally welcomed at the time by everyone except the chain store discounters. A 1988 French government study found that the independent stores had not in fact benefitted significantly from the law. Protected by the restrictions on discount, the chain stores and book departments in supermarkets, and so on had continued to use their volume to get better discounts from the publishers and had used some of their improved profit margin to bring their level of service closer to that of the independent stores. A comparison to Sweden, which does not have price maintenance, seems to show that the Swedish book trade, after an initial period of chaos, is now in better shape than the French book market.[23] Britain has resisted several attempts to abandon its Net Book Agreement, but the chain stores have become increasingly powerful in recent years and in 1989 reopened the issue. The French experience suggests a likely compromise: a limited, strictly regulated discount.

In court cases involving the Netherlands and Belgium and Britain and Ireland, the EC has rejected price agreements across national boundaries in Europe as being against the principle of unrestricted movement of goods. Some publishers and booksellers will probably try to take advantage of this, and the debate will continue. As countries move in and out of retail price maintenance, there can be some impact on American libraries. There is already a trend for smaller dealers to merge, be bought out, or go out of business, and increased pressure to provide discounts favors the larger vendors and could accelerate the trend. Also, when prices are effectively set by the vendor, it can be difficult for a library to determine that it is getting a fair price. There is even some danger, especially in countries where most library exports are in the hands of a few vendors, that foreign customers will end up paying more than the normal price within the country. When discounting is regulated and list prices are advertised, as in France today, spot checks against in-print lists and publishers' catalogs can provide pricing information. When discounts are not regulated, the situation is much more difficult. Publishers' discount policies to booksellers may differ greatly and it will be difficult for the vendor to quote a standard, verifiable

---

23. Herbert R. Lottman, "Traditional Booksellers Suffer by French Price-Fix Law, Study Shows," *Publishers Weekly,* 235 (March 24, 1989): p. 16, summarizes the report. Several French publishers who were unhappy with some of his conclusions sent in a letter of rebuttal, "Price-fixing in France," *Publishers Weekly,* 235 (May 19, 1989): 10.

James Campbell

discount to customers. Splitting orders between two vendors and comparing prices in their selection lists or for similar sorts of titles may be the only way to monitor the situation. Still, most libraries will probably not be aware of changes in retail price maintenance. Where it exists, the vendor is not allowed to discount or can discount only within a narrow range. Where it does not exist, it is the vendor who acquires many copies of a book at the same time who will get the largest discount. Few vendors who work with North American libraries can qualify for the big discounts unless they have many approval plan accounts, and the book dealers to whom that applies are mainly in the countries where sentiment for price maintenance is strong.

VAT

Value-added tax (VAT) on books is another issue that varies greatly from country to country and is in a period of transition. VAT is an indirect tax used in every Western European country. At each stage of production of an item, that producer is taxed on the value that has been added to the item. The producer of paper is charged for the price of paper as opposed to pulp; the publisher is charged for the price of the book as opposed to the raw materials and services that went into it. Depending on the country, the tax is collected either on the difference between the selling and purchase price or on the full price of the book, but the publisher can deduct any taxes that had been part of the price paid to the papermaker, printer, binder, advertising agency, and so on. VAT rates vary greatly across Europe and rates on books and other printed matter vary most of all. In some countries, all goods, including books, are charged at the same rate. This is the case in Sweden, which has the highest rate in Europe, 23.46 percent. In Britain, on the other hand, the standard rate is 15 percent, but books are "zero rated," that is, no tax is collected on them. Italy is changing from a zero rating to a tax of up to 4 percent. France has by far the most complex system; rates vary from 4 percent on some types of magazines to 33.3 percent on pornography. Some legislators in the United States have suggested the introduction of VAT, but there is another reason for librarians to be interested in it.

In every European country, exports are zero rated and no VAT is due. Some librarians have discovered this and also noticed that their vendors are charging them the full list price, a fact that leads to indignant complaints. If the book or periodical was published in Scandinavia, there is a basis for complaint. Elsewhere, the situation is unfortunately more complicated. The Scandinavian countries have a high VAT rate, make no reductions for cultural items, and collect VAT on the full purchase price. Their system is set up to allow sellers to discount the full VAT to retail buyers taking or having the item shipped out of the country. In the rest of Europe, books receive a reduced rate or (as in Britain) are zero rated, and, in some cases, the VAT is not collected on the full purchase price. This gives a much smaller amount to be considered. Usually there is not an agreed-upon system for dealing with exports. Some publishers specializing in exports list their prices without VAT and then add it on for domestic sales. Other publishers may factor the reduced VAT into the discount they allow export vendors, so that the publisher and not the dealer gains.

For the EC countries, all of this may be changing somewhat. As a part of harmonization, it has been recommended that all countries standardize their VAT rates, with one higher rate for general goods and a lower rate, in the range of 0 to 6 percent, for cultural goods such as books. If this suggestion is accepted, it will relieve some of the pressure on Britain to give up zero rating, but internal economic pressures may yet bring about a repeat of 1984's bitter fight against a "tax on knowledge." Some other countries will certainly benefit if their high VAT rates on books come down, and that will make it even more unlikely that VAT will be a negotiating point with any vendor. Remember, however, that Denmark is currently the only Scandinavian member of the EC, so harmonization may not have much effect there.[24]

Currency Conversion

Currency conversion is another area of occasional misunderstanding and even bad feeling between librarians and booksellers,

---

24. For an introduction to VAT, see Alan A. Tait, *Value Added Tax: International Practice and Problems* (Washington, D.C.: International Monetary Fund, 1988). There is a discussion of cultural activities, including books, on pp. 73–75. *Completing the Internal Market: White Paper from the Commission to the European Council* (Luxembourg: Office for Official Publications of the European Communities, 1985), pp. 46–50, presents the case for harmonization of VAT. Tait reviews briefly the case for not exempting cultural activities from VAT; Brenda White, "A Tax on Knowledge," *Journal of Information Science,* 10 (1985): 29–37, argues emotionally the British book trade's position against VAT on books and provides both a historical survey of earlier British taxation attempts and a review of the EC position.

James Campbell

especially in recent years as the value of the dollar has swung wildly. A vendor's invoice should state the prices in the original currency so that the library can compare them to the prices in publishers' catalogs and other book trade sources. As a matter of convenience for both vendor and customer, the price is usually also given in the customer's currency. The rate at which the currency was converted should be noted and libraries should monitor on a sample basis. A few dealers do in fact use artificially high rates. This is especially common with expensive sets, often reprints, offered by the publisher on a subscription basis. The high rate covers the overseas shipping costs and insures the publisher against any change in currency values between order and payment—good reasons to send offers of that kind through your regular vendors. Vendors should be encouraged not to hide shipping charges and bank fees for check conversion in the exchange rate but to list them separately, and most will indeed operate that way.

Currency problems commonly arise because of the time elapsed between invoice date and the date the vendor receives payment. Vendors with whom a library regularly does business will usually accept small losses on currency exchange, figuring that they will eventually make small gains when the market turns. Vendors who receive only an occasional order from a library, or any vendor who is supplying a single very expensive item or dealing with a rapidly falling currency and an institution that is very slow to pay, may send supplemental invoices to cover losses on the exchange rate. They're usually not anxious to do the additional paperwork, but they have to pay their suppliers the full sum in the now more valuable original currency. Librarians should examine requests for additional payment but should not resent the vendor's attempts to cover costs. Unfortunately, some libraries attempt to cheat on currency conversion; they use the vendor's rate when it is favorable and a rate from a newspaper or bank when they show a better rate. A library that is upset with supplemental fees or has had some bad experiences with vendor-supplied conversion rates may arrange to pay at a bank rate determined on the day the check is issued; libraries, however, should be consistent about how the payment amount is determined. It is important that the rate actually used is that of a bank. Exchange rates published in newspapers apply only to very large transactions, usually between banks. They are fine for estimating price on an order, but the rate used to convert a typical invoice payment will not be nearly so favorable.

KEEPING UP

Western Europe does not present the range of unexpected and sometimes insoluble problems encountered in dealing with less developed areas, but it does present a fast-changing environment that challenges the acquisitions librarian to keep up. Unfortunately, there has been relatively little on acquisitions from Europe in the library literature of recent years—a number of articles on serials pricing; a certain amount of information about the United Kingdom, much of it dealing with pricing; and a few articles on the French- and German-speaking areas, most of them written by vendors. Certainly there are plenty of other problems out there, but it is difficult to generalize about the whole of Western Europe and to find common factors between Sweden and Spain, Ireland and Italy. While Europe as a whole may play a large part in our acquisitions, each individual country has a much smaller role. The increasing importance of the English-language book trade and the harmonization efforts of the EC may make it easier to deal with Western Europe as a unit. Until then, the librarian trying to keep up with European events will find some coverage of trade publishing and bookselling in the news columns of *Publishers Weekly* and in its occasional articles by Herbert Lottman on book fairs, publishing centers, and important developments. Six European book trade journals—the British *Bookseller,* the French *Livres Hebdo,* the German *Borsenblatt,* the Italian *Giornale della Libreria,* the Dutch *Boekblad,* and the Spanish *DeLibros*—have agreed to exchange news and information, and a reader with access to any of them can get a good picture of current affairs. Discussion with colleagues and with vendors at library meetings remains the best way to keep current. Indeed, the best way to negotiate the problems of acquisitions from Europe is still to take advantage of its strong bookselling tradition and find the reliable vendors who suit the needs of the library.

Vendors

The Cost of Service: Understanding the Business of Vendors

Scott A. Smith

Bookselling has been variously described as an art, a science, and a business. The selling of books to libraries is an important part of a larger wholesale and distribution network. Bookselling of all kinds is a service industry. Vendors neither manufacture the products that they sell nor do they establish list prices (the recommended retail price set by the publisher). The complex process of handling library materials from the point when they leave the publisher to the point when they are acquired by a library and the nature of the adjunct services offered by the vendor to that library are the main determinants of the vendor's ability to earn a profit and to meet the needs of the market.

DISCOUNTS

The gross margin is the difference between the list price minus the discount that the publisher gives to the vendor, on the one hand, and the list price minus the discount that the vendor gives to the library, on the other. For example, if the list price of a book is $40.00 and the publisher gives the vendor a discount of 20 percent ($8.00) and the vendor gives the library a discount of 10 percent ($4.00) the gross margin is $4.00. The vendor pays $32.00 and the library pays $36.00. The vendor has to subtract the overhead and the variable expenses from this gross margin in order to arrive at his or her profit margin. Overhead consists of fixed expenses (lighting and heating, warehouse rental, and so on). Variable expenses consist of the costs related to volume of sales (advertising and convention expenses, wages of sales and customer relations staff, packing and shipping costs, and so on.) When overhead and variable expenses have been subtracted from the gross margin, what remains is the vendor's net profit (before taxes). If, in the example given, the sum of the vendor's overhead and variable expenses were $2.50, the net profit (before taxes) would be $1.50 (gross margin of $4.00 minus $2.50).

It is important to remember that gross margins are, essentially, the vendor discount minus the library discount. A trade publication (one issued by a commercial domestic publisher) may carry a high vendor discount but may have a low list price. If the price of such a book is, say, $7.95, and the vendor discount is 48 percent, the vendor has only $3.82 to work with. If, in such a case, the library discount is 25 percent, the vendor has only $1.83 as a gross margin. On the other hand, the discount on a university press title may be 20 percent, but, if the list price is $70.00 and the library discount is 10 percent, the gross margin is $7.50.

The discounts vendors give to libraries are influenced by two monetary considerations: the need to earn an adequate profit (that is, one that allows the company to pay its shareholders, reward its employees, and have funds to invest in the future) and the competitive pressures of the marketplace. In addition, vendors must pay attention to the order mix. Order mix is the combination of relatively profitable and unprofitable titles. Examples of the former are domestic trade and university press publications; examples of the latter are small press and association or society publications. There is a direct relationship between the vendor's discount policy and a library's order mix. Most vendors offer either a sliding-scale discount (wherein the library's discount is determined by the individual publisher's discount) or a flat discount (wherein the discount for each title is the same irrespective of the publisher's discount). A flat rate discount is easier to administer, but it can only be viable for the vendor if the order mix contains a significant percentage of profitable titles.

Order mix must also be considered in light of the quantity of copies ordered. Herein lies a major difference between academic or research libraries and public libraries. Academic libraries usually order one copy of each title and the titles come from a wide range of publishers. Public libraries often place large multicopy orders from a smaller range of publishers. In addition,

Scott A. Smith

public libraries order a higher percentage of trade and popular titles. Academic libraries, on the other hand, order many hundreds of esoteric and ephemeral titles. Hence, the vendor of books to academic libraries must maintain publisher files on a far greater number of suppliers of different types than do vendors who serve public libraries. Many of those suppliers will not extend discounts and require prepayment. Vendors to public libraries benefit from greater multicopy discount rates from publishers and are, therefore, able to support higher average discounts on the books they supply.

The fact that the two broad markets require different skills and services is illustrated by the small number of vendors that seek to compete in both; most vendors specialize in one or the other. Although there are a few vendors who do sell in both markets, the majority of their revenue is derived from one or the other.

Even though vendors to academic libraries cannot match the discounts offered to public libraries, all customers of vendors benefit from economies of scale. The consolidation of orders with a vendor works to the library's advantage. Despite the fact that a few publishers offer higher discounts to libraries ordering direct than they do to vendors, direct ordering has many drawbacks for the library. The disadvantages include the cost and inefficiencies in time incurred when generating individual purchase orders, when processing small shipments, and when handling multiple invoices and payments. To put it bluntly, the cost to the institution for cutting the check exceeds any discount that may have been gained. Resolving problems with individual publishers is much more time-consuming and expensive than it is with a small number of vendors. Consolidated shipments with invoices arranged to the library's specifications and single customer service departments are also part of the economies of scale.

Vendors benefit from processing efficiencies and from the combined buying power of many libraries. A vendor offering a standing order service, for example, will maintain a series file. An additional order will not increase costs but will contribute to order quantity. Because vendors deal in significantly greater quantities than individual libraries, the discounts and return privileges extended to vendors are, in general, more generous than those available to libraries. The discounts available to vendors are influenced by the type of publisher and the number of copies ordered. A list of common discount schedules is shown in Table 1.

TABLE 1 COMMON DISCOUNTS AVAILABLE TO VENDORS

Type of Publisher	Discount (%)
Trade	33 – 48%
Sci-Tech	20 – 38%
University press	20 – 35%
Reference book	0 – 19%

Most scholarly associations, societies, university departments, and small presses do not offer discounts. A few such publishers levy handling charges or require prepayment. Overall, the publisher discount to vendors dealing with academic libraries is 25 to 30 percent.

VENDORS' COSTS

Most vendors work within a gross margin of between 20 and 25 percent. From this, the vendor must cover fixed and variable costs, extend discounts to libraries, carry receivables (the sum due to the vendor from customers), and pay taxes. Given the nature of the industry, such margins are not excessive. Interest expenses for carrying the receivables can be considerable, particularly if publishers require payment before the libraries pay the vendor. Interest expenses alone can wipe out a profit margin. A vendor who is successful in controlling costs and maintaining his or her margin is likely to realize an after-tax profit of between 1.5 and 4 percent of total sales. (By comparison, sellers of automotive products, of beer, wine, and other alcoholic beverages, and of pharmaceuticals realize wholesale-distribution profits of between 7 and 8 percent.

Although vendors are sometimes successful in negotiating higher discounts and better terms with publishers, publisher discounts are fairly rigid. Market pressure to extend competitive discounts to libraries must also be respected if a vendor is to stay in business. Consequently, a vendor's control of costs is the main determinant of the achievement of profits.

An effective and profitable vendor is one who assesses resources properly and deploys them in the most effective manner. Planning, forecasting, and budgeting (which can be regarded as exercises in establishing and living within reasonable boundaries) provide a framework for maximizing service as well as profits. Periodic and careful review is required to insure adher-

Scott A. Smith

ence to performance standards and sustained levels of productivity. Internal control focuses on both fixed costs (for example, building maintenance and rent) and variable costs (for example, most labor costs, packing materials, and stationery such as invoice forms).

The range of services a vendor chooses to offer has a direct and immediate effect on operating expenses. Most vendors to libraries offer some, if not all, of these services: firm order service, approval plans, standing order service, full book processing, out-of-print searching, and electronic ordering.

Regardless of the range of services offered, every vendor needs customer service staff; order entry, billing, and shipping clerks; and marketing specialists. Approval vendors also require book profilers and editors; library profile specialists; and a returns desk. Standing order programs demand additional research and profiling staff. Full processing requires a source of MARC records and account managers to administer card profiles. Electronic ordering requires considerable data processing facilities and telecommunications experts.

Accuracy and efficiency in all aspects of vendor operations have a direct bearing on cost control and service levels. If a vendor ships a book to a library in error, the book will be returned. If the vendor fails to include an invoice, fails to follow library instructions, or fails to pack the books properly, costs go up and customer satisfaction goes down. Timely and comprehensive coverage of newly published titles is critical to a vendor who offers approval programs and standing order services; late treatment will almost certainly cause a duplicate order, claim, or return.

In addition to internal control, effective liaison with publishers (the suppliers) and libraries (the customers) is required. Close monitoring of publisher performance is mandatory. Most vendors operate with an error rate of one-fourth to one-half of 1 percent, whereas some publishers operate with an error rate of 5 to 7 percent. The vendor's inventory must be controlled; missed return windows (the time allowed by publishers for returns—usually 90 days) add to nonreturnable inventory, which in turn contributes to higher carrying costs. Library returns must be considered as well, especially if the vendor offers approval plans.

Because vendors have come to rely increasingly on automation to provide fast and effective service, their data processing costs have soared. A vendor's ability to maintain accurate files containing library requirements (customer master records detailing billing and shipping instructions, special handling, and so on), the names and addresses of publishers and distributors, and bibliographic files requires reliance on electronic data processing. Today, every major bookseller in the United States has either automated at least some elements of his or her operation or is in the process of doing so.

Vendor automation has improved operating efficiency and rendered additional benefits to libraries, such as management reports and machine-readable data to augment book supply. This has not been without a cost. Skillful management and control of data processing resources have become increasingly important to vendors, and new issues continue to surface. For example, market demand is changing as libraries look to vendors to provide additional support services. As more and more libraries move to automated acquisitions systems, demand for electronic ordering capabilities increases and vendor telecommunications costs rise.

MARKETING

Given the business constraints within which vendors operate, bookselling must be viewed as a long-term proposition. Profitability emerges only after, and as a result of, the establishment of capability. A good bookseller is one who can provide consistently good service, manage available resources, and remain flexible enough to respond to changing market demand. The ability to anticipate library needs and react effectively is central to the vendor's marketing division.

Marketing is the practice of linking a producer's or wholesaler's capabilities to a consumer's needs. Marketing may be done by one or a few people, or by a large department, but the mission remains the same: to pay very close attention to the library and its needs and act accordingly. Today's demand or need is tomorrow's product or service.

The ability to respond effectively requires good market intelligence. A vendor's customers provide invaluable feedback on the quality of service on its own merits and in comparison to competitors. The vendor may rely on sales representatives to relay information, may choose to conduct formal market research, or may do both.

Telephone surveys, questionnaires, and on-site interviews are primary methods of conducting market research. The objective may be to gather information on current market practices or to

Scott A. Smith

describe an envisioned product or service and measure response. The results of research are then analyzed. Over time, trends and opportunities emerge.

The vendor's response to trends and opportunities determines the products and services that will be developed and supported and the markets to be targeted. Whether through a structured marketing plan or by means of informal procedures, the marketing function sets the direction for the company.

Market identification stems from the practice of linking vendor capabilities to library demand. This process is essential to vendors. (For example, the academic vendors' decision to fill single-copy orders has defined, in no small measure, the institutions to be served.) A number of fundamental business questions affect market identification: Will all or only some publishers be handled? Will service be limited to firm orders or will approval programs, standing order services, out-of-print searching, and full book processing be offered? Will service be offered throughout the country or will service be limited to selected states or regions? Will service be offered to libraries in Canada and abroad? Marketing can answer these and other questions by examining the market: How many libraries exist? What is their buying power? Which services do they need, request, and require? What criteria determine buying patterns and vendor selection? Which methods of selling are called for? How should services be presented? What discounts are needed to compete? When vendor resources are matched to the answers to these questions, the range of possible responses is revealed. The marketer must then decide which course is best.

Marketing is an evolutionary process. As more information is obtained, as additional resources are developed or acquired, and as market needs change, vendors reevaluate their positions and adjust their offerings. The services they elect to support are modified and enhanced accordingly.

VENDOR-LIBRARY ARRANGEMENTS

In certain instances, the process of linking vendor to library is legislated by municipal, state, or federal agencies. At other times, a library may commit to a specified annual expenditure in return for concessions from a vendor. These arrangements are assisted by bids and special terms.

In several states the libraries in publicly supported institutions are governed by state purchasing guidelines, wherein all purchases are subject to official control. In a few states this control is extended to formal bid procedures for specified services, for example, approval programs. It is not uncommon for public and private institutions to enter into contracts with vendors in order to achieve more favorable discounts or better terms. In many states, including Florida, Minnesota, New Jersey, New York, Ohio, and Oklahoma, state purchasing offices require book dealers to apply for inclusion on an approved list of suppliers. The services and terms of supply are known as the state contract; the state generally assigns approved identification numbers to all vendors on the list. A state contract does not necessarily establish the terms of supply, but often it does require vendors to file discount schedules. Information on specific vendors is available to libraries from the state purchasing office.

Libraries not governed by such regulations may, nonetheless, establish a formal procedure for vendor selection. Unburdened by the frequent changes mandated by state bids of limited duration, these libraries seek to consolidate their business and achieve higher discounts. A library may, for example, agree to send all domestic firm orders to a selected bookseller in return for a guaranteed flat discount; or a vendor may agree to such a discount in return for an established annual expenditure. Discount may not be the only criterion; a library may agree to place all standing orders with a vendor in return for free microfiche or management reports, in addition to a discount.

Vendors enter into these arrangements for two reasons: to secure new or existing accounts and to increase volume. While the former point is straightforward, the latter requires some explanation.

A vendor already supporting an automated approval program may have an opportunity to bid on a large publicly supported university library's approval plan, valued at $300,000 annually. If the vendor can handle the increased volume without adding staff or otherwise increasing expenses (that is, if all costs associated with servicing the account are fixed), a sufficient profit can be earned even if the discount needed to win the bid is higher than usual. The economies of scale work in the vendor's favor.

The costs of carrying accounts are also of concern to vendors. As a result, many vendors now offer prepayment options, whereby a library pays a pro forma invoice for anticipated expenditures. In return for taking this money on deposit, and because it lessens carrying costs and eliminates uncertainty about payment, the

Scott A. Smith

vendor extends higher discounts or pays interest on the unspent balance.

Vendors hope that librarians understand their industry and the bookseller's need to make a profit. A good order mix is essential to profitability; if a library relies on a vendor to supply only esoteric and ephemeral material, high discounts should neither be expected nor demanded.

Vendors respect customer loyalty to other suppliers and appreciate the loyalty to their own accounts. When service problems do occur, vendors expect to be notified in a timely manner and to be given an opportunity to set things right. Bookselling, in general, is a low-profit business. Profitability, service, and satisfaction can only be the results of sincere commitment and skill.

The "E's" of Vendor Selection: An Archetype for Selection, Evaluation, and Sustenance

Gay N. Dannelly

John W. Gardner, former secretary of health, education and welfare and chairman of the public interest organization Common Cause, has stated that "the society which scorns excellence in plumbing, because plumbing is a humble activity, and tolerates shoddiness in philosophy, because it is an exalted activity, will have neither good plumbing nor good philosophy. Neither its pipes nor its theories will hold water."[1]

The literature of acquisitions and the selection of vendors is an example of very good plumbing indeed. It abounds in articles that suggest a variety of specific criteria to consider when selecting and evaluating a vendor of library materials. The checklists, diagrams, and prescriptions are primarily directed toward monograph or one-time orders of various kinds, but periodical and serial vendor evaluation is not neglected. Several of the most useful, and more recently published, works are included in the bibliography of this paper.

An even more specific tool for the evaluation of vendors has been published by the American Library Association as *Guide to Performance Evaluation of Library Materials Vendors*.[2] Although a very focused report, specific diagnostic points can

1. John Gardner, *Excellence: Can We be Equal and Excellent Too?*, rev. ed. (New York: W. W. Norton & Company, 1984), p. 102.
2. American Library Association, Collection Management and Development Committee and Acquisitions Committee, Resources Section, Resources and Technical Services Division, *Guide to Performance Evaluation of Library Materials Vendors* (Chicago: American Library Association, 1988.)

be extrapolated and amended to provide for a detailed evaluation of many kinds of vendors of many kinds of library materials and services.

Despite the plethora of literature on the selection and evaluation of vendors, the focus has been almost exclusively on specific plumbing concerns; there has been little if any discussion of a general approach to, or philosophy of, vendor relations. Therefore, this chapter will attempt to present a broader framework in which to view mutual concerns and to develop a construct in which to consider the selection, evaluation, and sustenance of the library-vendor relationship in the multiformatted world in which we find ourselves. To use John Gardner's analogy, it is hoped that the construct will "hold water."

To thoroughly examine the services offered to libraries by the vendor community, there are four general areas that must be evaluated in terms of the individual library's needs related to the options available. These areas are effectiveness, efficiency, economics, and the ethics of the proposed arrangement—the E's of this chapter's title and the structure within which every vendor's services could be usefully evaluated.

For the purposes of this discussion specific definitions will apply. Effectiveness is defined as the actual receipt of the materials ordered and the time frame in which receipt generally occurs. Efficiency is defined as the acquisition of materials with the minimum of activity on the part of the library. The economic issue, while directly related to effectiveness and efficiency in terms of patron and staff time and effort, is here focused on the cost of the materials. The issue of ethics involves not so much entertainment or other personal advantages offered to library staff, but rather those mutual responsibilities that the library and the vendor share if the relationship is to be productive for both organizations.

Specific issues addressed in the remainder of this chapter will fit into the framework of the E's of vendor selection. Once the pattern becomes implicit in the acquisitions librarian's approach, the detailed information to be considered takes on a more rational, quantifiable, and qualitative structure that is amenable to a relatively rigorous analysis and evaluation.

The many varieties of libraries within the basic groupings of school, public, academic, and special often have specific needs. Nevertheless, they should all be able to approach their vendor decisions within the suggested framework and thereby find more mutual concerns with libraries of different purposes. In the same way, the many kinds of vendors can be evaluated in parallel ways, thereby generalizing the process and contributing to a broader understanding of vendor functions and services.

To sell is defined by the *Oxford English Dictionary* as "to give up or hand over (something) to another person for money. . .; especially to dispose of merchandise to a buyer for a price; to vend." Clearly, the obverse is to buy, defined as "to get possession of by giving an equivalent, usually in money; to obtain by paying a price; to purchase." These definitions provide, essentially, a description of the basic business relationship between a vendor and a library. John Stuart Mill termed selling-buying "a social act"; and Louis Brandeis, U.S. Supreme Court Justice from 1916 to 1939, described such commerce as "a transaction which is good for both parties." These basic complementary needs of libraries and vendors result in a closely tied community of interests that extends far beyond the commercial basis upon which they were initially established.

The decision to use one or more vendors rather than to order materials directly from publishers is usually based upon economies of scale; that is, dealing with one or a few sources for many titles is nearly always more efficient than dealing directly with each publisher. As library support decreases, even as acquisitions funds may increase, and more is demanded of library services and resources, it is imperative that libraries seek a variety of methods to streamline their activities. This is particularly pertinent to the acquisitions process. The consolidation of acquisitions activities (as well as physical processing for many libraries) becomes even more appropriate when one considers the increasing rate of publication: an estimated 700,000 individual titles with more than 100,000 serial titles produced each year, worldwide.[3]

The use of vendors "automatically eliminates the necessity for finding and recording addresses for all sources and reduces the number of boxes to open, invoices to process, checks to issue, and people to contact about problem receipts."[4] In fact, a wholesaler's primary function is "to serve as one-half of any library's acquisitions program. . . . They sell, and we buy. True,

---

3. A. Robert Rogers, "College and University Libraries," in *The Library in Society,* edited by A. Robert Rogers and Kathryn McChesney (Littleton, Colo.: Libraries Unlimited, Inc., 1984), p. 94.

4. Marion T. Reid, "Acquisitions," in *Library Technical Services: Operations and Management,* edited by Irene P. Godden (Orlando, Fla.: Academic Press, Inc., 1984), p. 92.

they can't exist without us, but likewise, we can't exist without them."[5] This extension of the capabilities of an acquisitions department is, in reality, a search for simplicity with its attendant efficiencies and, presumably, increase in general effectiveness within the library.

A vendor is the intermediary who bridges the gap between the publisher—the physical producer of information and knowledge—and the library—the acquirer of specific, identified parts of that production. In generalizing the proposed structure, it is not productive or necessary to differentiate between wholesalers or dealers, jobbers or periodical agents. They are all suppliers of library materials and, as such, subject to general evaluative processes and analyses.

Just as materials are amenable to the E's, so too have services become an essential part of the product offered by the vendor and evaluated by the librarian. "The strength of a vendor's service centers around where he has chosen to concentrate his financial resources. Emphasis on large inventory, on approval plans, on firm-order single copy fulfillment, etc. . . ." vary from company to company.[6] Rarely, if ever, is one company able to handle all the needs of a library of any size. In fact, a variety of capabilities is actually an advantage to the libraries vendors serve, because it allows specialized materials and related services tailored to the specific needs of myriad library situations.

Despite the community of interests shared by library vendors, competition is still a fact of life. "Vendors adapt their procedures and services in response to the requirements of library customers. . . . The competition among American vendors forces them to be creative and sensitive to the needs of their customers and potential customers."[7]

The economic as well as the more general competitive climate in which all vendors operate influence their capabilities to varying extents. Among the variables to be considered by the vendor are availability of credit; varying currency conversion rates, which have fluctuated as much as 30 percent in a single year; the cost of loans, varying by as much as 10 percent during the

5. Scott Bullard, "Editorial," *Library Acquisitions: Practice and Theory* 2 (1978): 1.

6. Ed Lockman, "Panel Presentation: Truth in Vending," *Library Acquisitions: Practice and Theory* 9 (1985): 69.

7. Marcia Tuttle, *Introduction to Serials Management* (Greenwich, Conn.: JAI Press, 1983), p. 77.

Gay N. Dannelly

1980s; costs of initial automation of manual systems and the need for continuous upgrading; increasing personnel costs; varying publication rates; and varying library budgets. Unlike profit organizations and their libraries which most often operate on a calendar year, most libraries operate on a fiscal year, and the fiscal year time period may vary from institution to institution. Thus, a vendor's sales projections, with attendant personnel and equipment commitments, must span several library operating periods. It is no wonder that projections take on a sort of crystal ball character, at least to those outside the projecting organization. Like many service companies, the library materials vendor operates in a complex, and often seemingly random economic climate, and achieves a relatively low profit rate in comparison to many other types of businesses. The typical profit margin of "1½ to 2% of total sales after taxes is [considered to be] quite acceptable profit."[8] Just as one does not become a librarian primarily for monetary gains, neither does one go into the business of library materials wholesaling expecting to become wealthy.

THE PRELIMINARY REVIEW

Within the context of the library's knowledge of services and materials available, and the cost of such materials and services, it is the library's responsibility to define a preliminary list of wants and needs and the resulting priorities. In setting specific criteria and establishing their order of importance within the individual library's structure, it is imperative that the acquisitions staff realize that they bear primary responsibility for the success or failure of any vendor-library relationship established. Their responsibility is at least equal to that of the vendor and its agents. A successful library-vendor relationship has to be based on shared priorities and goals that define specified services to the library and frequent, honest, and effective communication between the organizations' representatives.

Following the development of an initial set of criteria and establishment of their relative importance, "each library... should shop for the combination of services and benefits that

---

8. Michael Markwith, "Panel Presentation: Truth in Vending," *Library Acquisitions: Practice and Theory* 9 (1985): 66.

will provide the greatest yield at the lowest financial and staff cost, and, *most* importantly, the service that will bring in the largest proportion of right books for the library's clientele."[9] Acquiring materials of many and varied kinds is, after all, the primary purpose of the vendor-library agreement, whether it is title-by-title selection, subject area coverage, or high proportional delivery of a list purchase order in which the total number of titles provided takes precedence over single works per se. The last arrangement is more commonly used by school or public libraries seeking to increase titles held in a general category; they define a universe of acceptable titles that are filled by the vendor on an as-available basis.

In order to evaluate the services offered in the library market-place, the acquisitions librarian has a number of methods available. Attendance at national, regional, and state meetings where exhibits form an important part of the program is an excellent way to begin. This allows the librarian to meet vendors' local representatives on neutral ground for initial discussion. Vendor representatives visit current and potential library clients on a regular basis and are usually more than willing to visit the library on request to present their company's programs for review. It is both courteous and wise to let the vendors know that the library is in the midst of a review process, that information is being gathered, and that the library is not yet ready to make decisions regarding the final establishment of any order agreement. Such understanding allows flexibility for the librarian and should ease any expectations on the part of the vendor and its representative.

It is also useful to talk with colleagues at similar institutions about their use of vendors in general and specific companies in particular. Do maintain a degree of skepticism, however, in evaluating opinions for "one library's perfect vendor can be another library's disaster."[10] In addition, "if the library contacts other customers and discovers dissatisfaction, it is important to listen to both sides of the story. A library may have experienced failure with a vendor because it made unreasonable demands that no vendor could reasonably expect to meet."[11] Each librarian

9. Paul H. Mosher, "Waiting for Godot: Rating Approval Service Vendors," in *Shaping Library Collections for the 1980s,* edited by Peter Spyers-Duran and Thomas Mann, Jr. (Phoenix, Ariz.: Oryx Press, 1980), p. 161.
10. Jennifer Cargill, "When Purchasing Commercially Available Technical Services Makes Sense," *Technicalities* 4 (February 1984): 9.
11. Ibid, p.9.

must evaluate evidence in the context of his or her own institutional needs and, of course, in relation to the information gathered from both library and vendor colleagues.

The review process can be fascinating and one of the most useful learning experiences a new acquisitions librarian can have. There are, however, a number of potential problems that the reviewer should anticipate and for which a strategy should be developed beforehand. (Unless otherwise indicated, the author is viewing these problems strictly from the librarian's point of view. Each vendor representative has undoubtedly had some reverse experience of the same type.) Among common problem areas, several are of concern.

A representative is responsible for selling the company's services to the library. The result can be, particularly if the vendor or the librarian is relatively new at the job, what the librarian might consider excessive pressure to make an immediate decision and to promise future orders to the vendor in question. Telling the representative up-front that the library is in a review process can prevent or limit this situation. An acquisitions librarian may also wish to establish a department policy that does not allow a decision to be made to use a vendor, place a subscription, or agree to order a specific title, while the representative is present. This allows for consultation with appropriate staff and time to weigh alternatives and defuse any undue influence.

In the current vendor marketplace, many representatives have years of experience either as librarians or in the library community. In many cases a representative may have useful suggestions to make concerning approaches to a problem, ways of streamlining procedures, or identification of specific areas or titles of interest. The representative may, however, try to tell a librarian how to do something. The "telling" approach is a clear matter of concern and indicates potential communication difficulties that should be solved with the representative and the company. Any acquisitions decision is the librarian's responsibility within the institutional setting; however, should the librarian be requesting a service or benefit outside the regular practice of the specific vendor, or the vendor community, it is clearly the representative's responsibility to make that known to the librarian.

With the increased number of female vendor representatives and the parallel increase of men in the library profession, instances of sexual chauvinism seem to have decreased considerably. There are still, however, occurrences of this nature that have no place in a professional relationship. A *Sally Forth* cartoon is an excellent example of this unacceptable approach. It depicts a sales representative entering Ms. Forth's office and asking, "Are you the cute little lady I'll be making a sale to?" Ms. Forth's response, most appropriate under the circumstances, is "Yes, I'm the cute little lady that has life and death power over your proposal."

Many other pressures can be brought to bear by both the vendor and the librarian. Even though pressuring is a normal part of the negotiation process, the librarian as well as the vendor representative must be sure that they do not pass beyond the professional bounds of effective and efficient bargaining. The acquisitions librarian should be aware of the potential for similar situations involving staff who deal directly with vendors. Should a problem develop in any vendor-library setting, it is the responsibility of the librarian to deal with it directly or, if appropriate, discuss the matter with the company's sales manager or vice president for sales. With the increasing emphasis on professionalism in business relations, such problems are rare, but it is best to be prepared to deal with them simply as a part of one's management responsibility.

When the initial phase of information gathering has been completed, the librarian, and perhaps key staff, should consider site visits to those vendors who seem to have the most appropriate services for the library's needs. Often visits are not possible, but if possible, the investment on the part of the library is well worth the effort. Vendors operate in such varied ways and with such different approaches to similar functions that the librarian can learn more on a site visit than is ever possible from a representative's visits. A site visit provides a clear picture of where the company's priorities lie and the way in which they are carried out.

For example, some vendors emphasize strong inventories; they backorder in groups, once a week, of titles not in stock. Other vendors operate with little or no inventory, but they issue a daily order to publishers reflecting that day's library orders. Different approaches may result in discount variance as well as variance in the kinds of orders vendors handle best. In addition, the quality of a vendor's staff can often be initially evaluated on site, providing a good estimate of what can be expected in an established working arrangement.

At this stage of vendor selection it should be clear to the librarian that the relationship with a vendor is, to carry Mosher's collaborative collection development model a step further, another example of a collaborative enterprise. The relationship is, in fact,

Gay N. Dannelly

a partnership from which each participant should receive considerable benefits and which is based on mutual interests and responsibilities.

EVALUATING VENDOR INFORMATION

In reviewing the information gathered from each vendor and prior to reaching a decision on which vendor(s) to use as primary source(s), specific services available and desired should be compared and evaluated. Staff who will regularly work with the aspects of the acquisitions process that are directly related to the vendor's performance should be active participants in the evaluation. Information that has been gathered from vendor representatives should be considered privileged. The information may be shared with other librarians, except for discounts, but it should not be shared with other vendors except in the most generic sense.

If each vendor under consideration is likely to provide a reasonable level of service and materials, then certain factors should be considered in the review of what have been called "value added services."[12] Unit, monograph, or one-time order dealers, approval dealers, and subscription agents each have general kinds of services that they offer. In specifics they may differ, and that's where the library may find its decision points.

Customer Services

What kind of customer service support is provided? Is there an assigned sales representative or in-house customer service representative? Are these individuals readily accessible or is the sales representative usually on the road? Is the attitude of the personnel one of positive problem solving?

Scope

When reviewing a monograph or one-time order vendor, specific questions may include any of these: What is the scope of the materials handled? What kind of stock is maintained—trade, university press, serial backfiles, media or microformat? Or does

---

12. Sharon C. Bonk, "Toward a Methodology of Evaluating Service Vendors," *Library Acquisitions: Practice and Theory* 9 (1985): 59.

the company specialize in rapid ordering, concentrating its assets in skilled personnel who order on a daily basis as orders require rather than relying on stock or batch orders? Does the vendor automatically back order titles not provided from the publisher from the initial order? Are rush or special handling orders treated as such? Can an out-of-print search be initiated automatically if the publisher's report indicates out of print?

Rate of Order Fulfillment?

Don't accept the vendor studies of other libraries as proof; the mix of orders and other vendors cited in such studies directly influence results. These studies may provide indicated areas of concern that need to be clarified, but all a vendor study can potentially accomplish is to evaluate services from specific vendors to a single institution.

Cataloging and Processing

If a library is interested in the cataloging and physical processing of materials acquired, what services are offered? Can all materials be cataloged and classified according to Dewey, Library of Congress, Sears, or some other scheme? Can card sets be supplied? Is a COM (computer-output-to-microform) catalog capability available? Can machine-readable tapes for addition to local online systems be provided? Can paperbacks be bound and can plastic covers be added to all or some titles? Are card pockets and date due slips included? Can the volumes be labeled? Can appropriate security or theft and detection devices be placed in the volumes?

Delivery

How are materials delivered: by United Parcel Service, U.S. mail, direct truck delivery? Are shipments made on a defined schedule, as materials come in, or as the library specifies? How are materials packed? Are they sufficiently protected and will any items damaged in shipping be replaced by the vendor?

Approval Plans

Are approval plans available? Can profiles be developed by subject and nonsubject, for example, by parameters such as format, level of complexity, and geographical origin? How often are materials shipped? What is the general time lag between publication date and receipt in the library? Is there a method for identifying titles that have been or will be treated on the plan? Are machine-readable records for addition to library systems available? Are preprinted bibliographic slips provided with each title supplied? Are similar slips provided for titles not shipped due to profile exclusions?

Out-of-Print Fulfillment

Does the antiquarian, out-of-print, or used book vendor specialize by subject area, time period, source of publication? Will searches for unavailable titles be established if so requested? Can searches be limited to a specific period of time? Will the dealer hold items requested by phone for a confirming order? Will the dealer respond to desiderata lists? Will the dealer serve as a consultant to the library in his or her area of specialization?

Serials Subscription Agents

Will a subscription agent place subscriptions for a specified starting date, particularly titles that may be ordered rush? Will common expiration dates be established? Does the vendor provide centralized claiming? Are subscription renewals automatic? Will the vendor try to distribute the incidence of multiple-year subscriptions to maximize savings and minimize unevenness of costs per year? Is a catalog or list of available titles provided? Can cost projection information be provided automatically or on request? Is updated information provided on title changes, frequency, cessation, and so on? Are materials consolidated for shipment? Are materials shipped to the library directly from the publisher?

Invoices

Is the invoicing system flexible enough to provide invoices arranged by author, title, library fund, library purchase order number, and other ways specified by the library? Are invoices produced to relate directly to one or more shipments? Can items supplied incorrectly be returned automatically by the library using free credit memos? Can invoices be addressed to institutional units other than the library? Are machine-readable invoices available?

Systems

Does the vendor have an online system or participate in biblio-graphic utility acquisitions systems? Can orders be transmitted electronically? Is the vendor's in-house system directly available for information purposes? Does it reflect the vendor's inventory?

Reports

What kinds of reports are available? How are the reports sup-plied: 3-by-5 inch slips, printouts, machine-readable formats? How often are claim or status reports supplied? With what fre-quency are general management reports supplied and what infor-mation do they include?

Costs

What does it all cost? What are the discount schedules for one-time and approval materials? Are there specific service or process-ing charges? Do subscription costs have discounts and when are service charges applied? Can significant prepayments be made and can interest be paid on the remaining balance, or can dis-count levels be improved? Can deposit accounts be established? Can the library verify application of specific invoices to prepay-ments or deposit accounts? Do management reports cost extra? Do machine-readable sources of vendor data cost extra?

Of course there are more questions that can be asked. Each library will have specific requirements and concerns that must be made clear to any vendor being considered.

INITIATING THE BUSINESS RELATIONSHIP

When the quest for information is complete and initial evalua-tion of those vendors who seem to be most appropriate has been finished, how does a library acquire a vendor? In the "real" world, acquiring a vendor usually means orders are sent to the vendor, with or without notification of an intent to begin a continuing business relationship. Proceeding this way almost guarantees that problems will develop.

To properly acquire a vendor, the library will, ideally, estab-lish written goals, preferences, and objectives that can be reviewed with the vendor, either generally or specifically, prior to the actual placement of orders. The library should include its preference for fulfillment or discount as the first priority. Sometimes the library can get the best of both worlds with high fulfillment and high discount, but such a result is usually dependent on the mix and number of projected orders. Specify the probable types of orders that will be sent to the vendor; for example, many libraries assign trade, university press, association, small press, and other special types of orders to specific vendors. Each of these types of orders has a different discount rate to the vendor and thus to the library. In order to adequately discuss discount rates, the vendor must know what to expect from the library.

In addition to a statement of goals, the library should provide a description of the institutional conditions in which the acquisitions process will take place. Include a description and sample of the purchase order: library, institutional, government, and so on. What kind of paperwork is required? Must vouchers be provided by the vendor for each purchase order or invoice? How many copies of the invoice are required? Must copies of the purchase order be returned in or with each item?

Provide information on the budget and payment processes of the library and the institution(s) responsible for issuing checks. What kind of budget year is used? When is the acquisitions budget established? Does this effect the ordering year; if so, how? Can the library carry encumbered funds forward from year to year or must all funds be expended by the end of the fiscal year? What kind of time lags should the vendor expect between shipment of materials and payment? Can the library pay for partial shipments or must a purchase order be completed or closed prior to payment?

BIDS

Although a bid approach may be used on a voluntary basis, more often it is a required procedure. To start the bidding process a statement of requirements of materials and services is developed, issued through the library's or institution's purchasing office, and announced through standard channels. The bid announcement may appear as a notice in the press, in published requests for proposals or requests for bids, or in a mailing to companies that may or may not be qualified. In the most advantageous situation, the library provides a list of vendors to the institution's purchasing office to whom the bid request is sent as part of the official announcement process.

Vendors

There are several kinds of bid situations. They may be based on the estimated expenditure for materials or simply on an agency requirement—be it school board, local, state, or federal government, or institution—for bids on all purchases over a specified amount. The purchasing arrangement can require anything from sole use of the vendor winning the bid to simple approval of all vendors replying. The latter procedure, in effect, provides a list of minimum sales conditions under which materials must be sold, but it allows the library to choose from the list, to choose vendors who may not be on the list, or to negotiate an even more favorable arrangement. The bid process for libraries does not usually extend to the purchase of foreign materials.

In many bid situations, the cost to the library of having to take the lowest bid with no opportunity to evaluate service can be significant. An even greater problem is the potential requirement to change vendors each bid period should a lower bid be entered by another company. This requirement is particularly cumbersome in approval plan programs and is even worse when subscriptions are involved. It may, of course, turn out to be a definite advantage to the library if it gains a high discount rate, good service, and enforceable requirements, but it can also be a costly proposition in terms of the staff time required to implement such changes.

Should an acquisitions librarian decide, or be required, to operate under bid conditions, he or she should be sure that the specifications accurately reflect all the library's requirements in materials, services, and communications and that they include an evaluation mechanism. When the bid responses are received, all of them should be forwarded to the library. Even in a situation that requires awarding the contract to the lowest bidder, the library should evaluate every bid conscientiously and notify the purchasing department of any anticipated problems or conditions that could make a contract unenforceable. For example, if a small dealer operating a manual system is required to provide machine-readable records, the dealer's capacity to perform must be investigated prior to awarding the contract. In such a situation, the best response on the part of the vendor, of course, is to install a new automated system with the bidding library as the first customer. Thus the library could advise on and request any special features that would assist that library and enhance the vendor's new system. In any case, careful review of all bid responses is a necessity.

Gay N. Dannelly

MAKING THE DECISION

If the library is not in a bid situation and is able to make its decision based on the library's needs as expressed to the vendor(s) considered, then the decision is easy. Consider the four E's: effectiveness, efficiency, economics, and ethics.

The decision to choose one or more vendors after a review of your needs and their capabilities is a most important one. The library may wish to concentrate its business with a single vendor. This is not unusual, especially when the majority of purchases are made from new or current domestic publishing. The decision also depends on the acquisitions budget. It is simply unrealistic to try to spread a small budget over several vendors, all of whom provide essentially the same type of services. Also, it is particularly costly in staff time for the library, and the vendors receive minimal incentive. For a large university library, however, it may be perfectly reasonable to use multiple domestic vendors. They can be selected based on specific services offered, location, or any of the other criteria that the library has established as essential. The author knows of one library that considered four domestic vendors to be essentially equal. Having a good sized budget, the library simply alternated, month by month, cycling through each vendor two or three times a year. The acquisitions librarian felt a strong commitment to support the vendor community and chose the sequencing approach to fulfill that commitment.

The decision to select a vendor or vendors is a professional one. It should be based on information, negotiation, and mutual expectations and responsibilities. The library's decision will have an economic impact, perhaps a significant one, on the selected vendor(s), so it is not a decision to be made lightly. The library and the vendor enter into a relationship that will develop over time and it is imperative that the decision be made on a rational basis with the expectation that the library's needs will be effectively and efficiently met within the available economic realities: "One does not establish himself with a wholesaler and move to another one immediately. The nature of the business is largely detail, which takes a long time to do correctly. It is based on agreement and interpretation of that agreement."[13]

---

13. Harold L. Roth, "The Book Wholesaler: His Forms and Services," in *Background Readings in Building Library Collections*, edited by Phyllis Van Orden and Edith A. Phillips (Metuchen, N.J.: Scarecrow Press, 1979), p. 312.

When the decision to work with a specific vendor has been made, then the real labor begins. Both parties have essentially approved the blueprints, but they have yet to lay the foundation and build the everyday framework of their working relationship. Henry Adams writes that "friendship needs a certain parallelism of life, a community of thought, a rivalry of aim." So too does a productive library-vendor partnership.

B I B L I O G R A P H Y

"ALA Ethics Committee Looks at Vendor-Library Relationships." *Library Journal* (September 1, 1984): 1584.

Berkner, Dimity S. "Communication between Vendors & Librarians." *Library Acquisitions: Practice and Theory* 3 (1979): 85–90.

Bonk, Sharon C. "Toward a Methodology of Evaluating Serials Vendors." *Library Acquisitions: Practice and Theory* 9 (1985): 51–60.

Bullard, Scott R. "Editorial." *Library Acquisitions: Practice and Theory* 2 (1978): 1.

Cargill, Jennifer. "Vendor Services Supermarket: The New Consumerism." *Wilson Library Bulletin* 57 (January 1983): 394–400.

Cargill, Jennifer. "When Purchasing Commercially Available Technical Services Makes Sense." *Technicalities* 4 (February 1984): 7–9.

Collection Management and Development Committee and Acquisitions Committee, Resources Section, Resources and Technical Services Division. *Guide to Performance Evaluation of Library Materials Vendors.* Chicago: American Library Association, 1988.

Duchin, Douglas. "The Jobber as a Surrogate Acquisitions Librarian." *Library Acquisitions: Practice and Theory* 7 (1983): 17–20.

Earnest, Patricia H. "What Can the Library/Information Manager Gain Through the Services of a Book Vendor?" In *Library Management in Review,* pp. 78-80. New York: Special Libraries Association, 1981.

Emery, C. David. "Efficiency and Effectiveness: Approval Plans from a Management Perspective." In *Shaping Collections for the 80s,* pp. 185–199. Edited by Peter Spyers-Duran and Thomas Mann, Jr. Phoenix, Ariz.: Oryx Press, 1980.

Fast, Barry. "Publishing and Bookselling: A Look at Some Idiosyncracies." *Library Acquisitions: Practice and Theory* 3 (1979): 15–17.

Gardner, John. *Excellence: Can We Be Equal and Excellent Too?* Rev. ed. New York: W. W. Norton & Company, 1984.

Gay N. Dannelly

Holmes, Lyndon S. "Systems Acquisitions and Vendor Expectations." *Library Hi Tech* 2, no. 2 (1984): 110–112.

Kidd, Tony. "Choosing between Suppliers: A British Perspective." *Library Acquisitions: Practice and Theory* 6 (1982): 313–328.

Landesman, Margaret. "Selling Out of Print Books to Libraries." *AB Bookman's Weekly* 74 (November 5, 1984): 3184–3192.

Lockman, Ed. "Panel Presentation: Truth in Vending." *Library Acquisitions: Practice and Theory* 9 (1985): 68–70.

Magrill, Rose Mary, and Doralyn J. Hickey. *Acquisitions Management and Collection Development in Libraries.* Chicago: American Library Association, 1984.

Markwith, Michael. "Panel Preservation: Truth in Vending." *Library Acquisitions: Practice and Theory* 9 (1985): 65–68.

Moore, Edythe. "Acquisitions in the Special Library." *Scholarly Publishing* 13 (January 1982): 167–173.

Morbey, John. "Libraries and Suppliers: 33 Steps Toward Peace." *The Bookseller* (January 19, 1980): 239–241.

Mosher, Paul H. "Waiting for Godot: Rating Approval Service Vendors." In *Shaping Library Collections for the 1980s*, pp. 159–166. Edited by Peter Spyers-Duran and Thomas Mann, Jr. Phoenix, Ariz: Oryx Press, 1980.

Reid, Marion T. "Acquisitions." In *Library Technical Services: Operations and Management*, pp. 89–131. Edited by Irene P. Godden. Orlando, Fla.: Academic Press, Inc., 1984.

Rogers, A. Robert. "College and University Libraries." In *The Library in Society*, pp. 91–97. Edited by A. Robert Rogers and Kathryn McChesney. Littleton, Colo: Libraries Unlimited, Inc., 1984.

Roth, Harold L. "The Book Wholesaler: His Forms and Services." In *Background Readings in Building Library Collections*, pp. 307–315. Edited by Phyllis Van Orden and Edith A. Phillips. Metuchen, N.J.: Scarecrow Press, 1979.

Safran, Franciska. "Defensive Ordering." *Library Acquisitions: Practice and Theory* 3 (1979): 5–8.

Schmid, Thomas M. Libraries and Publishers: The Uneasy Partnership." In *Background Readings in Building Library Collections*, pp. 289–292. Edited by Phyllis Van Orden and Edith B. Phillips. Metuchen, N.J.: Scarecrow Press, 1979.

Secor, John. "Panel Presentation: Truth in Vending." *Library Acquisitions: Practice and Theory* 9 (1985): 71–74.

Tuttle, Marcia. *Introduction to Serials Management.* Greenwich, Conn.: JAI Press, 1983.

Wolf, Milton T. "Approval Plan: A Paradigm of Library Economics." In *Shaping Collections for the 80s*, pp. 178–184. Edited by Peter Spyers-Duran and Thomas Mann, Jr. Phoenix, Ariz: Oryx Press, 1980.

Wulfehoetter, Gertrude. *Acquisition Work: Processes Involved in Building Library Collections.* Seattle: University of Washington Press, 1961.

Evaluating the Work
of a Vendor

Marion T. Reid

Acquisitions staff evaluate vendors on a daily basis. Every time they unpack a shipment, process an invoice, attempt to resolve a problem—indeed, every time they come in contact with a vendor's product or representative—they are making judgments and forming opinions of that vendor.

Occasionally, an acquisitions librarian will decide to check these judgments and opinions by making a more formal study of vendor performance. Results may be shared with the vendors evaluated and with colleagues, but rarely are they actually published.

WHY STUDY A VENDOR'S PERFORMANCE?

Vendor evaluation is a time-consuming process that is lauded by some (primarily those who have done it) and viewed by others as too inconclusive, ephemeral, or expensive to be worth the time invested.

There are several reasons to conduct a study of vendor performance:

1. A study facilitates communication with the vendor(s) involved. The results act as a specific basis for discussion of service and expectations.
2. A study confirms or contradicts the acquisitions staff's informal evaluation of the vendor(s) involved. It is reasonable

to occasionally check one's intuitive judgments with fact. Landesman and Gates found that their study results tallied with their perceptions of discount and general quality of vendor service, but it did not verify their impressions of speed of service and number of unfilled orders.[1]

3. A study can be used as a basis to establish or alter procedures. For example, as a result of their study, Bell and others determined more realistic claiming and cancelation dates.[2] After monitoring their approval vendor's performance, Hulbert and Curry were able to reduce the number of journals that they needed to review for selection.[3]

4. Study results may be used as a basis to determine when to use a vendor. Bracken and Calhoun[4] and Pickett[5] found that their studies gave them a good profile of the strengths and weaknesses of their suppliers' stocks.

5. Study results may be used as a basis to reduce the number of vendors used or to determine which vendor to use exclusively. Baumann ceased to use three of the vendors that she evaluated, since the data showed that they functioned below the level of the other eight.[6] Sumler, Barone, and Goetz devised their study in order to determine which of two vendors would get their business.[7]

6. Study results may be used as a touchstone for future studies. In doing a vendor performance study, the acquisitions librarian establishes a methodology for subsequent measurements of vendors.

1. Margaret Landesman and Christopher Gates, "Performance of American In-Print Vendors: A Comparison at the University of Utah," *Library Acquisitions: Practice and Theory* 4 (1980): 192.

2. JoAnn Bell and others, "Methodology for a Comparison of Book Jobber Performance," *Medical Library Association Bulletin* 70 (April 1982): 231.

3. Linda Ann Hulbert and David Stewart Curry, "Evaluation of an Approval Plan," *College & Research Libraries* 39 (November 1978): 490.

4. James K. Bracken and John C. Calhoun, "Profiling Vendor Performance," *Library Resources & Technical Services* 28 (April-June 1984): 127.

5. A. S. Pickett, "An Experiment in Book Buying," *Library Journal* 84 (February 1, 1959): 372.

6. Susan Baumann, "An Application of Davis' 'Model for a Vendor Study,'" *Library Acquisitions: Practice and Theory* 8 (1984): 83.

7. Claudia Sumler, Kristine Barone, and Art Goetz, "Getting Books Faster and Cheaper: A Jobber Acquisitions Study," *Public Libraries* 19 (Winter 1980): 104.

WHAT KINDS OF STUDIES CAN BE DONE?

The characteristics and results of vendor performance studies may vary according to the purposes of the study. Studies may measure feasibility of use of a vendor by type of material, age of material, discounts, additional vendor charges, and factors such as the location of the vendor in terms of speed of order fulfillment. In addition, vendor studies may look at the work of one vendor or compare two or more. Several types of studies have been done in the past few years.

Type and Location of Vendor

The ordering source can vary widely. All of the following qualify as vendors: publisher, distributor, wholesaler, and bookstore, each of which can be divided into subtypes. Some distributors and wholesalers specialize in a particular subject or clientele. Others are generalists. They may be located anywhere in the world. Most published studies focus on North American wholesaler performance. Lincoln provides raw data to show the speed with which Canadian publishers, publisher-agents, distributors, and wholesalers supplied titles to the Dafoe Library at the University of Manitoba.[8] As a result of his experience at the San Francisco State College Library, Pickett advocates that acquisitions librarians located in metropolitan areas with a number of scholarly and trade bookstores in close proximity utilize those bookstores as vendors.[9] Kim[10] and Veenstra and Mai[11] point out the advantages of ordering directly from the publisher.

Type of Material Ordered

Most published vendor performance studies address the ordering of in-print monographs. Lynden and Meyerfeld suggest six factors to consider when evaluating out-of-print (OP) dealers;[12]

8. Robert Lincoln, "Vendors and Delivery," *Canadian Library Journal* 35 (February 1978): 52−55, 57.

9. Pickett, "An Experiment in Book Buying," p. 372.

10. Ung Chon Kim, "Purchasing Books from Publishers and Wholesalers," *Library Resources & Technical Services* 19 (Spring 1975): 146−147.

11. John Veenstra and Lois Mai, "When Do You Use a Jobber?" *College & Research Libraries* 23 (November 1962): 524.

12. Fred C. Lynden and Arthur Meyerfeld, "Library Out-of-Print Book Procurement: The Stanford University Experience," *Library Resources & Technical Services* 17 (Spring 1973): 221−222.

Mitchell describes the specific methodology used for evaluating OP dealers at the San Fernando Valley State College Library.[13] Green describes his evaluation of serials agents through a detailed analysis of the number of claims sent to each.[14] Bonk discusses the thought process and analysis necessary to evaluate serials vendors.[15]

Ordering Method Used

The majority of studies in the literature analyze vendor performance in supplying firm orders. Grant and Perelmuter analyze performance of three vendors in supplying items on approval.[16] Hulbert and Curry review the performance of one approval dealer.[17] Leonhardt presents several analyses done by research libraries on approval vendor performance.[18] As part of their report on the results of a questionnaire filled out by more than 100 academic librarians using approval vendors, Reidelbach and Shirk analyze rating of vendors by acquisitions departments, collection development departments, bibliographers, and faculty.[19]

Number of Vendors

Most studies evaluate the performance of more than one vendor. Exceptions are the Bracken and Calhoun study[20] which analyzes one vendor's performance with firm orders by subject and by publisher and the Hulbert and Curry evaluation of a single approval dealer.[21]

13. Betty J. Mitchell, "A Systematic Approach to Performance Evaluation of Out-of-Print Book Dealers: The San Fernando Valley State College Experience," *Library Resources & Technical Services* 15 (Spring 1971): 216–221.

14. Paul Robert Green, "The Performance of Subscription Agents: A Detailed Survey," *The Serials Librarian* 8 (Winter 1983): 8–21.

15. Sharon C. Bonk, "Toward a Methodology of Evaluating Serials Vendors," *Library Acquisitions: Practice and Theory* 9 (1985): 54–59.

16. Joan Grant and Susan Perelmuter, "Vendor Performance Evaluation," *Journal of Academic Librarianship* 4 (November 1978): 366–367.

17. Hulbert and Curry, "Evaluation of an Approval Plan," pp. 486–490.

18. Thomas W. Leonhardt, comp., *Approval Plans in ARL Libraries*, OMS Systems and Procedures Exchange Center Kit 83 (Washington, D.C.: Association of Research Libraries, 1982), pp. 21–72.

19. John H. Reidelbach and Gary M. Shirk, "Selecting an Approval Plan Vendor. III: Academic Librarians' Evaluations of Eight United States Approval Plan Vendors," *Library Acquisitions: Practice and Theory* 9 (1985): 255–260.

20. Bracken and Calhoun, "Profiling Vendor Performance," pp. 120–128.

21. Hulbert and Curry, "Evaluation of an Approval Plan," pp. 485–491.

Marion T. Reid

Number of Libraries

Most vendor evaluations to date have been conducted by staff members in a single library. The literature identifies two studies done by more than one library. Sumler, Barone, and Goetz describe the method by which the directors of eight small public libraries and one regional library on the eastern shore of Maryland analyzed the performance of two vendors.[22] Miller and Niemeier, who work in different libraries, explain parallel comparison of four vendors.[23] Leonhardt describes the joint surveys done by more than thirty members of the North Carolina Center for Independent Higher Education, Inc., in connection with obtaining across-the-board discounts for firm orders from book vendors.[24] Having multiple acquisitions staffs adhere to the same study procedures is an arduous task, for staff must strive for consistency on as many variables as possible. Being able to compare data of libraries of different sizes can result in a meaningful experience for the acquisitions librarians involved, as Lindsey points out.[25]

Combination of Factors

Two studies incorporate a variety of the factors cited. Joseph compares the effectiveness of receipt of foreign serials in two libraries in India.[26] One library acquires serials directly from the publisher; the other receives materials through an agent. Thorton and Bigger analyze the varying costs charged by serials vendors to a group of eighty-six British libraries for a list of forty-three journals.[27]

22. Sumler, Barone, and Goetz, "Getting Books Faster and Cheaper: A Jobber Acquisitions Study," pp. 103–104.

23. Ruth H. Miller and Martha W. Niemeier, "Vendor Performance: A Study of Two Libraries," *Libraries Resources & Technical Services* 31 (January-March 1987): 60–68.

24. Thomas W. Leonhardt, "Vendor Performance Studies," unpublished text of a paper delivered at the ALA RTSD Conference-within-a-Conference on Research in Library Resources and Technical Services, Philadelphia, Penn., July 11, 1982, pp. 6–7.

25. Jonathan A. Lindsey, "Vendor Discounts to Libraries in a Consortium," *Library Acquisitions: Practice and Theory* 5 (1981): 151.

26. Rosamma Joseph, "Procurement of Foreign Periodicals Direct and Through Agents: A Comparative Study Based on a Cost-Benefit Analysis," *Library Progress* 3 (June-December 1983): 37–42.

27. S. A. Thornton and C. J. Bigger, "Periodicals, Prices and Policies," *ASLIB Proceedings* 37 (November-December 1985): 437–52.

WHAT FACTORS SHOULD BE ANALYZED?

What should be measured? The two most common factors measured are delivery rate and discount. Before initiating a vendor performance study, the acquisitions librarian must determine which factors of vendor performance are important in a particular library setting. Various libraries will rate the importance of speed over discount and vice versa, but what other factors are important?

The following list of factors that others have measured can be used as a starting point to identify factors important in a given library situation:

- list price
- discount
- effective discount (actual rate of discount with postage and service charges included)
- average cost per volume
- number of titles ordered
- number of titles received
- number of days required for receipt
- number of days from order placement until the vendor initiated shipment or issued a report or cancellation notice
- amount of time between receipt of book and receipt of invoice
- number of reports
- number of claims
- number of cancellations
- imprint dates of titles canceled by vendor
- number of titles not received, reported on, or canceled by vendor
- number and type of vendor-related problems
- information included on the invoice
- publisher category according to *Literary Market Place*
- bibliographic accuracy of approval slips

WHAT FORMULAS OR MODELS ARE AVAILABLE?

Most authors of published vendor performance studies have simply presented their results in the form of raw data with a bit of narrative. Very few formulas or models have been suggested.

Bell and others rank the vendors they studied by four variables: percentage of orders received, mean receipt period, time lapse between receipt of book and invoice, and number of vendor-related problems.[28] In each area, the vendor with the best performance was given a 1, and when more than one vendor demonstrated identical performance, each was given the same rank. The vendor considered to have performed best is the vendor with the lowest cumulative ranking. The authors point out that, "if certain jobber characteristics are considered more important than others, weighted rankings should be used."

Kim[29] and Rouse[30] each provide a method of combining the two factors of discount rate and delivery time. Kim offers a simple formula to compute the relative efficiency value. The acquisitions librarian must decide which factor, discount or speed, is more important to his or her library and weigh the factors accordingly. Rouse sets forth a more complex scheme; he uses a technique called decision analysis to analyze past vendor performance in order to predict the vendor most suitable for new orders. Each new order must be characterized as trade or nontrade with a rush or nonrush status.

Henshaw and Kurth describe the system developed at the Library of Congress to evaluate vendors who are authorized to supply certain categories of newly published materials.[31] This scheme analyzes dealer performance in four areas, each of which has a set number of possible points to score:

1. coverage (degree of coverage achieved)
2. quality of materials supplied
3. understanding (clearness and intelligibility of dealer's correspondence and reports)
4. acceptability of invoices

Prices are also analyzed. First, one of the following three is scored:

1. discount on domestic prices
2. domestic prices
3. service charge on domestic prices

Then, one of the following two is scored:

1. library pays postage
2. dealer pays postage

28. Bell and others, "Methodology for a Comparison of Book Jobber Performance," p. 227.

29. Kim, "Purchasing Books from Publishers and Wholesalers," pp. 145–146.

30. William B. Rouse, "Optimal Selection of Acquisition Sources," *Journal of the American Society for Information Sciences* 25 (July-August 1974): 228–30.

31. Francis H. Henshaw and William H. Kurth, "Dealer Rating System at LC," *Library Resources & Technical Services* 1 (Summer 1957): 133–136.

In order to fairly compare one vendor to another using this scheme, it is imperative that the same qualitative judgment be used in assigning the score in each category.

Davis sets forth the most viable vendor performance evaluation model to date; she presents a how-to prescription for determining the sample, recording the data, and compiling results.[32] Davis offers formulas for computing the portion of points earned by each vendor in the areas of discount, speed, fulfillment, and service. She defines service, the most nebulous area, as an aggregate of the following: reporting, lack of errors, invoicing, handling orders without sending them back for prepayment or for further information, ease of returns, and settling of problems. Although Davis sets forth one way of assessing points, she does not consider it definitive, since formulas will vary from library to library according to each library's unique needs.

WHAT GUIDELINES CAN BE USED FOR A VENDOR PERFORMANCE STUDY?

In 1981 a subcommittee of the Collection Management and Development Committee of ALA's Resources and Technical Services Division/Resources Section began formulating guidelines to assist an acquisitions librarian in conducting a study of vendor performance. The resulting publication, *Guide to Performance Evaluation of Library Materials Vendors*, offers guidelines for planning a study; outlines both qualitative and quantitative variables to consider; offers some basic data analysis considerations including how to compute such measures as mean discount, claims means, and mean cost per volume; and offers hints in using vendor evaluation data provided by an automated system. As the introduction points out:

> The purpose of these guidelines is to assist librarians in designing vendor performance studies. They suggest methods of applying quantitative measurements to book vendors' performance in supplying libraries with in-print monographs. Rather than prescribing a standard valuative

---

32. Mary Byrd Davis, "Model for a Vendor Study in a Manual or Semi-Automated Acquisitions System," *Library Acquisitions: Practice and Theory* 3 (1979): 57–59.

Marion T. Reid

study, the guidelines list various elements of vendor performance and suggest ways to measure them. These suggestions may be adapted to the needs and circumstances of each
individual library.[33]

An acquisitions librarian can best prepare to do a vendor performance study by following these guidelines and by adapting por-
tions of previous studies and models.

SHOULD A VENDOR PERFORMANCE STUDY BE SHARED?

The results of a vendor performance study should be shared with
each of the vendors evaluated. Each vendor should be told how
his or her firm performed in relation to the other vendors in
general. Each vendor may be able to assist with the interpretation of the data by suggesting another way to compute the results
or by suggesting additional factors to consider. Through discussion of the results, both the acquisitions librarian and the vendor will more clearly understand the complexities of the
operation of the other. If problems with vendor performance are
evident, the vendor will most likely adjust procedures in order
to improve service. The librarian should allow a reasonable
length of time for the results of those procedural changes to take
effect.

Colleagues will be interested in hearing the results of a vendor performance study. The ALA guidelines indicate that

> Because acquisitions procedures vary widely from library
> to library, both in their form and their efficiency, librarians
> should exercise caution in sharing their own vendor perfor-
> mance studies with their colleagues or in accepting the
> results of others as appropriate for their own libraries.[34]

If the study is valid in terms of the factors measured, in how
they are measured, and in how the results are interpreted, then
the study may be considered for publication. Care should be taken

---

33. American Library Association, Collection Management and Development
Committee, *Guide to Performance Evaluation of Library Material Vendors*
(Chicago: American Library Association, 1988) p. 1.
34. Ibid., p. 2.

to describe the study methodology in detail, pointing out flaws and areas for further study. Prior to submitting the report of such a study for publication, the author should discuss the study with each vendor involved in order to provide opportunity for comment and to consider the results from as many angles as possible.

Lengthy discussion has ensued over this question: Should the vendors evaluated in a study be identified? Alley reports on an ALA meeting in which panel participants advocated anonymity of vendors in published findings.[35] Bullard, a member of the audience at that meeting, stated then and later wrote that each vendor *should* be identified by name so that acquisitions librarians can be better informed.[36] The published studies identified at the end of this chapter are divided on this topic in practice. Eight of them identify vendors by name, while fifteen refer to the vendors generically. The reasons that many authors elect *not* to identify the vendors in print are many. Each library has unique requirements, so the favorable rating of a vendor in one library may not equate to the evaluation of that vendor in another library even if the vendor is performing in the same manner. Quirks in time and location may cause results for one library to be quite different from results for another library. For example, a dealer's warehouse may flood or a mail strike may effect speed of supply. A library located away from large cities and main transportation routes may experience quite different performance from a vendor than that which a library located in a large metropolitan area might experience. And the same library might experience quite different performance from the same vendor now than it experienced two years ago. Rather than tending to cast a study in stone by identifying the vendors by name, it is best to identify them in print generically; they may be identified by name orally with qualifications on the age and methodology of the study.

HOW DOES ONE FOLLOW UP
A VENDOR PERFORMANCE STUDY?

As mentioned earlier, the performance study should serve as a basis for continued communication with each vendor studied. It

35. Brian Alley, "What Ever Became of Vendor B?" *Library Acquisitions: Practice and Theory,* 4 (1980): 185–186.

36. Scott R. Bullard, "Where's Ralph Nader, Now that Acquisitions Librarians Need Him?" *Library Acquisitions: Practice and Theory,* 3 (1979): 1–2.

can form the basis for changes in acquisitions procedures or for the choice of which vendor is to be used in a certain situation.

SHOULD MORE STUDIES BE DONE?

The ALA guidelines are a beginning point for vendor studies. They were written with the intention of stimulating acquisitions librarians to conduct studies and to undertake future revisions of the guidelines themselves. As Leonhardt pointed out at the Conference-within-a-Conference on Research in Library Resources and Technical Services, "the greatest research need [in the area of vendor performance studies] is to keep earlier studies and conclusions up-to-date."[37]

Vendor performance studies done in an acquisitions department using manual procedures are cumbersome and a drain on staff time. When appropriate vendor performance information is gathered by automated systems in many libraries, it will be more realistic for acquisitions librarians to analyze vendor performance on a regular basis. And when many libraries using the same automated system analyze vendor performance data for the same time period in the same manner, a more meaningful profile of vendor performance will exist.

B I B L I O G R A P H Y

Alley, Brian. "What Ever Became of Vendor B?" *Library Acquisitions: Practice and Theory* 4 (1980): 185–186.

Baumann, Susan. "An Application of Davis' 'Model for a Vendor Study.'" *Library Acquisitions: Practice and Theory* 8 (1984): 83–90.

_____ . "An Extended Application of Davis' 'Model for a Vendor Study.'" *Library Acquisitions: Practice and Theory* 9 (1985): 317–329.

Bell, JoAnn, and others. "Methodology for a Comparison of Book Jobber Performance." *Medical Library Association Bulletin* 70 (April 1982): 229–231.

37. Leonhardt, "Vendor Performance Studies," p. 8.

Bonk, Sharon C. "Toward a Methodology of Evaluating Serials Vendors." *Library Acquisitions: Practice and Theory* 9 (1985): 51–60.

Bracken, James K., and John C. Calhoun. "Profiling Vendor Performance." *Library Resources & Technical Services* 28 (April-June 1984): 120–128.

Bullard, Scott R. "Where's Ralph Nader, Now that Acquisitions Librarians Need Him?" *Library Acquisitions: Practice and Theory* 3 (1979): 1–2.

Collection Management and Development Committee. *Guide to Performance Evaluation of Library Materials Vendors.* Chicago: American Library Association, 1988.

Davis, Mary Byrd. "Model for a Vendor Study in a Manual or Semi-Automated Acquisitions System." *Library Acquisitions: Practice and Theory* 3 (1979): 53–60.

Grant, Joan, and Susan Perelmuter. "Vendor Performance Evaluation." *Journal of Academic Librarianship* 4 (November 1978): 366–367.

Green, Paul Robert. "The Performance of Subscription Agents: A Detailed Survey." *The Serials Librarian* 8 (Winter 1983): 7–22.

Hanson, Jo Ann. "An Evaluation of Book Suppliers Used by the University of Denver Library." Master's thesis, University of Denver, 1977. ERIC no. ED 156 132.

Henshaw, Francis H., and William H. Kurth. "Dealer Rating System at LC." *Library Resources & Technical Services* 1 (Summer 1957): 131–136.

Hulbert, Linda Ann, and David Stewart Curry. "Evaluation of an Approval Plan." *College & Research Libraries* 39 (November 1978): 485–491.

Ivins, October. "The Development of Criteria and Methodologies for evaluating the Performance of Monograph and Serials Vendors," *Advances in Serials Management* 2: 185–212 (Greenwich, Conn.: JAI Press, 1988).

Joseph, Rosamma. "Procurement of Foreign Periodicals Direct and Through Agents: A Comparative Study Based on a Cost-Benefit Analysis." *Library Progress* 3 (June-December 1983): 37–42.

Kim, Ung Chon. "Purchasing Books from Publishers and Wholesalers." *Library Resources & Technical Services* 19 (Spring 1975): 133–147.

Landesman, Margaret, and Christopher Gates. "Performance of American In-Print Vendors: A Comparison at the University of Utah." *Library Acquisitions: Practice and Theory* 4 (1980): 187–192.

Lawson, Clinton D. "Where in Hell Are Those Books We Ordered?; A Study of Speed of Service from Canadian Publishers." *Ontario Library Review* 55 (December 1971): 237-41.

Leonhardt, Thomas W., comp. *Approval Plans in ARL Libraries.* OMS Systems and Procedures Exchange Center Kit 83. Washington, D.C.: Association of Research Libraries, 1982.

_____ . "Vendor Performance Studies." Unpublished text of a paper read at the ALA RTSD Conference-within-a-Conference on Research in Library Resources and Technical Services, Philadelphia, Penn., July 11, 1982.

Lincoln, Robert. "Vendors and Delivery." *Canadian Library Journal* 35 (February 1978): 51–55, 57.

Lindsey, Jonathan A. "Vendor Discounts to Libraries in a Consortium." *Library Acquisitions: Practice and Theory* 5 (1981): 147–152.

Lynden, Fred C., and Arthur Meyerfeld. "Library Out-of-Print Book Procurement: The Stanford University Experience." *Library Resources & Technical Services* 17 (Spring 1973): 216–224.

Miller, Ruth H., and Martha W. Niemeier. "Vendor Performance: A Study of Two Libraries." *Library Resources & Technical Services* 31 (January-March 1987): 60–68.

Mitchell, Betty J. "A Systematic Approach to Performance Evaluation of Out-of-Print Book Dealers: The San Fernando Valley State College Experience." *Library Resources & Technical Services* 15 (Spring 1971): 215–222.

Pickett, A. S. "An Experiment in Book Buying." *Library Journal* 84 (February 1, 1959): 371–372.

Reidelbach, John H., and Gary M. Shirk. "Selecting an Approval Plan Vendor. III: Academic Librarians' Evaluations of Eight United States Approval Plan Vendors." *Library Acquisitions: Practice and Theory* 9 (1985): 177–260.

Rouse, William B. "Optimal Selection of Acquisition Sources." *Journal of the American Society for Information Sciences* 25 (July-August 1974): 227–231.

Stokley, Sandra Lu, and Marion T. Reid. "A Study of Five Book Dealers Used by Louisiana State University." *Library Resources & Technical Services* 22 (Spring 1978): 117–125.

Sumler, Claudia, Kristine Barone, and Art Goetz. "Getting Books Faster and Cheaper: A Jobber Acquisitions Study." *Public Libraries* 19 (Winter 1980): 103-05.

Thorton, S. A., and C. J. Bigger. "Periodicals, Prices and Policies." *ASLIB Proceedings* 37 (November-December 1985): 437–452.

Uden, Janet. "Financial Reporting and Vendor Performance: A Case Study." *Journal of Library Automation* 13 (September 1980): 185–195.

Veenstra, John, and Lois Mai. "When Do You Use a Jobber?" *College & Research Libraries* 23 (November 1962): 522–524.

Vendor-Library Relations:
The Ethics of Working with Vendors

Donna Goehner

What do acquisitions librarians want from their relationships with vendors? What do vendors expect from their associations with librarians? How could the current state of relations between the two groups be characterized? Who decides what is appropriate conduct for librarians and vendors in their dealings with each other? Answers to these questions must be contributed by both librarians and vendors, not only because their roles create a state of interdependency, but also because they have much in common. Each serves an intermediary role in an arena where service is the primary function and information the primary commodity. Furthermore, there is a growing trend for librarians to turn to vendors, not only for supplying materials for their library collections, but also for providing them with sophisticated automated products and systems for administering their acquisitions programs. In fact, the symbiotic relationship that exists between acquisitions librarians and vendors has been acknowledged by members of both groups.

Speaking at the 1986 Conference on Issues in Book and Serial Acquisition held at the College of Charleston, Christian Biossonnas, acquisitions librarian at Cornell University, said he was bothered because he didn't know what the limits of that symbiotic relationship were. He suspected that "it is much deeper and complex than we think."[1] Boissonnas went on to say that it seemed to him that

---

1. Christian Boissonnas, "The Cost Is More than That Elegant Dinner: Your Ethics Are at Steak," paper presented at the Conference on Issues in Book and Serial Acquisition: External Influences on Acquisitions and Collection Development. College of Charleston, Charleston, S.C., November 6-8, 1986.

librarians should know these limits and should be concerned about the ethical implications of their affiliations with vendors. Avenues for exploring the behavior of librarians and vendors exist within the American Library Association by way of at least two committees: the Professional Ethics Committee and the Publisher/Vendor-Library Relations Committee. The charge of the latter is

> to serve as the review and advising committee on all matters of vendors of library materials-library relationships; to investigate these relationships; and to prepare recommendations and develop guidelines of acceptable performance for libraries and vendors for ordering and supplying of library materials.[2]

A growing awareness of the need for more dialogue concerning the ethics of working with vendors is found in the article by John Lindsey which appeared in the May 1984 issue of *Technicalities*. In that paper, Lindsey briefly outlined the evolution of the current code of ethics adopted by the American Library Association in 1981, focusing on the portion of the document that addresses the concepts of relationships and responsibilities. Librarians are expected to avoid "situations in which personal interests might be served or financial benefits gained at the expense of library users, colleagues, or the employing institution."[3] Lindsey notes that these concepts raise interesting questions when one considers some of the dynamics of library and vendor interaction: librarians approaching vendors for contributions, prizes, and awards; vendors sponsoring meal functions for librarians at conferences; and vendors providing shuttle bus service during conferences. In the same vein, Lindsey lists a number of questions relating to vendor-library relations which have been the topic of discussions at meetings of the Professional Ethics Committee of ALA:

1. To what extent should a librarian accept vendor invitations?
2. How do you differentiate between personal and professional relationships among vendors and librarians?

2. American Library Association, *Handbook of Organization 1986/1987* (Chicago: American Library Association, 1986), p. 136.
3. Jonathan A. Lindsey, "Appreciation and/or Motivation—Ethics and the Library/Vendor Relationship," *Technicalities* 4 (May 1984): 12.

Donna Goehner

3. Do vendors as businesses operate on one ethical level and librarians on another?
4. Should you give a contract to a personal friend who has a higher bid?
5. Is the professional judgment of a librarian enhanced by accepting no vendor social invitations?

He concludes by relating a comment made by a vendor representative on the question pertaining to social invitations. "That person said, 'Well, it's a mixture of issues: appreciation and motivation. How do you differentiate?' This encapsulates a dilemma in need of articulation from both the vendors' and librarians' perspective."[4]

SURVEY QUESTIONS

Questions similar to those listed were suggested as a departure point for this chapter. Since there are librarians and vendors who have already been considering the ethical aspects of their relations, it was decided to involve some of those people in helping to define acceptable behavior. Six experienced acquisitions librarians and six successful vendors were contacted and asked to respond to the same set of questions pertaining to ethics. The librarians were from academic institutions of various sizes: small, medium, and large. Vendor respondents were from companies that handle book orders and from companies providing subscription services. Nine questions were used for the survey:

1. Do social events obligate a library or acquisitions librarian?
2. Is it fair to compare your vendor contracts with those of other libraries?
3. What information should vendors reveal among themselves about libraries?
4. What information should vendors reveal to libraries about other vendors?
5. What are legitimate promises on both sides?
6. What do you consider to be the most serious ethical issues facing the library-vending community?
7. What do you believe is the greatest incentive to high ethical behavior in organizations?

---

4. Ibid.

8. What do you believe is the major cause for ethical lapses?
9. What other comments would you care to make?

Since answers to questions dealing with ethical behavior are based primarily on personal opinions and value judgments, nuances in replies were more likely to be noticed in face-to-face discussions. Therefore, individual interviews were scheduled with all participants to talk about the questions, which they had received previously through the mail. After the interviews were completed, the answers and related comments were transcribed and compiled. Because the participants were assured anonymity prior to the interviews, their observations are not identified by name. Since ethical reflection means, among other things, thinking about the question of what expectations others may have of us, the respondents' replies should help clarify what behavior is anticipated. The legitimacy of those expectations can be assessed to determine if, and to what degree, they are, or might be, accommodated in the librarians' code of ethics.

SURVEY RESULTS

Obligations of Social Events

The first question participants were asked to address was: Do social events obligate a library or acquisitions librarian? Although everyone interviewed said that social events should not obligate librarians, the operative word is *do*. Several librarians believed there was, at least in theory, general agreement among their peers that accepting an invitation to lunch or attending a social mixer at a vendor's hospitality suite during conventions does not obligate a person in any way. Nonetheless, there is a point at which social entertaining does tend to create a sense of indebtedness. The likelihood of librarians allowing their decisions to be affected by social activities was believed to be directly related to the amount of money involved. The more elegant the dinner, the more lavish the social event, and the more frequent the invitations, the more likely one was to feel subtle pressure to reciprocate by placing orders with the more generous vendors. Even one of the vendors indicated that when the question is *do*, rather than *should* social events obligate librarians, the answer would be "in some cases, yes."

Donna Goehner

Nonetheless, among those interviewed, there was consensus that it is a common practice for vendors and librarians to interact socially, and no one expected that behavior to change. Social activities can, and often do, help both parties understand each other better and can lead to improved working relationships. Vendors mentioned that a more productive discussion can frequently take place over breakfast or lunch when librarians are away from the distractions and interruptions in their work environments. To prevent matters from getting out of hand, it was suggested that vendors set reasonable fiscal guidelines for social activities and stick to them. Many corporations have established certain criteria for business entertaining that are to be adhered to by employees. Yet the values held by individuals, as well as personal motivations, determine how consistently such rules are followed.

If vendors could agree, collectively, to reduce the amount of money they spend on social activities, libraries might be better served. The high costs associated with entertaining are simply passed on to the library consumer in the form of lower discount rates, higher handling or transportation charges, and similar cost-recovery strategies. Librarians who are genuinely interested in seeing vendors set limits on expenditures for social events should be encouraged to say so. Beyond that, however, several of the respondents in both groups said that there must be a commitment on the part of librarians to behave accordingly by declining invitations to extravagant events that could be compromising. As one vendor said during the interviews, "What fuels all this behavior is what works. If it doesn't work, it won't be continued." As long as vendors perceive that financial outlays for social events "pay off," they will continue to sponsor them. When one vendor raises the ante by increasing the amount spent for entertaining current and potential customers, other vendors are obliged to meet that challenge. In this game of one-upmanship, library users may be the ones who suffer the consequences in the form of fewer resources, because libraries' acquisitions dollars are partially subsidizing vendors' expenses for costly social activities.

Librarians and vendors agreed that as long as social events are kept at a modest level, librarians do not obligate themselves in any way by accepting such invitations. However, when librarians accept a vendor's invitations to costly social events, and the result is increased orders to that vendor out of a sense of obligation, librarians have been compromised.

Comparing Vendor Contracts

The second question pertained to contracts: Is it fair to compare your vendor contract with those of other libraries? One acquisitions librarian replied that one of the things that contributes to keeping the library profession honest is that this type of information *is* shared, even though specific names might not be used. Although other librarians agreed, they also believed that the librarians making the comparisons should exercise care and strive for equity. If there are special conditions that could affect the outcome of the assessments, these qualifications should be noted. Few of the librarians thought it was unfair to discuss costs. If there were specific stipulations negotiated with a vendor that were unique to a single institution, however, they questioned whether cost information should be shared with other libraries. Although describing vendor contracts was not viewed as a breach of ethics by most of the librarians as long as factors figuring into the comparison were actually similar, one librarian drew the line at sharing particular discounts received from vendors.

The responses from vendors reveal that attitudes toward this question differ. One vendor said that contracts between a library and a vendor were considered by his company to be private documents and that confidentiality should be maintained on both sides. The reason given for this position was that a contract is a vendor's response to a set of library-specific needs and requests. Such specifications are rarely the same in other libraries. Exceptions to that position are bid situations or cases where the contract is uniform for all customers.

Another vendor said it was all right for librarians to compare contracts unless there had been a specific agreement with the vendor not to reveal the details of the contract. A third vendor stated that his company believed that a well-informed customer is a better client. Moreover, since there should be nothing to fear from an honest and fair comparison, information sharing among librarians was not viewed as a problem. Other comments made by vendors echoed the concern expressed by librarians regarding comparisons, that is, that conditions in the respective institutions be taken into account. It is not fair, for instance, to compare contracts between two libraries when the commitment to volume, the mix of their orders, or the amount of special handling required are different for each. Several vendors mentioned that contracts with state-supported institutions should be available as public information. And most conceded that even a pri-

Donna Goehner

vate institution's contracts might be made available to other libraries. One vendor remarked (paraphrased here): What is there to hide? If a librarian's negotiating skills are so good that exceptional terms of sale are granted, more power to him. The librarian who is reluctant to talk about business dealings may be allowing the personality of the vendor, rather than a factual evaluation of costs and services, to determine from whom his library acquires material.

Even though there was less consensus on this question than the first, it was evident that most respondents were more concerned about the way contractual comparisons were made than with whether librarians should make them. Many factors help determine the terms of a library's contract with a vendor. Librarians were expected to make an effort to identify and examine as many of the relevant elements as possible whenever contractual analyses were undertaken.

Exchange of Information

The third and fourth questions on the list were more general in nature. The third question—what information should vendors reveal among themselves about libraries?—received brief and similar replies from the vendors. They all said, in effect, that vendors should reveal to other vendors only information about libraries that is common knowledge. In their personal experiences, vendors reported that little specific information was actually shared with colleagues. Even when it was, as one respondent indicated, "it is pretty superficial information generally. Pricing or discounts are never discussed because this could be construed as price fixing. Personnel changes, staffing levels, and library programs are examples of the type of information that is generally shared."

There was also considerable agreement among the respondents in their answers to question four: What information should vendors reveal to libraries about other vendors? Vendors may share nonproprietary or public information about other vendors. One of the vendors said that he would not reveal any information that was not clearly stated in a competitor's literature or that was not in the public domain (for example, a new service or product that had been announced at large and for public consumption). Political struggles within the vending community were judged off-limits as were discussions involving the economic health or status of a competitor. Two respondents, one librarian and one vendor, said that no information should be revealed about one's competition. It is difficult to reconcile this opinion with the comment expressed by the vendor who felt that vendors ought to be free to ask or raise questions about the performance of the competition if only to offer reasons for differences in performance among vendors. Finally, one of the librarians pointed out the need for her colleagues to exercise care and to be as fair and objective as possible when talking to other librarians about vendors.

Legitimate Promises

This last observation leads to a broader concern, which was posed in the fifth question: What are legitimate promises on both sides? Since this question generated a great deal of discussion, the responses were difficult to summarize. There was as much description of behavior that was disliked when legitimate promises were not kept as there was in identifying the promises. What follows is a combination of what librarians expect from vendors, what vendors expect from librarians, and which business practices both groups prefer.

Vendors expect librarians to be as good as their word when they indicate the volume of orders that will be placed. Other considerations vendors appreciate are a fair mix of orders, good preorder searching to reduce the number of duplicates and returns, and prompt payment when goods and services have been delivered as promised. Librarians should recognize a purchase order as a legal, contractual obligation representing a product or service that is going to be accepted and paid for in accordance with the vendor's terms of sale. One vendor elaborated, "Librarians must recognize that their vendors must receive fair pay for services provided. Vendors are under tremendous strain to constantly reinvest profits back into their business, particularly regarding emerging technologies. Unrealistic demands for increasing discounts only fuel the discount gamesmanship of some vendors. In today's competitive environment we find vendors according discounts that are deemed necessary to buy a particular account. And, librarians encourage this unethical happening." One of the librarians interviewed was also uneasy about the attitude of some librarians toward the vendor's predicament. She explained, "I am particularly concerned about delays in payment to small vendors who may already have a cash flow problem. Carrying a long overdue account may result in the fail-

Donna Goehner

ure of a small organization having limited reserves. Librarians have to be sensitive to the effects of their actions in these matters. Many librarians seem to think they deserve a lot of favors from vendors, and, yet, they have little understanding of what it takes to run a business these days."

Both vendors and librarians emphasized the importance of keeping one's word. When either party does not live up to its promises, the library-vendor relationship is damaged. When a librarian negotiates a certain volume of business with a vendor who quotes a discount based on that volume, this is considered a legitimate promise. If the librarian reneges on that agreement by failing to place the specified volume of orders, is it ethical for the librarian to expect to receive the discount originally negotiated? The respondents thought not.

What are legitimate promises that vendors should make to librarians? Respondents had less difficulty answering this part of the question. The vendor should offer the library the best possible terms of sale. Terms should be similar, if not identical, to those offered to other libraries with comparable operations. Additionally, vendors should clearly define their policies regarding invoicing, pricing, discount structure, service charges, returns, claims, and other business practices unique to their company. For example, they should adhere to the delivery schedules stated in their informational literature or promised by a representative of the company.

Ethical Issues

Turning from questions dealing with the conduct of librarians and vendors on circumscribed issues, the respondents were asked to react to questions of a more general nature. The sixth question was: What do you consider to be the most serious ethical issues facing the library-vending community? Honest representation of vendor services was viewed by more than half of the respondents as one of the most serious issues facing vendors as well as librarians. One individual stated that "some vendors are deliberately misleading in describing the nature of their services and products." Another said that vendors should "provide libraries with a complete explanation of costs—what is included and what is not—and with the short- and long-term benefits and shortcomings of their services." A third deplored the practice of "promising librarians discounts that have no reality base to the fair profit that a vendor must realize for success."

Vendors

   Two of the respondents expressed concern regarding the growing level of competitiveness in the vending community. The
librarian believed there would be fewer vendors in the near future
and that increased competition would lead to a lowering of standards for ethical behavior, less attention to requests for cus-
tomized services, and lower discounts. The vendor who spoke
about the effects of competition explained it in these words: "I
anticipate an increase in ethical lapses as vendors move to position for success. The pie is shrinking and too many vendors are,
literally, buying market position. Vendors are promoting technical services and librarians are demanding increasing technical support from vendors. Yet, librarians are unwilling to pay for
such 'support' and the vendor is being forced to operate more stra-
tegically in a world of shrinking profit margins."
   Other ethical issues that were considered serious included
defaulting on contracts, abusing policies on book returns, over-
encumbering and overspending by libraries, and expecting financial support from vendors for activities unrelated to libraries.
Such practices strain the library-vendor relationship and can lead
not only to criticism but also to termination of the business affiliation. Numerous examples were given to illustrate the awkward
position in which vendors and librarians have found themselves
when the limits of probity were exceeded.
   The description that follows depicts one vendor's dilemma in
a case where canceling a contract was considered the appropriate course of action. Library X told vendor Y that a certain
amount of money would be spent for material from a variety of
trade, university press, and science-technology publishers. Vendor Y wrote a two-year contract that included a good discount
based on the volume and mix of orders projected by library X.
When the mix of orders was not at all as indicated by the library,
vendor Y's contract became unprofitable. The vendor had to
decide whether to honor the contract or default and cut its losses.
The company decided to fulfill its obligation for one year but to
cancel at the end of the first year rather than to let the contract
run the intended two-year period.
   Another situation that can affect a vendor's profit margin is
the abuse of return privileges by libraries. Vendors can legitimately return books to publishers within 90 to 100 days. When
libraries keep books longer than the publisher's return agreement specifies, the vendor again is in a quandary. If the vendor
accepts the late return to maintain a good relationship with the
library, the profit on the sale is forfeited. By refusing the late

Donna Goehner

return, the vendor jeopardizes future orders from the library. One vendor remarked that it seemed to be the same libraries abusing this policy on a routine basis.

A related occurrence involves the return of material because of poor quality. Vendors said they ought not to be placed in the role of judges in the publishing arena and be expected to evaluate the quality of material. As one vendor explained, "If inferior material is returned to us because of its content, and if the publisher will not accept the return, the vendor should not have to absorb the cost. The library should keep the book. It is not our job to see that standards of quality meet the library's expectations." On the other hand, material that is physically damaged is of concern to both parties.

Although there were numerous examples given of ethical infringements, the practice of overspending or overextending library materials budgets was selected as the last illustration because it is serious and because it was reported to occur with some degree of regularity. Some are libraries that not only over-encumber their materials budget but also overspend their allocation. They then expect the vendor to "carry" them or bail them out. Degrees of seriousness associated with this problem were noted. One vendor described a situation in which a library ordered $200,000 of processed books. After the vendor had placed the orders and received and processed them to the library's specifications, the librarian called to say there was only $100,000 in the book budget. Who was asleep at the wheel? Was it fair to expect the vendor to hold invoices for those books until the library's funds for the next fiscal year were released? Unfortunately, this was not an isolated instance. The vendor's position in cases such as these was outlined in the following statement: "We have had several experiences with libraries and business offices who have overspent, promised payment, and failed to make payment over a long period of time. We have been put in a difficult situation because of such unscrupulous practices. Business officers and institutional fiscal agents should know better." One librarian who acknowledged that this practice was more prevalent than she liked to admit added that she did not want her library to subsidize those institutions that did not pay their bills on time.

Ethical Behavior

Since respondents recognized the damaging effects of unethical conduct on their working relationships, they were willing to attempt answers to the seventh question: What do you believe is the greatest incentive to high ethical behavior in organizations? There was virtually unanimous agreement that the ethical tone of an organization is established and fostered at the top. Management has to assume responsibility for defining and maintaining the value system. Mutual respect and high expectations were incentives mentioned by several respondents. Fairness, honesty, and respect were values respondents considered prerequisites to ethical behavior. If high standards are demanded and practiced by those in positions of leadership, other people in the organization will be more inclined to follow suit. In the words of one librarian, proper behavior is more likely to occur "just by knowing that ethical behavior is what the other person expects, by letting each other know when these expectations have not been achieved, and by indicating how severe the lapse was judged to be." Another respondent said that a good reputation is built up over a long period of time and that consistency in doing the right thing is how respect is earned. Avoiding short-term, quick-fix solutions to problems was considered a good approach to establishing the necessary climate for success. As one individual noted, perhaps the greatest incentive to high ethical behavior in organizations is "the clear indication that unethical behavior is intolerable. Moreover, the environment should be such that others within the organization would be shocked if unethical acts had been committed."

Ethical Lapses

The flip side of this issue was addressed in the eighth question: What do you believe is the major cause for ethical lapses? As might be expected from previous responses, one reason given for ethical lapses was the failure of leaders within the organization to have clearly defined and communicated the expectation for high ethical behavior. Lack of concern on the part of leadership does make a difference in how people behave. If an executive officer does not exercise internal control by telling staff that ethics is an important issue, the business practices of some employees may deteriorate. An organization is defined ultimately by the caliber of people it employs, not by mission statements or advertising claims. Therefore, if the ethical conduct of an individual degenerates, the good name of the organization also suffers. When the bottom line becomes the prime consideration for vendors, the company is jeopardizing its reputation. Based on those

Donna Goehner

observations, it was not surprising that most respondents said that greed was the major cause for ethical lapses. This reason would apply more to vendors than librarians in the context of bottom-line considerations. Yet, librarians put themselves in a similar position when they ask vendors for donations knowing that the vendor's interest will not be served. For instance, how does a vendor benefit when agreeing to make a donation toward a university's fund drive for a new field house? Vendors reported cases even more flagrant. Some university development officers telephone vendors who have major accounts with their institution and ask for substantial donations to their development programs. If the company does not contribute, the institution implies that the library might select another vendor for the services being provided. Often such actions take place without the knowledge of anyone in the library.

While activities centering around money were mentioned most often as ones that can lead to questionable conduct, other causes for ethical lapses were identified: naiveté, thoughtlessness, egotism, and exploitation. The majority of respondents, however, thought that vendors and librarians were, for the most part, an ethical group of people. Commenting on the conduct of both parties, one librarian observed: "I think in some ways we are to be complimented because the number of cases we see that involve unethical behavior on the part of librarians or vendors is minimal."

Additional Comments

It would be possible to end this chapter with that positive statement. There are, however, a few concluding remarks, made in answer to the last question on the sheet sent to respondents, that should be recorded. Participants were asked if there were other comments they would like to make pertaining either to ethics or to the relationship between librarians and vendors that were not covered in the previous questions.

Several of the respondents noted that few library schools teach students much about the publishing world, the acquisitions process, or how to be a good consumer. Many librarians accept positions in an acquisitions department with little firsthand knowledge of basic bookkeeping practices, contract negotiations, financial reports, or accounting principles. They know even less about how vendors operate. This void in their program of studies has to be filled on the job and can result in a less-than-optimum business relationship with seasoned vendors.

Some respondents thought that librarians are becoming more businesslike in their approach to acquisitions. As fiscal agents for their institutions, acquisitions librarians are responsible for monitoring the expenditure of many thousands of dollars. To build quality collections, they should make every effort to insure that they are acquiring the most appropriate material money can buy. They should be able to provide valid reasons for their choices and indicate how the selections they make contribute to quality and value for library users. One vendor went so far as to say that he thought it was unethical for a librarian to spend large sums of money for books and not expect to be held accountable for where the money was spent or for the value of the items received. With more access to the products of automation, the potential exists for better management information to monitor the performance of vendors and librarians. While this could lead to more scrutiny and more competitiveness, the general consensus of respondents was that having better data is essential to evaluate effectiveness.

Librarians expect vendors to be familiar with the programs, policies, fiscal procedures, and budget constraints in each of the libraries with which they do business. In addition, vendors are expected to be aware of the vagaries of the publishing world and to serve as a library's link to that market. In return, vendors believe that acquisitions librarians should reciprocate by managing their operations efficiently and objectively, and by being sensitive to vendors' needs for a return on their investment in order to remain solvent. By responding to unique requests and tailoring services to precise specifications, vendors are hampered in their ability to generate savings which could be realized if library acquisitions practices were more uniform. Vendors are not asking that libraries modify their practices to conform to a particular standard simply to cut down on the amount of time and effort they expend on an individual account. They do want librarians to acknowledge that special requirements and exceptions increase the vendor's operating costs.

CONCLUSION

In the opening paragraph of this chapter, four questions dealing with expectations and behavior were posed. The librarians and vendors interviewed have provided some answers to those questions as well as to other more specific queries. They have explained

Donna Goehner

what they expect from their relationships with one another. They have characterized the current state of these associations as cordial and basically ethical, although they noted some of the more obvious exceptions. They have expressed the belief that it is the responsibility of individuals in both groups to determine if certain conduct is appropriate. When conduct is considered inappropriate, they want to be told. In short, librarians and vendors were concerned about their relationships, their behavior, and their expectations of one another. Furthermore, they indicated that many vendors and acquisitions librarians have developed personal as well as business relationships with one another because they often have similar backgrounds and interests. It is precisely for this reason that extra care should be taken to insure that those friendships do not bias judgments. In business dealings that meet the expressed needs of both groups, the participants simply cannot afford to jeopardize a mutually beneficial arrangement. Librarians and vendors are more likely to maintain a healthy and profitable affiliation by taking seriously the advice offered by one of the respondents: "Don't make promises lightly, and deliver what you promise."

Approval Plans:
The Vendor as Preselector

Joan Grant

Approval plans as a means of acquiring books were first introduced in the early 1960s. Since that time, they have been the subject of a series of conferences and many presentations at professional meetings and discussion groups. Library literature is replete with both articles and monographs that discuss the history of approval plans, argue for and against their use, describe the experiences of specific libraries, and suggest models for selecting, establishing, and evaluating approval plans. Librarians who are considering or are already involved with such a plan are fortunate to be working at a time when so much documentation exists. They are also in the happy position of being able to draw upon the now quite sophisticated experience of their colleagues at other libraries and the vendors who offer approval plan services.

While it is wise to glean as much as possible from the experiences of others via the literature and personal contacts, it is also essential that every library consider the advisability of establishing an approval plan and the evaluation of an ongoing plan within the context of its own situation. Local staffing, organization, budget, collection development practices, and politics and personalities all are important factors that will have an impact on the success or failure of an approval plan. The same variables should be borne in mind when selecting or evaluating vendors. There are a good number of competent vendors who have successful approval plan programs. Choosing the right vendor for a specific plan will have much to do with how well that vendor's plan meshes with the library's local needs.

The librarian who wishes to explore approval plans should embark upon a research project designed to gather information in three areas:

1. The business of approval plans: What are the general principles behind the operation of approval plans? What is it that a plan can and cannot do? What can reasonably be asked of a vendor?
2. Library's requirements: What are the library's acquisitions and collection development goals and objectives? How will an approval plan enhance the library's ability to reach these goals?
3. Vendor selection and evaluation: What services are offered by the vendors? How well do the vendor's services meet the library's requirements in all areas, including collection development, organization, and procedures?

There is a natural progression in these steps. Knowing which services can be expected from the marketplace and what the library needs can greatly facilitate decisions about specific plans.

DEFINITION OF APPROVAL PLANS

An approval plan is a contractual agreement between a library and a vendor. The vendor uses a profile (the vendor's coded description of the library's needs) to determine the library's collecting interests. Using the profile, the vendor agrees to make regular (usually weekly) shipments of current imprints in those subjects or from those publishers which the library has indicated it wants. The books are shipped on approval; that is, the library reviews the books on receipt and reserves the right to return any that it deems unsuitable. There are many variations on this admittedly general definition:

1. Breadth of coverage: Plans may be broad enough to cover all the humanities, sciences, and social sciences; limited to a single subject, such as art; or limited to a special aspect of a subject, such as avant-garde poetry. Plans may also be limited to a type of material, such as music scores, or to a list of publishers, such as all publications from university presses.
2. Selection slips: Most plans offer some combination of automatic shipment of books and provision of selection slips to be reviewed by the library staff. Slips may be preferred for

Joan Grant

subject areas in which the library wishes to be very selective or in which initial monitoring of the publishing output is desired. The vendor may also provide slips on those titles that cannot be sent on approval because of price limitations set by the library, questionable content such as textbooks or workbooks, or the publisher's refusal to accept returns. Some plans consist exclusively of slips, in which case the vendor may treat orders on these slips as firm orders and restrict the library's return privileges. Several vendors will assist with retrospective selection projects by using their approval databases to supply back runs of slips in areas the library wants to strengthen.

3. Publisher-based plans: Plans with vendors can be publisher-based rather than subject-based. For instance, some plans are limited to university presses, small presses, or major commercial publishers. In addition, subject plans may be limited to an agreed upon list of key publishers. A number of publishers offer approval plans of their own. They have subject profiles and supply their books directly to the library, frequently for a substantial discount.

4. Foreign imprints: Approval plans are not limited to vendors or publications from the United States. Varieties of book and slip plans are available from vendors in many countries including Britain, France, Germany, the Netherlands, Spain, Italy, Latin American, Australia, Canada, and the Middle East.

VIEW FROM THE VENDORS' SIDE

Approval plans represent a means of doing business that is very attractive to vendors. Successful plans develop into long-term relationships between the library and the vendor, giving the vendor sales that are predictable and dependable. Although libraries have return privileges on approval plans, the vendor and library will wish to set limits on returns, which are a costly use of staff time for both. A generally agreed upon outside limit on returns is 10 percent of a shipment, although less than 5 percent is the most desirable. Any return percentage higher than 10 percent is a warning that the approval plan profile is inaccurate and should be carefully reexamined.

Firm order business for vendors is less dependable, since a library can change its vendor for firm orders relatively quickly and easily. In fact, it is not unusual for staff changes in an acquisitions department to lead to a sudden loss of firm order business to another vendor—one that the new acquisitions librarian is accustomed to using. Changing approval vendors is a far more complicated matter that involves both acquisitions and collection development staff in the operation of a complex project. Fine-tuning the profile and developing effective library-vendor communication concerning the plan requires time and careful, hard work. These factors, combined with the inevitable inadvertent gaps and duplication that occur with new plans, make capricious vendor changes quite rare.

Approval vendors not only can depend upon a certain volume of sales but also can predict the nature of these sales. The subjects and publishers to be covered are agreed upon in advance, so the vendor can concentrate on providing full coverage in those areas. Responding to firm orders on the other hand requires that the vendor devote a good deal of staff time to tracking down elusive small publishers, claiming and reporting out-of-print titles, and dealing with each title in a more individual way. In addition, regular high-volume orders with publishers for approval plan books will, in many cases, allow the vendor to negotiate greater discounts. The discounts can be passed along to customers and eventually lead to an increase in the vendor's approval business.

The ways in which vendors identify publications, match them against the library profiles, and monitor their own performance vary from vendor to vendor. It is important to look at the way in which a vendor handles these three functions.

1. Identification and acquisition: The size of the vendor is one factor in differentiating the ways vendors can identify and acquire the books to be supplied on approval. Large vendors may have a staff of buyers who meet regularly with publishers' representatives, while small vendors may need to rely on less personal forms of identifying potential approval titles. These other methods of identification include examination of prepublication announcements, subscription to LC MARC tapes for CIP (cataloging in publication) information, and maintenance of blanket orders with publishers. Vendors will use some or all of these methods depending upon the size of their staff and the extensiveness of their publisher lists. All of these methods can be highly successful ways of identifying and acquiring publications. It is important to note that it is not always a vendor's

Joan Grant

size that makes it successful in identifying publications; the consistency of the vendor in following through on the information at hand is just as important.

2. Subject analysis: Coding titles in order to match them with library subject profiles may occur at the point of identification or with the book in hand. Titles also may be reviewed at both points, with greater refinement in coding done at the second stage. Many vendors employ librarians or subject specialists with academic backgrounds to do both the selecting and profiling of titles. Publisher-based approval plans can override the need to examine each title more than once, thus enabling the vendor to process the book more quickly.

3. Monitoring the plan: The sources a vendor uses to monitor the coverage of the plan again depend on the size of the company and the scope of the plan. All vendors use publishers' catalogs and customer claims for this purpose. Many also use the *Weekly Record,* reviewing sources such as *Choice, Library Journal, Booklist,* and the *New York Times Book Review,* professional journals, and specialized bibliographies. Reviewing with potential vendors their particular methods and time frame for monitoring what they supply to the library can be revealing.

In 1984, Reidelbach and Shirk published the results of a survey they conducted of eight U.S. approval plan vendors.[1] Data were gathered in nine areas: company background; employee background; customer service; profile and title selection; profile maintenance; materials, forms, slips, and returns handling; financial practices; statistical reporting; and miscellaneous data. While their data should not be used for the purpose of selecting a vendor in lieu of up-to-date information gathered by the library, they do provide a useful overview of the ranges of services offered by vendors. Read in conjunction with papers such as those by Alessi,[2] Frye and Romanansky,[3] and Stave,[4] the article gives the

1. John H. Reidelbach and Gary M. Shirk, "Selecting an Approval Plan Vendor: A Step-by-Step Process," *Library Acquisitions: Practice and Theory* 7 (1984): 182–183.

2. Dana L. Alessi, "Coping With Library Needs: The Approval Vendor's Response/Responsibility," in *Issues in Acquisitions,* edited by Sul H. Lee (Ann Arbor, Mich.: Pierian Press, 1984), pp. 91–109.

3. Gloria Frye and Marcia Romanansky, "The Approval Plan—The Core of an Academic Wholesaler's Business," in *Issues in Acquisitions,* pp. 111–119.

4. Donald G. Stave, "Approval Book Acquisitions: Some Vendor Requirements and Practices," in *Shaping Library Collections for the 1980s,* (Phoenix, Ariz.: Oryx Press, 1980), pp. 159–166.

librarian who is unfamiliar with the vendor's side of approval plans insight into factors that influence approval plan performance.

Other than the books themselves, the profile is the most visible and tangible evidence to the library of the way the vendor manages the plan. A profile consists of a subject thesaurus and a set of nonsubject parameters. The thesauri in use as reported by Reidelbach and Shirk consist of either the LC classification outline or vendor-developed thesauri. In either case, the thesaurus lists subjects in hierarchical order and allows a library to receive publications in part or all of any given subject. For example, a library may not wish to have medical books in general, but may wish to receive all titles available on sports medicine. The subject thesaurus part of a profile will delete every medical topic except sports medicine. Nonsubject parameters allow the library to refine the plan beyond subjects by specifying acceptance or rejection of titles based on level of work, series, edition, price, format, language, place of publication, or other needs. Libraries use nonsubject parameters to block series titles for which the library already has a standing order. Or a library may ask to have slips sent instead of books for all titles costing more than $100, or any reprint editions, or juvenile literature. Using the subject thesaurus in tandem with nonsubject parameters allows for an almost limitless number of permutations in a library's profile. Obviously, the simpler the profile, the less the margin for error in the vendor's ability to supply wanted titles. If a vendor uses the profile correctly, and the library understands and has correctly appraised the vendor of its needs in terms of the profile, there is little chance for error.

DECIDING TO HAVE AN APPROVAL PLAN

There are many reasons why a library might choose to initiate an approval plan. Theoretically, the ideal plan would insure that the library has the subject coverage it wishes at a lower cost. In the process the library would save on acquisitions and selection staff time and also get the books on the shelves faster. While no plan will solve all of the library's selection and acquisition problems so felicitously, a plan will certainly have an impact on existing procedures, staff, budget, and selection practices. However, approval plan "services are not always needed by or relevant to particular libraries, and . . . these potential advantages can be

Joan Grant

nullified by certain internal operations within the library."[5] The decision to implement a plan should, therefore, be preceded by a self-study of sorts that examines the following factors and determines that an approval plan is suitable for the library:

1. Acceptance by selectors: Responsibility for selection may be vested in one or several librarians. In academic libraries, it may also be shared to varying degrees with the teaching faculty. Regardless of the configuration of selection responsibility or the type of library, for an approval plan to be appropriate and successful it is important for those involved to understand and support the plan. They should view the plan as a reliable and effective tool, not an obstacle to be overcome. Everyone concerned with the approval plan should be involved in the review of approval plan vendors from the beginning. Logistics are an important consideration as well. Selectors must be able to review the shipments on a regular, usually weekly, basis. This can be a serious problem for a library that depends upon teaching faculty for its selection decisions.

2. Budgeting: One of the first questions to be asked is whether the library can afford the plan it wants. There will be other demands on the budget, for example, for standing orders, foreign material, retrospective selection, and current imprints not covered by the plan. The cost of these commitments should first be assessed. Then the vendor can help by providing an estimate of the annual cost of the proposed plan. Local budgeting practices should also be analyzed. Political problems may arise if the budget for the plan must be drawn from funds previously set aside for another purpose such as selection of materials by teaching faculty. Will expenditures for the plan be charged to a single fund or to book funds for the various subjects or disciplines? It may be easier to do the former, but the latter will provide potentially useful information about the way the collection is growing. The vendor's management reports can be helpful in this regard, and the vendor should be queried about the company's ability to provide a variety of management reports either on a regular basis or on demand. Some types

---

5. Dimity S. Berkner, "Considerations in Selecting an Approval Plan," in *Shaping Library Collections for the 1980s,* p. 144.

of reports that may be useful are reports by subject, that list areas of slip selection, and reports by publisher. If the detail these reports provide is sufficient for the library's local use, they can be consulted to determine the amount spent by subject.

3. Acquisitions procedures: An ongoing approval plan requires a complex set of procedures to keep it running smoothly. Although not difficult to devise, these procedures will be different from those required for placing and receiving firm orders and should be carefully thought through before a plan is undertaken. Those involved in administering the plan should examine the new workflow and make certain that there are no staffing or procedural problems that might prevent the plan from reaching its full potential. Examples of areas to be examined include support staff responsibility and procedures for sorting and searching the books received; record keeping for orders placed from selection slips; approval claims; invoices, credits, and returns; ordering of second copies; and volumes previously published in a series or set. In addition, acquisitions and selection staff need to communicate regularly on matters ranging from notice of a late shipment to changes in personnel or procedures.

4. Selection practices: For an approval plan to succeed, a library must first define its collection development policies and then communicate them clearly to the vendor via the profile. If a written collection development policy statement does not already exist, it may be that preparation for writing the profile will provide the impetus for discussing policy within the library. Regardless of the order of events, questions such as how interdisciplinary areas will be treated, which subjects are to be collected most intensively, and what are general library policies on collecting types of materials, such as textbooks, should be answered clearly early on. The library should not, after all, expect the vendor to follow policies that are not uniformly understood and followed by the library's own selection staff. The selectors must be willing and able to switch from making choices based on reviews and faculty recommendations to book-in-hand decisions. This provides an opportunity for the selection staff to exercise independent judgment in evaluating the merits of a book and its suitability for the local collection.

Joan Grant

SELECTING AND EVALUATING
AN APPROVAL PLAN

The selection of a vendor for an approval plan and the later evaluation of that vendor's performance are two areas that are covered quite well in library literature. The librarian facing the first of these tasks will benefit from reading Mosher[6], Reidelbach and Shirk,[7] and Berkner[8] on steps to follow in selecting a plan. For the second project, Shirk's suggested model for evaluating vendor performance on approval plans[9], as well as numerous articles by others on the evaluation of specific plans would be useful sources of information. The objective of this research is to cull from the literature the principles and techniques that have worked for others and then to modify them as necessary for application locally.

The selection process involves identifying vendors who offer the kind of plan the library is considering and investigating those vendors' services. The investigation will involve requesting information from the vendors, interviewing the vendors' customers in similar libraries, scheduling on-site presentations by the vendors' representatives, and perhaps even scheduling a visit by library staff to the vendors' offices. The questions to be asked of others at this point are the same ones the library will ask of itself later on when it evaluates its experience with its own plan. Typical factors to examine in judging an approval plan include the following:

1. Profile: Is the profile structured in a way that is compatible with the library's selection policies? Does it have an appropriate degree of detail? How quickly can profile changes be implemented? Is the vendor's acceptable return rate reasonable?
2. Selectivity and coverage: Does the vendor interpret the profile as expected? What sort of monitoring has the library done using regular selection tools, and what were the results? Have gaps been noticeable? Is the number of claims reasonable? How does the vendor handle these claims?

6. Paul H. Mosher, "Waiting for Godot: Rating Approval Service Vendors," in *Shaping Library Collections for the 1980s*, pp. 135–142.
7. Reidelbach and Shirk, "Selecting an Approval Plan Vendor," *Library Acquisitions: Practice and Theory* 7 (1983): 115–122 and 8 (1984): 157–202.
8. Berkner, "Considerations in Selecting an Approval Plan," pp. 143–158.
9. Gary M. Shirk, "Evaluating Approval Plan Vendor Performance: Toward a Rationale and Model," in *Issues in Acquisitions*, pp. 11–31.

3. Publishers: Is the list of publishers the vendor regularly handles extensive enough? Are the publishers suitable to the objectives of the plan?
4. Cost: What discount is offered? Are shipping charges or service charges levied? Are prepayments accepted as a means of increasing the discount? Who pays for returns?
5. Slips: Do selection slips have accurate and complete bibliographic information? Are they coded by subject in a useful way? Does the same discount apply for slips as for books?
6. Management reports: Are management reports useful and easy to interpret? Are they issued in a timely fashion? What special reports could be issued on request?
7. Staff: Does the acquisitions librarian have a good working relationship with the vendor? Are both the representative and the customer service staff responsive and helpful?
8. Acquisitions procedures: Do shipments arrive on a regular schedule? Do returns, invoices, credits, statements, and claims move smoothly or are there nagging problems? Is there an interface to prevent duplication with firm orders and standing orders?

It is wise to look at all these factors when examining a plan rather than to let a single one, such as discount, determine the plan's fate. The importance of the various criteria will differ from library to library. Those engaged in selection and evaluation should think not only about how well the plan compares on each point but also about how important each point is to the library.

THE EFFECT OF AN APPROVAL PLAN ON SELECTION

The most controversial aspect of initiating an approval plan is usually consideration of the effect the plan can be expected to have on selection in the library. Fears of the deleterious effects of plans run from believing that selectors will assume an "as long as it's here, let's keep it" attitude, to concern that their lack of confidence in their ability to make book-in-hand decisions will lead to a tendency to reject too many titles. The potential does exist for situations such as these to develop; the library must clearly understand that having an approval plan in no way shifts responsibility for selection from the library to the vendor. Kevil writes about

Joan Grant

> the old myth that a library with an approval plan lets a ven-
> dor do its selection for it. This is simply untrue. The job the
> vendor wants to do is preselection, not the actual selection,
> which is done at the library. This preselection is accom-
> plished by the library's profile which, of course, is a record
> of its collection development policy. To the extent that this
> record is accurate, preselection will simply exclude those
> titles library policy would have excluded,...and will send
> for consideration those titles the library has determined its
> selectors should see. Selection can then be done at the library
> in the best way, with book-in-hand.[10]

The responsibility of the library to retain control of selection
notwithstanding, approval plans can provide a safety net for some
libraries. For example, when a vacant position or other staff short-
age leaves the library without the expertise to select in an area,
having an approval plan to rely upon is a significant convenience.
Some libraries have chosen to rely upon the approval plan on a
long-term basis, trusting that the vendor with a staff of specialists will be better able to cover the publishing output than the
library is. This option is particularly tempting for libraries that
must collect in esoteric subjects or languages but do not have
specialists on staff to cover them all. Those who choose this option
should realize that great care must be taken to insure that the
vendor understands the library's collecting priorities.

Selection practices could change after a plan is underway. The
library selectors who have an opportunity to judge for themselves
the scholarship and the physical quality of books being added
to the collection gain knowledge about publishing in their fields.
As they gain confidence that the books they want will come automatically, they can spend less time scanning catalogs and book
reviews and turn their attention to selection of retrospective
material and current imprints not covered by the plans. The test
of the success of an approval plan should be in the nature of samples and spot checks of lists of books published. A situation should
not be allowed to develop in which the "bibliographers spend as
much time monitoring approval receipts as they would have spent
on initiating orders for the same books.[11]"

---

10. Hunter S. Kevil, "The Approval Plan of Smaller Scope," *Library Acquisitions: Practice and Theory* 9 (1985): 16.
11. Berkner, "Considerations in Selecting an Approval Plan," p. 149.

CONCLUSION

While approval plans are not a panacea, well-managed ones can contribute to an effective collection development program. Through a careful process of defining local requirements and matching them with vendors' services, a library can use approval plans to insure a steady flow of prescreened books, and to enable selectors to allocate some of their time to other collection development projects.

Out-of-Print and Secondhand Markets, Domestic and Foreign

Gifts and Exchanges

Mae Clark

The two most popular ways of acquiring library materials indirectly are gifts and exchanges. Certain types of materials are unavailable by the usual means of purchase. For example, some publications of nonprofit institutions, museums, libraries, university departments, labor unions, and churches can only be acquired as gifts. Foreign government agencies and universities often distribute their publications only through noncommercial channels (that is, exchange). This chapter will describe the ways and means of acquiring and handling gifts and exchanges. It also will establish criteria for determining the relative advantages and disadvantages of these two methods of acquisition.

ORGANIZATION AND MANAGEMENT

The gift and exchange section of libraries has undergone many changes in policies and procedures in the past decade. Some of the most important changes have been caused by automation, the advent of collection development as a subdiscipline, and changing tax laws. Automation has required that gifts be processed in the same way as purchased items and that procedures be streamlined. Bibliographers are consulted about which gifts are appropriate to add to the collection as well as about which exchanges should be pursued. The 1984 tax law's reporting requirements have had a major impact on gifts operations. Additional duties sometimes have been assigned to the gifts and exchange staff. Checking the incoming gifts against the library's missing books list or searching for out-of-print desiderata are responsibilities often assigned to the gifts and exchange section. Rather than being an isolated part of acquisitions, the gifts and exchange personnel need to be involved in almost every aspect of the library's operation.

For example, gift and exchange personnel must be familiar with any preorder searching procedures so that gift and exchange material enters the normal workflow without causing disruption. Knowledge of basic monograph and serial cataloging may be helpful in choosing the correct bibliographic record, searching for title changes, or setting up the initial exchange records. The gifts and exchange staff must be knowledgeable about special collections as well as about the needs of subject specialists in order to do preliminary sorting of large gifts. In addition, they must know the basis of the 1984 tax law, must be able to keep detailed records of gifts for years, and must be able to correspond with colleagues around the world, in addition to dealing with local donors.

With all of these demands, how are gifts and exchanges managed? According to Kovacic, who studied gifts and exchange operations at eighteen U.S. academic libraries,[1] there are essentially three ways to organize these activities. They can be centralized, they can be separated into a gifts division and an exchange division, or they can be integrated into other work units. He found that while there is no consensus as to the ideal organization for a gifts and exchange section, the pattern has been for the larger collections (those of 2 million volumes and over) to have a centralized gifts and exchange section, while those libraries with smaller holdings tend to integrate gift and exchange activities in other units.

ADVANTAGES AND DISADVANTAGES

What are the advantages and disadvantages of a gift and exchange program? Why allocate several people to pursuing gifts and setting up exchanges? Why are libraries offered gifts and why do they accept them?

---

1. Mark Kovacic, "Gifts and Exchanges in U.S. Academic Libraries," *Library Resources & Technical Services* 24 (Spring 1980): 159.

Mae Clark

Gifts

Libraries receive gifts from many different sources. Some are the result of being placed on a corporation's mailing list so that annual and research reports, as well as histories of the corporation, are received gratis. Other gifts are received when a faculty member retires and needs to vacate his or her office. Gifts also can come from students at the end of a term, townspeople moving away, an alumnus who wants a tax deduction, and many other sources. The size and content of gifts to libraries are as varied as their donors. Gifts can be one item or a whole collection. They can be items such as sound recordings, videotapes, periodicals, maps, photographs, and manuscripts.

What advantages do all these gifts offer to the library? Often gift collections are donated by scholars who have carefully selected the materials in their collection over many years and from several different countries. These collections are complete representations of a specific period or style. Today, even if money could be allotted to this particular topic, most of the books would be unobtainable because they are out of print. A gift collection that arrives intact and that focuses on a particular topic complements the library's existing holdings by filling in gaps or by broadening the area of emphasis. If the library already has a substantial collection in this field, the gift can provide replacement copies for missing items or additional copies of heavily used items. Often gifts contain older periodical runs, which can be used to supplement current subscriptions or replace damaged or missing volumes.

Gifts also are accepted by libraries for reasons other than their content. Some gifts are accepted only if no constraints are placed on their handling or disposition. In many such cases, the library hopes more valuable gifts will follow. One reason for accepting gifts is to raise money for the library through book sales. Many libraries have a lenient gift policy of accepting almost any item in good condition without constraint and will use surplus items in book sales. These sales can be handled in many ways. A library with an active gifts program can establish something like a used book store, in which staff members or volunteers handle sales. Another way to handle book sales is an annual sale on a particular subject or for a particular price. If a library's gift activities are too small for a used book store or too large for an annual book sale, the third choice is to have book sales periodically throughout the year.

A library may sell gifts of periodical issues or volumes to back issue dealers. They are primarily interested in complete volumes, bound or unbound, with at least five years' run. Subject matter is of great importance to such dealers.

If it conducts some or all of the preceding activities, a very active gifts section could add between $15,000 and $25,000 to the library's budget per year. If, at the same time, the gift section is able to add replacement volumes to the collection from incoming gifts and thereby save the cost of buying materials from secondhand dealers, a gifts section can justify its existence within the library organization.

If gifts can be justified because they strengthen the library's holdings, fill in gaps in collections or find replacements, and make money for a library, why not concentrate all activity in the gifts section and not bother with exchanges? Why have an exchange program at all?

Exchange Programs

The main purpose of an exchange program is to acquire materials that are available in no other way or for which exchange is more economically advantageous than purchasing.[2] Often materials are not available through regular purchasing channels.[3] Little bibliographic information exists within many countries, and that which does often does not get outside those countries. National bibliographies often are outdated by the time they are published. Sometimes the publications are published in limited quantities and commercial dealers might not be able to obtain a copy. If approval plans have been established to try to obtain these materials, often the dealers are unreliable and the coverage is not satisfactory. Should a dealer be able to supply an item from a Third World country, the price frequently is inflated. Some Third World countries prefer to exchange governmental or institutional publications for similar information from other countries.

There are other advantages of an exchange program. Some libraries have had exchange agreements with European insti-

---

2. Mark Kovacic, *"Acquisition by Gift and Exchange," in Acquisition of Foreign Materials for U.S. Libraries,* edited by Theodore Samore (Metuchen, N.J.: Scarecrow Press, 1982): 39.

3. Priscilla C. Yu, "International Gift & Exchange: The Asian Experience," *Journal of Academic Librarianship* 6 (January 1981): 331.

tutions since the beginning of this century. Amicable relationships between the institutions offer a sense of continuity and friendship. When a need arises, one partner can ask the other for assistance. For example, an out-of-print missing volume was replaced free of charge by the exchange partner that published the journal in question.[4] Often information received through serial exchanges is of high caliber and assists research. Faculty need to know what others in the field are doing. By publishing the latest discoveries at its own institution, and offering these publications as exchanges, the faculty and institution gain in prestige. An extensive serials collection augmented by exchanges also may help to attract outstanding faculty and, therefore, grants.[5]

One further advantage of exchanges is that once established they require less maintenance than gifts.[6] The material to be exchanged must be mailed, but if serials are being exchanged, the selection and cataloging is done once. Except for occasional claims for missing issues, correspondence is minimal. In contrast, each gift item must be reviewed, selected, and cataloged and records must be maintained.

While there are advantages to an active gifts and exchange section, there are disadvantages as well. Personnel must be assigned to support these activities, and today, such staff may not be available. In many large research libraries with centralized gift and exchange activities, Kovacic reports, staffing may include an average of one librarian and two paraprofessionals who are assisted by part-time clerical and student help.[7] Although some of the staff may be paid for by money raised from book sales, the institution must make a commitment to gifts and exchange operations if it is to be successful.

Another disadvantage to an active gift and exchange program is space. If a large number of gifts come in more quickly than bibliographers can review them and dissemination can occur, a lot of space can be required. The situation has been aggravated by the 1984 tax law changes, which will be discussed in detail later. Briefly, before the 1984 law, items that arrived in large ship-

---

4. Pamela Bluh and Virginia C. Haines, "The Exchange of Publications; An Alternative to Acquisitions," *Serials Review* 5 (April-June 1979): 105.
5. Priscilla C. Yu, "Cost Analysis: Domestic Serials Exchanges," *Serials Review* 8 (Fall 1982): 80.
6. Kovacic, "Gifts and Exchanges in U.S. Academic Libraries," p. 157.
7. Ibid., p. 159.

ments and were not selected for inclusion into the collection could be sold or disposed of as desired. Now, if the gift is valued at over $5,000 and the donor has claimed a tax deduction, no materials may be sold, exchanged, or disposed of within two years of receipt without completing IRS Form 8282. Since tax laws change frequently and librarians are required to follow them (even when regulations are not finalized), many institutions' attorneys are recommending storing for two years everything not added to the collection.[8] One can readily see that if several large gifts are received and they contain items the library cannot use, additional storage space may be required.

Time must be allotted for unpacking and sorting gifts in an active gift and exchange program. If exchange lists of duplicates are made and sent to exchange partners for selection, staff and time must be allocated. Packing and labeling materials and communicating with the shipping agent require time and staff. One of the most time-consuming activities in gifts and exchange is the sorting of large gifts of several thousand items, arranging for the subject specialists to review them, and handling any precataloging searching.

Even with these potential disadvantages, Kovacic found in his survey of eighteen academic libraries that none of the people interviewed believed that his or her library could adopt a policy of not accepting gifts. Also, sixteen of the eighteen library staffs he interviewed maintain exchange programs.[9] Since all indications are that gifts and exchanges are important and do improve the collection, how does an institution establish a gifts and exchange program?

ESTABLISHING GIFT PROGRAMS

Before accepting gifts, most libraries inform donors that they reserve the right to decide whether or not the gift is to be retained. No promises are made that the entire gift will be added to the collection. The accepted items must fit the collecting policy of the library, and restrictions on gifts should be kept to a minimum. Only in exceptional circumstances should a library accept a special collection with the condition that the items not circu-

8. John J. Kominski, "Effect of the Tax Reform Act of 1984 on Library Operations (PL98-369)," Library of Congress Memorandum L085-104 [1984?].
9. Kovacic, "Gifts and Exchanges in U.S. Academic Libraries, p. 155.

Mae Clark

late, or that they be housed together in a special area, or that they be cataloged and maintained in specific ways.[10]

Most libraries have a gift policy, whether stated or not. Since the Tax Reform Act of 1984, several libraries have reviewed and rewritten their policies. A policy must include the following: (1) a general acceptance statement, noting that not everything donated will be added; (2) a statement of what will and will not be accepted; (3) brief information about what is tax deductible and what must be done before a deduction can be claimed; and (4) the name of the person with whom contact is made for the donation.

Once a gift is received, certain records must be created and kept. Records should include the name and address of the donor as well as the date and size of the gift. If the gift is large, a general count or count by type of material (for example, paperbacks, maps, textbooks) is sufficient. Restrictions or special conditions placed on the gift (such as special bookplates or special requirements) should be noted. If appraisals have been submitted such information should be attached to the records so that all information concerning a gift is recorded in one place.[11]

It is important that timely acknowledgments be sent to donors. All acknowledgments should be sent by December 31st of the tax year. Acknowledgments can be form letters, preferably individualized, or engraved cards. Not only is it important to send an acknowledgment soon after the gift is accepted but also to address the donor correctly, including titles. Remember that acknowledgments may be scrutinized by the Internal Revenue Service or other officials. Often donors call when preparing their tax returns to say that acknowledgment was not received or has been lost. Therefore, it is important to keep a copy of the acknowledgment.

Once the gift has been received and acknowledged, the next step is to sort it into broad categories so that subject specialists can review the collection and make decisions. Searching for duplicates can occur before or after the gifts are reviewed.

If the gifts received are fairly small, the library may adopt the policy of searching all books in good condition. This preselection searching can be a matter of checking the library's catalog and various files, or it can include actually comparing the gift volume to the one on the shelf. Such depth of searching gives

10. Alfred H. Lane, *Gifts and Exchange Manual* (Westport, Conn., Greenwood Press, 1980), p. 30.
11. Ibid., p. 41.

the searcher a chance to compare the bindings of the books to see which is in better condition. Preselection searching also gives the subject specialist all the necessary information for reviewing the books.

When gifts are large, libraries often have bibliographers review the material before searching. While the method described for small gifts provides subject specialists with all the information necessary to decide whether or not to add an item to the collection, it is too labor-intensive when a library is dealing with thousands of items. Bibliographers must decide many things: whether to add one edition only or the latest edition only, add if the only copy, or add as an extra copy. The costs of cataloging, processing, and storing must be kept in mind so that only significant contributions to the collection are added.

Bibliographers' decisions can be recorded on a form placed in each item. The form should contain the name of the donor or the gift number, the title, the library's holdings, any special instructions, and the subject specialist's decision.

For those items not chosen for addition to the collection, there are several methods of disposal. Some items can be used in book or journal sales or given to other institutions such as prisons, hospitals, or public schools. Often such places have limited funds for books and are grateful for titles from other libraries. Public schools are interested in encyclopedias in good condition. They can be used as circulating copies or replacement volumes; therefore, sets do not necessarily have to be complete.

The ALA Duplicate Exchange Union, composed of approximately 520 members, is another possibility for disposing of unwanted items. To belong to this group one contacts the chair of the group or writes to ALA/ALCTS Headquarters for an application form. There are no dues for the organization, but any library that joins must agree to send out at least one list per year to every member. There is no minimum or maximum number of titles and either books or periodicals may be offered on the list. When a member library finds a title it needs, it contacts the library that sent the list. The receiving library reimburses the sending library for postage over one dollar. Lists generally have a time limit noted; items are disposed of after that time.[12]

12. June Breland, chair, American Library Association Duplicate Exchange Union, telephone call, May 1986.

Mae Clark

In addition to the ALA Duplicate Exchange List, another possibility for disposing of unwanted items is USBE (Universal Serials and Book Exchange). Originally incorporated in 1948 as the United States Book Exchange, USBE's headquarters are in Cleveland, Ohio. USBE is a membership cooperative in which libraries support other libraries and information centers by sharing their unwanted books, periodicals, and other materials. A regular membership allows libraries to purchase USBE serials for a low rate, plus shipping, and entitles members to a vote on their advisory board.[13]

Not all of these suggested disposal methods are used at every library. Gifts staff must decide, based on time, space, and personnel constraints, which of these methods is cost-effective for their library. Sometimes the most cost-effective method is simply to discard the material. Often librarians are reluctant to resort to this method, but when one is faced with a continuing influx of gifts and a few alternatives have been tried, including a book sale, the dumpster is often the best place for some items.

INTERNAL REVENUE
SERVICE REQUIREMENTS

The Tax Reform Act of 1984 placed new requirements and responsibilities on donors to substantiate charitable contributions. At the same time, it affected many existing library procedures and made the library accountable as the recipient of certain properties for which donors-taxpayers have claimed a charitable deduction. The following sections are synopses from a Library of Congress memorandum written by their general counsel, John Kominski,[14] and from a talk given by Wiley C. Grant, senior art appraiser, IRS.[15]

---

13. "USBE Rises Again," *American Libraries* 21 (May 1990): 402.

14. Kominski, "Effect of the Tax Reform Act of 1984 on Library Operations (PL-98-369)."

15. Wiley C. Grant, "Substantiation Requirements for Donations Made After December 31, 1984," talk given at the October 31, 1985 meeting of the Mid-Atlantic Chapter of the Antiquarian Booksellers Association of America, New York.

Donor Responsibility

Although gifts and exchange personnel primarily deal with individual donors, donors under the tax laws can be individuals, closely held corporations, personal service corporations, partnerships, and corporations. A significant aspect of the law after December 31, 1984, is that a donor is no longer allowed to claim a charitable donation for noncash gifts over $5,000 unless the donor has: (1) obtained a qualified appraisal of the donated property from a qualified appraiser; (2) attached a Noncash Charitable Contributions Form (IRS Form 8283) to the tax return; and (3) included on the return whatever additional information the regulations may require, including the costs and acquisition date of the property.

A qualified appraisal cannot be made earlier than sixty days prior to the date of donation; it must be prepared, signed, and dated by a qualified appraiser and it must not involve a prohibited type of appraisal fee. It should also include:

1. a description of the property
2. the condition of the property
3. the date of the contribution to the donee
4. any known terms of any agreement between the donor and donee
5. the name, address, and Social Security number or Employer Identification number
6. the qualifications of the appraiser
7. a statement that the appraisal was prepared for tax purposes
8. the date on which the property was valued
9. the appraised fair market value
10. the method of valuation used to determine the fair market value
11. the specific basis for the valuation, such as any specific comparable sales
12. a description of the fee arrangement between the donor and appraiser

A separate qualified appraisal is required for each item of property that is not included in a group of similar items of property. "Similar items of property" are defined as stamps, coins, books, photographs, and so on.

The appraiser may group together any items whose aggregate value is appraised at $100 or less for which a group description

Mae Clark

rather than an individual description will suffice. An appraisal is not treated as a qualified appraisal if all or part of the fee paid to the appraiser is based on a percentage of the appraised value of the property.

Specifically excluded as a qualified appraiser for the property donated is the donor, a party to the transaction in which the donor acquired the property (seller or seller's agent), the donee, and any employee or relative of these. A person whose relationship to the donor would cause a reasonable person to question the appraiser's independence is also excluded.

For each item valued at $5,000 or more that is not included in a group of similar items of property, the donor must attach a separate Form 8283 (the appraisal summary). However, if during a tax year, a contribution of similar items of property is made to the same donee and totals more than $5,000, only one Form 8283 is required.

Should similar items of property be given to more than one donee and the total be more than $5,000, a separate Form 8283 must be attached for each one.

Donee Requirements

As far as a library is concerned, the most significant provision of the new regulations affects disposition of donated property. If a donee of donated property for which a charitable deduction is taken disposes of such property, or any portion of it, within two years after the date of receipt, the donee must complete Form 8282, Donee Information Return. Among other information required on that form are:

1. a description of the property disposed of in sufficient detail to identify it as donated property
2. the date the gift was made
3. the date the property was disposed of and the amount received, or if exchanged, the exchange value

The donee must furnish a copy of the information to the donor and must file the return with the IRS not later than ninety days after disposing of the property.

Form 8282 is only filed when disposing of donated property for which Form 8283 has been filed indicating that a deduction has been claimed by the donor. This presumes knowledge that the library may not have unless it secures a copy of the appraisal summary at the time it executes one. If the donee can obtain a copy of the Form 8283 filed, this would serve as actual knowledge of a claimed deduction. Gift acceptance forms often acknowledge that materials not needed for the collections are found in donated property. The reporting requirement then becomes a problem in those instances where a summary appraisal fails to identify specifically the excess property and the library is uncertain as to whether some of it has been included in a deduction.

If the property donated is evaluated below the $5,000 threshold, reporting requirements still apply if the property was part of an aggregate donation of similar items of property to several donees, the appraisal value for which exceeds $5,000. If the donor intends to claim a deduction for those donations, he or she will have to submit the required appraisal summary form, which is completed in part by a library officer so designated. A copy of Form 8283, made at the time it is submitted to the donee library, should provide the information needed to effectively make decisions regarding the disposition of donated property.

When offers of gifts are made, the library should inform the potential donor of the library's responsibilities and make reference to the donor's own possible responsibilities. Failure on the part of the library to file the Donee Information Return (Form 8282) will subject the library to a penalty of $50 per failure, up to a maximum of $50,000 per year, unless the failure was due to reasonable cause and not to willful neglect.

The IRS has modified existing regulations that impose reporting requirements on certain dispositions of donated property. In these regulations, no reporting will be required on sales of donated property, "provided the donor properly informs the donee that the appraised value of the property is not more than $500." Also, no reporting is necessary on an item disposed of for no consideration provided the disposition "is in furtherance of the donee's exempt purpose."[16]

Appraiser's Penalties

If an appraiser of donated property is found to have produced an appraisal that overvalued items which enabled a taxpayer to pay less tax than was due, the appraiser could be subject to a civil penalty of not less than $1,000 per return.

While the current regulations place stringent requirements on all parties involved in donating or accepting gifts, the tax laws are not static. Since the Tax Reform Act of 1984 was passed there

---

16. Internal Revenue Service, Reg. 1.170A-13(b).

have been continuous changes. One must always be on the alert for changes in procedures and requirements and be in continuing contact with institution counsel.

ESTABLISHING AN EXCHANGE PROGRAM

Unlike gifts, most libraries do not have a formal written exchange policy. Decisions should be made, however, about which types of material are to be received on exchange, in which subject areas, from which geographic locations, and in which languages. The kind of materials to be used for exchange must also be decided since the type of material offered affects the type of material received.

Sources for exchange items can be monographs or periodicals from the institution's presses. Sometimes these publications can be obtained free or at reduced rates. Gift items not selected for addition to the collection can be listed and made available to exchange partners. For the list of possible exchange items to be useful, it must include basic bibliographic information (including author, title, publication information, and date). It should give the exact addresses to which replies should be sent. Some kind of identifying code or list number should also be given. Instructions about how to request items should be specified. If postage is to be refunded, specify whether it should be in stamps or cash. If lists are to be filled as requests are received, that information should be noted.[17]

Another decision concerns the extent to which the library will purchase materials to be used for exchange. Bartered exchanges occur when a library pays for American publications to be sent to foreign exchange partners. In such cases, the publisher or vendor ships the desired material to the exchange partner and sends the invoice to the library for payment.[18]

Exchange of Periodicals

The majority of exchanges involve periodicals. This is the most difficult kind of exchange to monitor. If lists of titles available for exchange are sent, it is easy to balance an exchange on a piece-

17. Lane, *Gifts and Exchange Manual,* p. 15.
18. Kovacic, "Gifts and Exchanges in U.S. Academic Libraries," p. 157.

for-piece basis. If a barter exchange is established, invoice receipts must be made available so a dollar value can be placed on the exchange. With periodical exchanges, each title must be reviewed individually to ascertain its value.

Once these decisions have been made, the mechanism of requesting periodical exchanges can begin. Potential exchanges can be suggested in many ways: library users suggest periodicals, new periodical titles are sent as sample issues to serial or gift and exchange sections, and bibliographers discover gaps in the collections that need to be filled. The subject specialist should decide whether the title will be cataloged, whether it will be permanently retained, and if so, whether it will be bound. These decisions may be changed later if use differs from what is anticipated.

After the decision is made to request an exchange, the exchange personnel verify the bibliographic information, check the local library's files to confirm that the title was not recently ordered, and then contact the institution or journal. A written statement must clearly state the exact mailing address for each partner, what is to be exchanged, and how the exchange is to be monitored. Often the exchange personnel instigate the exchange, but the items are received by a branch library or the serials area. The ship-to address should be clearly differentiated from the correspondence or claim address. If a specific title is being requested, it should be clearly identified. When one offers periodicals, it is helpful to include sample issues if possible.[19] Otherwise, the exchange partner must make its decision based on a list that may only give the title offered, the number of times a year it is published, and perhaps a sentence or two describing the periodical.

If a response to the initial letter is not received within a reasonable length of time, a second request is sent. The mail, especially for Third World countries, is sometimes unreliable.

A file must be maintained so that when a response is received, it can be matched to the requested item. The easiest method is to keep a copy of the exchange request filed in an open correspondence folder. Sample copies can be shelved nearby. When a response is received, the request form can be returned to the requestor with a note specifying what action was taken. If the item is only available through purchase, the subject specialist needs to know so that alternate methods for procuring the item

---

19. Lane, *Gifts and Exchange Manual,* p. 11.

can be tried. In their article "Coordinated System of Processing Gift or Exchange Serials at the University of Utah Library," Stevens and Swenson offer practical suggestions and copies of forms used for exchange purposes.[20]

Close cooperation between serials and exchanges is important for periodicals. The records of the two sections must agree. If exchange personnel are not notified of nonreceipt of issues or title changes, the exchange is soon in trouble. Conversely, if the exchange staff fail to notify the serials staff of changes of address or titles no longer available on exchange, serials staff may needlessly claim issues that will never come.

The records pertaining to an exchange must be kept permanently. Without these records, it is not uncommon for the library to be removed accidentally from a mailing list. The records need not be complicated but they must be complete and accurate. They should list the mailing address, titles of serials sent and received, and dates and numbers of monographs sent and received. Routine form requests, claims, and acknowledgments need not be kept.[21]

With so much correspondence involved in exchanges, form letters can be a significant help. Requests for an exchange can be written in several different languages and sent out as necessary. Other types of form letters include a multiple-answer query from a partner who wants to know what is being sent, identification of the latest issue, requests to be removed from the mailing list, or advisement of cessation or change of address. Acknowledgments and claims also can be handled by forms. Foreign institutions tend to acknowledge every issue of a periodical received with either a postcard or letter. Often they include postcards for notification of receipt in periodicals sent on exchange. If the cards are not returned, the exchange could lapse.

Using form letters may simplify record keeping and correspondence, but without careful monitoring the exchange effort could be wasted. In the past, exchange programs had been viewed as a generous gesture by affluent libraries. This was particularly true through the 1960s when more money for libraries was available and there was little assessment of material received on exchange and little concern for the costs involved. With the infla-

20. Jana K. Stevens and Jennifer Swenson, "Coordinated System of Processing Gift or Exchange Serials at the University of Utah Library," *Library Acquisitions: Practice and Theory* 4 (1980): 159.
21. Lane, *Gifts and Exchange Manual*, p. 14.

tion of the 1970s, however, many libraries with extensive exchange programs found themselves overcommitted. Large amounts of money were no longer available and ways to reduce spending had to be found immediately.

In their article "The Exchange of Publications: An Alternative to Acquisitions," Bluh and Haines describe the procedure used at Johns Hopkins University Library to evaluate exchanges.[22] Serials received on exchange were subjected to the same evaluation as paid subscriptions. While each title was being evaluated for its relevance to the academic program, each exchange agreement was also evaluated. Before this analysis began, Johns Hopkins had agreements with 390 exchange partners and received more than 800 titles on the basis of these agreements. Afterwards they had 250 exchange agreements and received 555 titles.

Bluh and Haines report that in reviewing the exchange agreements and when making cancelation decisions, a strictly monetary approach was used. They found that only eight of their more than 500 titles were available only on exchange. The usual reasons for instituting exchanges—the partner's lack of Western currency or the nonavailability of the title on subscription—are not the common factors today that they were thirty years ago. The hidden costs of exchanges (the item, postage, processing, binding, and shelving) must be weighed against the contents of the item to determine if the exchange should be continued. If the publications received are not relevant to the academic needs of an institution, the exchange should be terminated.

Yu listed several difficulties that must be overcome in order to financially monitor an exchange program; her study is based on a cost analysis done on domestic serials exchanges of the University of Illinois at Urbana-Champaign (UIUC) Library in 1980.[23] Yu found many of the journals exchanged have no price value attached to them and are not found in bibliographic sources. Many serials are issued irregularly and priced individually, and a title may be published only every three years. Unless a cost analysis study is done for several years, it is difficult to get a complete picture. Rather than finding the cost of each single title, Yu suggests taking a sample of the exchanges.

How should one assess an exchange program? One needs to

22. Bluh and Haines, "The Exchange of Publications," p. 104.
23. Yu, "Cost Analysis: Domestic Serials Exchanges," p. 79.

look not only at the fiscal aspect of exchanges but also at the subject areas and materials exchanged. At UIUC, Yu found that the library had many publications to offer in scientific fields, and the departmental librarians agreed that those exchanges should be continued. The exchanges were needed for research purposes and the publications chosen were related to the university's academic programs, so it was reasonable to continue expansion of the exchange program in these areas.[24]

For an institution to have a successful exchange program, suitable materials must be available to exchange. If items are not available in all subject areas from the university's own publications, it may be necessary to effect the bartered exchange. If monies are not available to purchase items for exchange partners, it is advisable to limit the exchanges to those subject areas in which exchange titles are available locally.

Finally, to have a dynamic exchange program it must be continually reassessed. Although many of the reasons for an exchange program that were relevant in the past no longer apply, exchanges that adhere strictly to monetary values and consider need and use as criteria for acquisitions continue to have a place in libraries. If the exchange program reflects the university's fiscal and collection development needs, there is no reason for it to become stagnant. New exchanges should be added if they are fiscally beneficial and will add important new information to the collection.

FOREIGN AND DOMESTIC GIFT AND EXCHANGE PROGRAMS

Handling foreign gifts requires many of the same steps as domestic gifts. Foreign gifts must be acknowledged, and any special requirements for book plating or shelving must be followed. A decision must be made about whether or not they should be added to the collection. If they are to be added, they must be searched to make certain they are not currently held in the collection. At this point particular care must be taken. Familiarity with foreign languages is helpful. Regardless of their disposition, there is no reason to separate foreign gifts from domestic ones and to treat them differently. They can all go through the same decision-making and processing procedure together.

---

24. Ibid., p. 80.

The potential problem with foreign exchanges is that of language. If exchange personnel are not fluent in several languages, help must be sought from other sections within the library. Sometimes form letters in several different languages help solve the problem. It is best to limit exchanges with foreign countries to those for which there is sufficient language support within the library. It is advisable not to overcommit to a language when there may be no bibliographic help available. In the academic library, collection needs related to the needs of the disciplines being taught also have to be considered. If the institution teaches little or no courses in an area, there should be less effort expended to obtain gifts in this discipline.

If language barriers can be overcome and the exchange has been agreed upon, there are several ways the exchange items can be shipped. The quickest but most expensive way is for the institution to send each item as it is published to the exchange partner. While this allows the exchange partner to receive current information, it is more costly for the sending institution.

One way to avoid some of the postage costs is to hold issues of a periodical and send them only when a volume is complete. The disadvantages to this method are that the information sent is less current, and issues must be stored for a period of time. If the disadvantages can be overcome, this method may be worth the savings.

A less expensive and slower manner of transmittal is to send the exchanges through the Smithsonian Office of Publications Exchange, which was begun in 1850 as the International Exchange Service Organization. Originally, the organization was intended to encourage the exchange of publications between the Smithsonian and scientific societies abroad by shipping and receiving exchange materials via clipper ship.

Recently, this program at the Smithsonian has been undergoing a review. The Gramm-Rudman Act, the purpose of which is to cut the federal deficit, has affected the program adversely. Essentially, the Smithsonian is subsidizing postage to foreign countries. Material is received at the Smithsonian in large packages from U.S. libraries. Within these packages each exchange partner's items must already be wrapped and labeled. Personnel at the Smithsonian apply the necessary postage and the package is forwarded. Approximately 80,000 items are sent out and 20,000 are received through this office per year. Before beginning to use this system, it is advisable to make arrangements with the Smithsonian office so that exact directions concerning packing can be obtained.[25]

CONCLUSION

Gifts and exchanges are a valuable and viable method for bringing unique material to the library. Gifts provide an excellent method for renewing contacts with alumni and for enriching collections through donations from faculty, students, and the community. Librarians need to be cognizant, however, of the staff time and space requirements needed to maintain an active and aggressive gifts program. Of equal importance is an awareness of current tax laws and of the record keeping involved in supporting a gifts program. Exchanges likewise serve an important function in gathering ephemeral and unique titles so important to a research institution. Like gifts, exchanges require a commitment on the part of the library to adequate staffing, space, and record keeping. Exchanges with foreign countries are a particularly valuable source of materials that are difficult to obtain. Both gifts and exchanges can be an important addition to a library's acquisitions and collection development program.

---

25. Dr. Richard Conroy, deputy director, Office of International Activities, Smithsonian Institution, Washington, D.C., telephone call, May 1986.

Out-of-Print and Secondhand Markets

Margaret Landesman

The out-of-print market is often avoided. It tries the patience and the budget. It is hard on those requesting out-of-print titles—they may wait, and wait, and wait. It is hard on acquisitions staff, being among the more labor-intensive ways devised to spend one's time. It is hard on the business office, which doesn't understand the rush about paying or why the library insists on leaving orders outstanding for years. Can't they just buy some other book? And when the books do arrive—lacking appealing book jackets and looking sometimes old and faded—nobody thinks such mundane objects ought to cost very much. But they do. The out-of-print market is a trying experience all round.

On the other hand, it's rewarding. There are bargains to be had if one works at it. Dealing with small and individualistic operations can be a pleasant change from the anonymity of library wholesalers. And coming up with a really obscure book one never thought could be found can quite make your day.

Libraries are not buying as much on the out-of-print market as they used to. A number of reasons are cited; the most important is the drying up of acquisitions budgets and the heavy shift to the serials budget due to the incredible level of inflation there. The growth of OCLC, RLIN, WLN, and UTLAS and the resulting improvement in interlibrary loans have lessened the reliance on ownership. The reprint and microfilm industries have provided alternatives to the out-of-print market for some titles. And improvements in photocopying and interlibrary loans have probably increased the tendency for individuals and libraries to photocopy what is needed from a borrowed copy.

Many libraries never bought much from the out-of-print market, but larger academic libraries in the past spent a considerable percentage of the acquisitions budget there. This is no longer the case.[1] In some ways the decline complicates the situation for acquisitions. With a substantial amount of out-of-print buying, expertise was developed naturally within the library. A library now is less likely to be able to afford someone who devotes enough time to the out-of-print market to develop expertise, and selectors are less likely to be knowledgeable about an area for which they lack funds. Yet libraries still do need out-of-print books and must find ways to buy them in a timely and cost-effective fashion. While libraries have less money for retrospective purchases, the increasing speed with which books are going out of print means that even libraries with few retrospective interests need to enter the out-of-print market from time to time for current titles or replacements.

The problem of buying from the out-of-print market is analogous to trying to buy in-print books, but without wholesalers and publishers who will take direct orders. Add to this the suppositions that only a few copies of each book exist and that publishers charge bookstores wildly differing prices from day to day, and one has a sense of the out-of-print market. In such a market, it is easy to find as many good books as the collection needs. But if a particular title is desired and no other will do, a certain amount of ingenuity and effort is required.

When purchasing an out-of-print book, the library is not only paying for the book. It is paying for its location—on the library shelf—and the time and effort it took both the library and the vendor to get it there. The combined effort is higher for out-of-print books than for in-print books.

---

1. Thomas D. Kilton, "Out-of-Print Procurement in Academic Libraries: Current Methods and Sources," *Collection Management* 5 (Fall-Winter 1983): 113–34. Kilton's 1983 survey of ARL libraries showed that the average expenditure for out-of-print titles (both rare and nonrare) was 6.1 percent of the acquisitions budget. This contrasts with articles from the 1960s and early 1970s which indicate much higher figures and are concerned with handling actual or expected heavy volumes of out-of-print material.

Margaret Landesman

THE NATURE OF THE OUT-OF-PRINT MARKET

Types of Dealers

Out-of-print dealers are an extraordinarily varied lot and are not subject to any very useful classification. The following groups, however, give some idea of the varieties to be found:

1. Bookscouts, working part time or full time, search out desirable books and sell them to dealers or collectors.
2. Out-of-print dealers usually work from home and do not maintain a shop, although they often did own a shop while getting established. As overhead expenses go up, working from home has become more popular among dealers whose primary sales are by mail.
3. Many small specialized out-of-print shops issue catalogs and often do searching in their specialty.
4. General out-of-print dealers have a rather large stock in varied areas and may have specialties as well. Some offer search services, some do not. Some issue catalogs, some do not.
5. In-print stores that also have an out-of-print section can be small subject-specialized concerns or larger general bookstores. Some do out-of-print searching and some offer catalogs.
6. Some library in-print wholesalers also offer out-of-print search services.
7. Rare book dealers deal in rare and expensive titles. Most established rare book dealers do not handle the more ordinary scholarly out-of-print titles, but many out-of-print dealers will also handle some rare books.

Out-of-print dealers differ from in-print dealers. Except for wholesalers and those associated with in-print bookstores, they tend to be smaller, frequently one-person, operations. It is critical for libraries to keep this in mind, because it means that libraries have to pay them promptly. Larger wholesalers, on the other hand, sometimes seem not to notice overdue bills for months. For many out-of-print dealers, each day without payment can be critical. And, it is harder for the smaller dealer to absorb returns, although many do so gracefully, far beyond reasonable bounds.

Out-of-print dealers have a personal involvement with their books. In-print dealers act as the intermediary between the library and the publisher, and if the library doesn't like a book, the dealer can return it to the publisher. Out-of-print dealers tend to be bookmen; that is, they deal with books in subject areas that interest them and about which they are knowledgeable. They have to be knowledgeable because they are selecting and purchasing their books: they choose from the mass of older published material that which is still worthwhile. Often their knowledge is extensive, and they frequently know more about the bibliography of an area than the faculty does. One can complain of the quality of titles bought from an in-print dealer without hurting the dealer's feelings, but the same is not true for out-of-print dealers!

Out-of-print dealers are notoriously fine packers. One often finds even inexpensive books individually wrapped. Perhaps such care reflects the personal interest in each title as well as the greater financial investment that each represents.

How does a library find dealers? There are subject guides to dealers. Shepperd Press in London publishes them for most of the world, and *AB Bookman's Yearbook*[2] has a geographical section each year. More informal ways are often useful. Watch *AB Bookman's Weekly*[3] ads to see who is active in fields of interest to the library. Call other libraries of similar size and interests. Advertise for needed titles and see which dealers respond. A dealer the library already works with may be the best person to make a recommendation. Good dealers are knowledgeable about other dealers and their specialties and can be extremely helpful when a dealer with a particular location or specialty is needed. Especially if money is involved—for example, when a dealer is needed to inspect a prospective purchase or to appraise material for the library—it is best to get a recommendation from someone the library knows and trusts.

Dealers are useful to libraries in many ways. Libraries can sell duplicates and other good but unneeded titles to many out-of-print vendors, often at more advantageous prices than can be obtained otherwise. Many dealers will do appraisals for donors, although the library needs to be aware of all provisions of the current tax law. Sometimes dealers are responsible for sending potential donors to the library. It is well worth putting effort into building a good relationship with a dealer whose material is of

---

2. *AB Bookman's Yearbook* (Clifton, N.J.: AB Bookman's Weekly, 1954–), annual.

3. *AB Bookman's Weekly* (Clifton, N.J.: AB Bookman's Weekly, 1948–), weekly.

Margaret Landesman

serious interest to the library. When a dealer has choice material, he or she is naturally likely to offer it first to a reliable customer with known interests in the area. Dealers often send advance copies of catalogs to some libraries and will quote on materials expected to be of interest, if a good relationship has been built up between the dealer and the library.

Book Sources

Librarians are always curious about where dealers get books, and dealers, perhaps somewhat suspicious of librarians' motives or perhaps just in the interests of professional mystique, may not be forthcoming on the matter. The popular conception seems to be that dealers lurk. Just where this lurking takes place is unclear, but it seems to have a lot to do with attics or perhaps with widows and orphans. The reality is more prosaic. Sources of books vary from dealer to dealer depending on the type of material, the geographical location of the dealer, the sources developed, the size of the dealer's stock, and so forth.[4]

Established dealers have developed a network of contacts and may be offered individual titles and collections of books from many sources, including individuals, estates, and libraries who have come to know of the dealer and his or her interests. Many out-of-print books come from other dealers. Dealers often do not like to admit this because libraries resent paying the increases involved in moving books from one dealer to another. If a book could go directly from the retiring professor to the one library missing that particular title—preferably, of course, as a gift—efficiency would prevail. But of course acquisitions do not occur this way, and a book bought from another dealer costs just as much as it does from any other source. Dealers visit one another's shops and read one another's catalogs. A book that one dealer has at a very low price because of few or no likely customers, may be one for which another dealer has several customers. Dealers also buy duplicates and discards from libraries. They buy from individuals wishing to dispose of a few books or of collections. They buy at auctions and estate sales. Buying for the dealer is

---

4. For a description of the procedures used by dealers to obtain books see Blackwell's Staff, "Acquisition of Retrospective Material: A View from Blackwell's" and Richard W. Dorn and Jane Maddox, "Acquisition of Retrospective Material: A View from Harrassowitz," in *Acquisition of Foreign Materials for U.S. Libraries,* edited and compiled by Theodore Samore (Metuchen, N.J.: Scarecrow Press, 1982), pp. 52−58, 75−79.

at least as important as selling, and dealers consequently get very good at buying if they are to survive.

Many dealers will search for books on the library's want list. Where do these books come from? Dealers use many of the same sources as libraries in finding wanted titles, but they are able to devote more energy and expertise to the search. They advertise, check other dealers' holdings and catalogs judiciously, use bookscouts, and so forth.[5] Obviously, books that involve this extra labor will cost more than books supplied from stock. Searching is not a financially rewarding pursuit. Not all dealers are willing to do it, and those who do often see searching more as a service to their customers than as a main part of their business.

Pricing

How does a dealer establish a price and how does a library know prices are fair? Dealers cannot spend time researching the price of each book; they must rely on experience and memory, and in most instances these serve well. Many dealers maintain records of previous sales and many maintain files of the catalogs of similar dealers. *American Book Prices Current*[6] and *Bookmans' Price Index*[7] are useful tools for dealers as well as for librarians.

The buying price may be the least important element in the selling price. Dealers buy more books than they sell, and the time between buying and selling may be years. A catalog is an expensive proposition if there is only one of each item to sell. In addition to what they pay for the books, dealers must add enough to pay the rent and taxes and feed the children. Generally, dealers must sell books for at least twice as much as they pay and must average considerably more.

It is not remarkable that prices vary a great deal for any individual title,[8] but the situation leaves the library with the problem of deciding what is a fair price to pay.

---

5. A study of how dealers obtain wanted titles was conducted by Ernest R. Perez, "Acquisitions of Out-of-Print Materials," *Library Resources & Technical Services* 17 (Winter 1973): 42−59.

6. *American Book Prices Current* (New York: Bancroft-Parkman, 1895−), annual.

7. Daniel F. McGrath, *Bookman's Price Index* (Detroit: Gale Research, 1964−), annual.

8. Fred C. Lynden and Arthur Meyerfeld, "Library Out-of-Print Book Procurement: The Stanford University Experience," *Library Resources & Technical Services* 17 (Spring 1973): 216−24.

Margaret Landesman

Is a book worth the price? The first criterion, as always, is to judge the book against the rest of the collection, dollar for dollar, as one would any other proposed acquisition. Is the book worth what it costs in terms of the benefit it brings? Would the library buy it if it were a new book or information in another format? The library, of course, wants to know if the book is likely to be cheaper from another dealer. There is no point in paying more than necessary, but checking prices is difficult. One can check price guides, but it is no more practical for librarians than for dealers to research every price.

The best bet is to know the dealer. If the dealer is offering material at consistently reasonable prices, then buy. A few titles may be priced high and others low, but the library will come out about even in the end. What a book would have cost if the library had the prescience to buy it new or if a selector had found a copy in the basement of the local used book store is not relevant. It is important to weigh the cost of staff time, however, and consider this administrative aspect when making a decision about out-of-print purchases.

Prices are a major source of distrust between librarians and dealers. The wide range of prices for out-of-print materials leaves librarians feeling ill at ease with the market. It is hard to know what a fair price is, and if the librarian is not familiar with the out-of-print market, prices tend to seem awfully high. Dealers, all too familiar with the economics of the trade, feel understandably disturbed at being the target of the resulting suspicion. While there are dealers whose prices are higher than others, librarians should note how few people ever have become rich selling out-of-print books.

It is a good idea (at least in theory) to evaluate dealers' timeliness and pricing periodically, but this is an area in which care should be taken.[9] Do not look at the prices of individual titles. Every dealer is going to be off now and then, and the same book will cost one dealer more than another. Look at the average price in light of the sort of material you are getting. For smaller libraries, this is difficult because the number of titles bought from many dealers will not be enough for fair appraisal. In such cases, there is little alternative but to rely on an intuitive judgment.

9. A model for dealer evaluation is described by Betty J. Mitchell, "A Systematic Approach to Performance Evaluation of Out-of-Print Book Dealers: The San Fernando Valley State College Experience," *Library Resources & Technical Services* 15 (Spring 1971): 215–22.

BUYING ON THE OUT-OF-PRINT MARKET
GENERAL RETROSPECTIVE BUYING

The whole nature of the way out-of-print books surface, bob about for a bit from dealer to dealer, and finally are absorbed into some person's or institution's collection—perhaps to reemerge in another generation and perhaps not—makes generalized out-of-print buying to strengthen a library's collections far easier than locating particular wanted titles. General retrospective buying to build in broad subject areas—for example, to build a strong American fiction collection—is different from buying specific, fill-in items. The two situations have little in common. General retrospective buying costs less per title. Both the dealer and the library have less labor invested. Usual purchase procedures can be used, though often they must be speeded up. The usual methods and sources of retrospective buying include catalogs, quotes (titles a dealer has available which may be of interest to a library), dealer visits, buying trips, auctions, and collections.

Catalogs Catalog purchases make up the bulk of retrospective buying. Acquisitions departments, faculty, and selectors are daily deluged with catalogs. Orders returned and marked "sold" are inevitable; the cost in labor for searching, placing, and then canceling orders is high. To hold down wasted expenses as well as to get needed materials, speed is important.

To speed the process, the following procedures are suggested:

1. Get catalogs to the right person quickly. Ask to have selectors' names put directly on mailing lists. Make sure the person sorting mail can recognize out-of-print catalogs and knows to rush them. Develop good relationships with dealers so that those who are important send advance copies of catalogs or quote items of special interest.
2. If the catalog is old, it may pay to phone and find out what is still available.
3. Rush search the library holdings.
4. Phone or cable dealers and ask that wanted items be held until the purchase order comes. Most dealers will tell the library if items are sold, saving the issuing of useless purchase orders.
5. To maintain a good ongoing relationship with a dealer, order fairly regularly.

Quotes Dealers will often quote items they suspect are of interest to a library. It is courteous to respond promptly, whether one wants the item or not. It may be helpful to include the reasons for accepting or rejecting the quote, so that the dealer can adjust future quotes. Be sure quotes do not bypass normal search procedures or the library may end up buying duplicates.

Dealer Visits Some dealers like to visit libraries and bring stocks of books. Some libraries encourage this practice, others do not. The advantages are that the librarian can look at material firsthand and can learn a lot from dealers. If a library is located in an area where out-of-print sources are rare, a dealer's visit can be particularly helpful. The librarian may, for example, be able to sell the library's duplicates or ask the dealer for help with gift appraisals. A disadvantage is that the library may need to buy a certain amount and on occasion may not wish to. A visit also necessitates having searchers available for possible purchases.

Buying Trips Buying trips can range from having selectors visit local bookstores to sending a selector, cash in hand, to some distant place. Buying trips tend to be labor intensive for acquisitions personnel but very worthwhile in the material they bring in.

The most frequent nasty side effect when buying away from home is unwanted duplication. This can be avoided by having the selector pick the books and asking the dealer to hold them while sending an invoice or list to the library. The library can cross off duplicates and return the invoice to the dealer, who ships and invoices in the usual way. The selector does not have to physically deal with the books and does not take personal responsibility for the money. The library avoids unwanted duplicates.

On rare occasions this procedure will not work and the selector needs to carry money and bring back the books. If the price of the materials is low enough to offset the duplicates and the extra paperwork, this approach can be useful.

When a library sends enthusiastic selectors to a bookstore with a sizable out-of-print stock, it is almost guaranteed that the selectors will locate a dozen titles in the dollar bin for which they believe the library would happily pay substantial amounts. By the time the library determines which of the dozen valuable books are missing from the library's collection, the library has paid substantial amounts in staff time. Nevertheless, the value to the collection makes the time spent worthwhile. Going to library sales can also be an inexpensive way to acquire books.

If one library sells its duplicates, another library can inexpensively replenish worn-out copies of titles.

Auctions Only the largest libraries seem to buy regularly at auctions. The reason commonly given is the mysterious and intimidating nature of auctions, but it may have more to do with impracticality. Most libraries are located a long way from the few cities with most of the auctions, and library travel budgets are seldom ample. Books sold at auction are frequently sold in groups, or lots, and auction catalogs often do not specify the titles of all the books in a given lot. This means the library may have to buy books it does not want to get those it does want. If the library decides to enter an auction, the material being auctioned must be searched and a high and low bid must be decided. Ways of having the material inspected prior to the auction, bid for, paid for (cash usually required), and picked up after the auction must be established. By far the most sensible thing is to ask a dealer trusted by the library to take care of the whole procedure for a 10 percent commission. Dealers do not make a lot of money on such commissions but are willing to undertake them for customers.

Collections Collections are often offered to libraries both by dealers and by individuals. They pose difficulties for established libraries because the duplication rate is almost always unacceptably high. Collections from individuals also pose problems because the owners may not be disposed to wait the time required for institutional decision making and payment. For these reasons, libraries tend to buy only those collections they want quite badly. A good relationship with a dealer may again be helpful as a dealer may be willing to purchase a collection of interest and give the library first pick.

Locating Wanted Titles

Alternatives to the out-of-print market
Rule 1. Be sure the title is really out of print.

It is a well-known phenomenon that a library that takes titles canceled by one vendor as out of print and orders them from another vendor or direct from the publisher will get a large percentage of the books on the second try. Why? A number of reasons are given. The publisher may believe a title is out of print

but later gets returns from bookstores. The publisher may choose
not to deal with vendors for the last few copies of a title. The publisher's inventory system may report out-of-print titles when
there are a few copies still in stock. Whatever the reason, if a
title has a recent imprint date, it is worth ordering direct from
the publisher before moving to the out-of-print market.

Remember also that many smaller publishers do not list in
Books in Print.[10] Check the publisher listing to be sure the title
is actually out of print and not just too ephemeral to be listed.

Remaindered books are a special source of frustration. These
titles are available, if only the library could get at them. *Best
Buys in Print,*[11] also called the Buckley-Little Catalogue, is an
attempt to solve this problem. Authors buy remaining copies of
their books rather than let them be remaindered and list them
in the catalog. The catalog has recently been purchased by Kraus,
which plans to improve and expand the program.[12]

Rule 2. Consider reprints.

A great many more titles are available in reprint than was
once the case, although the reprint market is not expanding as
rapidly as it did in the era of larger acquisitions budgets.
Reprints, when available, have two major drawbacks: they are
expensive, and reprint publishers are notoriously unreliable
about asserting that a book is available when they are only test-
ing the waters to see if there is enough interest to reprint. Check
OCLC to see if there are holdings statements.

Reprint publishers seem worse than most about advertising
prepayment deals and then supplying the prepaid materials slug-
gishly. The quality of some reprints is poor in terms of print legibility and illustrations. On the other hand, the paper is often
better than that of the original. Weighing advantages and disadvantages, some libraries try first for a copy on the out-of-print
market and others check first for a reprint. The most useful
sources for reprints are *Guide to Reprints*[13] and *Out-of-Print
Books*[14] (previously Books on Demand).

10. *Books in Print: Authors* and *Books in Print: Titles.* (New York: R.R. Bowker),
annual.

11. *Best Buys in Print* (Ann Arbor, Mich.: Pierian Press, 1978–), monthly.

12. Edwin McDowell, "Buyer Planning to Expand Out-of-Print Books List,"
New York Times (August 11, 1986): Sec. 15N, p. C14, col. 1.

13. Anne Davis, ed., *Guide to Reprints: An International Bibliography of Scholarly Reprints* (Kent, Conn.: Guide to Reprints, Inc., 1967–), annual.

14. *Out-of-Print Books: 1984–85: Author and Title Guide* (Ann Arbor, Mich.:
University Microfilms International, 1984).

Rule 3. Look for microfilm copies.

As with reprints, many more titles are available in microfilm than used to be, and it may be worthwhile for the library to check for microform editions in *Guide to Microforms in Print*[15] and the *National Register of Microform Masters*[16] (watch for copyright problems). The price of microfilm is often reasonable, but the format may be unacceptable to patrons. Microform publishers are frequently the source of choice for periodical backrun requests.

Rule 4. Try photocopying or microfilming.

There is little in the literature to indicate how often libraries produce photocopies of out-of-print works needed for their collections. Photocopying is expensive and the result is never wholly satisfactory. Before the national networks made interlibrary loan so effective, it was time-consuming to find a copy to photocopy. Photocopying is more common today, but libraries are reluctant to comment in print, perhaps because of the fuzzy copyright issues involved. Under exactly which conditions it is legal to photocopy an out-of-print title still under copyright is not clear, but if efforts have been made to contact the publisher or author for permission and there is no reprint or microform edition available, it is reasonable to make a single copy for the library. The advantages of photocopying a book (preferably on acid-free paper) needed urgently for class use are obvious. The drawbacks in terms of copyright issues and products that are less than satisfactory are also obvious.

Microfilming, if a library has access to it, can be more satisfactory. Copyright problems remain. More libraries probably have access to microfilming than realize it. Many universities and government bodies have microfilming capabilities in their records centers and may be willing to microfilm for the library. There are also commercial services available that will microfilm titles for a reasonable fee.

Locating a copy in the out-of-print market Having eliminated titles that can be dealt with in other ways, the library is left with a list of books to be searched on the out-of-print market. It is worthwhile to check again with the selector to make sure the title wanted is important enough to justify an out-of-print search. Selectors need to be familiar with the library's usual

---

15. *Guide to Microforms in Print* (Westport, Conn.: Meckler, 1961–), annual.
16. *National Register of Microfilm Masters* (Washington, D.C.: U.S. Library of Congress, 1965–), annual.

Margaret Landesman

fill rate on out-of-print orders and with the likely cost. Few libraries can fill more than 50 percent of their out-of-print requests in a year.

Once the library decides to search for a title, it goes into what has traditionally been called the desiderata file. Arguments exist about the merits of a library's holding desiderata files centrally versus having specialists maintain small subject files. There are also arguments as to whether or not desiderata should be interfiled with the main order file. However a library chooses to arrange its files, it should be able to produce a list of titles currently out on search and should be able to tell from the main order file that a given title is being searched.

There is no single answer to the question of how best to search for out-of-print books and no consensus on the question among librarians. Each library must determine which methods best suit its needs. Most libraries use a mixture of approaches, depending on the type of material and the urgency with which it is needed.

There are two basic types of searching: the library does it or the library asks someone else to do it. If the library chooses to do its own searching, it advertises for wanted titles through a trade journal or by circulating multiple copies of a title list to dealers. Multiple quotes are received and compared and orders are placed. If the library chooses to ask someone else to do its searching, it sends title lists to a dealer or a search service which is responsible for locating the books and quoting located titles to the library.

AB Bookman's Weekly and *The Library Bookseller*[17] (formerly *TAAB: The American Antiquarian Bookman*), are journals devoted to circulating lists of out-of-print titles desired by libraries, bookstores, and dealers among dealers interested in supplying the books. *AB Bookman's Weekly* has a circulation of approximately 8,000 and the library pays for advertisements by the line or page. *The Library Bookseller* has a much smaller circulation. Ads are free to libraries.

The library's procedure is similar for either journal. A list of wanted titles is made up. Full bibliographic citations are not necessary. Short author-title lists with additions as required to specify editions are commonly used. It is best to keep lists relatively short.

---

17. *The Library Bookseller: Books Wanted by College and University Libraries* (West Orange, N.J.: Albert Saifer, 1949–), biweekly.

The list is published in the chosen journal and the library receives quotes from dealers. The library must devise a system for comparing and responding to quotes. Purchase orders are issued for desired items. Some libraries reply to unsuccessful quotes, while others do not; some note in their ads that quotes for which purchase orders are not received in a given time are to be considered declined. Some dealers supply on a CWO (cash with order) basis, and it may be wise to so state if the library only wants quotes that can be invoiced.

Advertising is most successful for relatively common books. Other methods work better for technical and scientific books, textbooks, foreign titles, and older rare materials. The advantages of advertising are speed—if a quote is going to come, it will be received within two to four weeks—and lower prices, with dealers quoting from stock and investing labor in searching. Advertising can also be a good way for a library to identify new dealers in areas of interest to the library. The disadvantages are that advertising is more labor intensive than some other methods and that the search is short-lived. If a quote is not received, the library must readvertise or try another method.[18]

A method similar to advertising is to make up a want list of desired titles and send it simultaneously to a list of dealers with a request for quotes. This method has much the same advantages and disadvantages as advertising through *AB Bookman's Weekly* or *The Library Bookseller.* The labor required on the part of the library is similar. Multiple quotes may be received and will need to be compared and answered; then orders are placed. Although want lists reach fewer dealers than an ad, they can be tailored to suit the specialties of a group of dealers. Some dealers who do not find it worth their while to read *AB Bookman's Weekly* may read a want list of titles in their specialty.

Dealers particularly and emphatically dislike nonexclusive lists. The depth of the dislike is somewhat difficult to understand given how little want lists differ from quoting on *AB Bookman's Weekly* or *Library Bookseller* lists, but many dealers have had unpleasant experiences working with them. They believe the practice of issuing want lists creates an artificial market wherein several dealers, not realizing that the list is not exclusive, adver-

18. Good results with this method are reported in a useful article covering all the methods of out-of-print searching by William Z. Schenck, "The Acquisition of Out-of-Print Books," *AB Bookman's Weekly* (December 7, 1981): 4015–32.

Margaret Landesman

tise for the same titles at once, thereby pushing prices up. Dealers feel they are unlikely to supply as high a percentage of wants on such a list, and they do not want to devote time to looking for titles that may be rejected. They dislike being pitted against other dealers. Some will not deal with lists except on an exclusive basis.

Though many libraries do advertise their wants in this way, it is only fair to do so if the library makes it clear that the list is being circulated to several dealers at once and that dealers should quote from stock only.

Another method is to send a want list to one dealer with exclusive rights to search for a specified period of time, usually from six months to one year. At the end of this period, unsupplied titles can be rotated to another dealer.[19] This method is probably the preference of most libraries; it is certainly the method preferred by dealers. The dealer takes over the job of collecting and coordinating quotes. Considerably less work is involved for the library. Once a good working relationship is established, guidelines can be set so that titles under an agreed upon price are automatically supplied without quoting.

Exclusive lists are particularly well suited to specialized titles that are not good candidates for advertising. Several small lists can be made and tailored to dealer specialties, which usually results in a higher find rate. The disadvantage is that the average price may be somewhat higher because the library is paying for more labor and, perhaps, because dealers are not competing against each other on individual titles. Initial response is not as fast as with advertising, but as the dealer continues to search actively, the eventual fill rate should be substantially higher.

Dealers and search services range from highly specialized individuals to large operations with or without stock. Some in-print library vendors in this country and abroad also offer out-of-print searching services.[20] The large general search services are convenient for a library with a small-to-medium size want

19. An excellent and still timely description of this procedure is an article by Eldred Smith, "Out-of-Print Booksearching," *College & Research Libraries* 29 (July 1968): 303–309.

20. Blackwell North America's out-of-print department issues a monthly publication, *Richard's Reference*, listing titles wanted by libraries. The publication is sent to a large group of interested dealers. Each title is advertised every four months for a year. Similar services are offered by Baker and Taylor, B. H. Blackwell's, Harrassowitz, and other vendors.

list; the library's entire out-of-print list can be placed with one source. Drawbacks are that prices may be higher and that the return rate, even for searching services that claim to go on searching indefinitely, seems to fall off. It is best to rotate all lists from time to time or at least to reconfirm with the dealer or search service which items are still being searched.

Another source of out-of-print titles is USBE, the United States Book Exchange. USBE is a nonprofit membership cooperative established in 1948 for the purpose of stockpiling surplus books and periodicals from member libraries and redistributing them to other member libraries in need of the material. Member libraries pay an annual membership fee and a handling charge for each periodical issue or monographic title supplied. The USBE serials collection has approximately 40,000 titles and 4 million issues. Libraries submit lists of their needs to be matched against this inventory. Monthly selection lists of monographs available are issued.[21]

Checking incoming dealers' catalogs against the library's desiderata file was considered a useful method by some libraries in the days of large desiderata files. It is difficult to imagine that such a method would be practical now, but some libraries evidently still find it useful, mostly on an occasional basis.[22] The amount of labor involved relative to the number of titles successfully located is great.

BIBLIOGRAPHIC SOURCES FOR OUT-OF-PRINT BUYING

Library literature does not deal extensively with the out-of-print market, and what there is deals primarily with the question of search strategies. Little has been published on the topic in the past decade, but as computerization has had relatively little impact as yet on the out-of-print market, the older articles are still useful. [A more extensive bib-

---

21. Kilton's 1983 survey, cited previously, showed 47.4 percent of ARL libraries using USBE frequently or occasionally.

22. Many older articles mention and even advocate this method. Ung Chon Kin, "A Comparison of Two Out-of-Print Book Buying Methods," *College & Research Libraries* 34 (September 1973): 258–264, documents the costs involved. Kilton's 1983 survey, cited previously, showed 15.2 percent of ARL libraries using this approach frequently and 31.6 percent occasionally.

liography of earlier but still useful references can be found in Felix Reich-mann's, "Purchase of Out-of-Print Material in American University Libraries," *Library Trends* (January 1970): 328–353.] The more useful articles have been cited in this chapter's notes. There is, however, a rich literature on the history of the book trade and book collecting. The memoirs of a number of dealers and bookmen make particularly entic-ing reading. This bibliography lists a few personal favorites from each category.

GUIDES TO DEALERS

AB Bookman's Yearbook. Clifton, N.J.: AB Bookman's Weekly, 1954–____. Annual. Contains a list arranged geographically and by subject. *AB Bookman's Weekly,* indexed in *Library Literature,* also fre-quently carries articles on dealers in specific cities and specialties.

American Booktrade Directory. New York: Bowker, 1952–____. Annual. Antiquarian dealers are interspersed with other sorts, making this list less convenient than the others.

Antiquarian Booksellers Association of America Incorporated. *Mem-bership List.* New York: Antiquarian Booksellers of America Inc. A list of members indexed geographically and by subject. Send a self-addressed stamped (56 cents) #10 envelope to ABAA at 50 Rockefeller Plaza, NY, NY 10020.

Modoc Press, Inc., comp. *The Collector's Guide to Antiquarian Bookstores,* with an introduction by Leona Rostenberg and Madeleine B. Stern. New York: Macmillan; London: Collier Macmillan, 1984. Arranged geographically and indexed by subject. Fun to read as it gives details and history on each store.

Robinson, Ruth Eleanor, and Daryush Farudi. *Buy Books Where-Sell Books Where: A Directory of Out-of-Print Booksellers and their Special-ties.* 4th ed. Morgantown, W.Va.: Robinson Books, 1984. There are also a number of guides for specific subject and geographic areas.

Sheppard's Book Dealers in North America: A Directory of Dealers in Secondhand and Antiquarian Books in Canada and the United States of America. 10th ed. London: Europa, 1986. The standard guide. New edition every few years. Arranged geographically and indexed by sub-ject. Sheppard guides are also available for Great Britain, Europe, and India.

PRICE GUIDES

American Book Prices Current. New York: Bancroft-Parkman, 1895–. Annual. Cumulates with five year indexes. Auction prices of books sold in United States and abroad.

Book-Auction Records, a Priced and Annotated Annual Record of London Book Auctions. Kent, England: Wm. Dawson, 1902–. Annual.

Bradley, Van Allen. *The Book Collector's Handbook of Values.* 4th rev. ed. New York: G. P. Putnam's Sons, 1982. A convenient one-volume reference compiled from dealer catalogs. Unfortunately, out of print and publisher reports no plans for a new edition.

Connolly, Joseph. *Modern First Editions: Their Value to Collectors.* London: Orbis, 1984. An update of his 1977 *Collecting Modern First Editions.*

Mandeville, Mildred S. *The Used Book Price Guide: An Aid in Ascertaining Current Prices.* 2 vol. Kenmore, Wash.: Price Guide Publishers. (*Five Year Edition,* 1972; *Supplement,* 1977; *Five Year Edition,* 2 vol. 1983.) Compiled from dealer catalogs.

McGrath, Daniel F. *Bookman's Price Index.* Detroit: Gale Research, 1964–. Annual. Compiled from American and British dealer catalogs.

REPRINTS AND MICROFORMS

Best Buys in Print. Ann Arbor, Mich.: Pieran Press, 1978–. Monthly. Supplement. 1982–. Bimonthly. Recently purchased by Kraus which plans to expand the program.

Davis, Anne, ed. *Guide to Reprints: An International Bibliography of Scholarly Reprints.* Kent, Conn.: Guide to Reprints, Inc., 1967–. Annual.

Guide to Microforms in Print. Westport, Conn.: Meckler, 1961–. Annual.

National Register of Microfilm Masters. Washington, D.C.: U.S. Library of Congress, 1965–. Annual. Lists masters retained solely for purposes of making other copies.

Out-of-Print Books: 1984–85: Author and Title Guide. Ann Arbor, Mich.: University Microfilms International, 1984. Most recent hard-copy listing from UMI. Contains about 10,000 of the newest titles. A complete catalog of the 100,000 available titles is published on microfiche. It was formed by the merger of *Books on Demand: Author Guide and Books on Demand: Title Guide.* Both are available free from UMI.

Serials in Microform. Ann Arbor, Mich.: University Microfilms International, 1972–. Annual.

ADVERTISING JOURNALS

AB Bookman's Weekly. Clifton, N.J.: AB Bookman's Weekly, 1948–. Weekly. Contains also substantive articles on the out-of-print market, which are cumulated annually in the *AB Bookman's Yearbook.*

The Library Bookseller: Books Wanted by College and University Libraries. West Orange, N.J.: Albert Saifer, 1949–. Biweekly. Previously called *TAAB: The American Antiquarian Bookman* and mostly still referred to as *TAAB.* Recently taken over by Mr. Saifer's grandson: Scott Saifer, Box 9544, Berkeley, CA 94709.

GENERALLY USEFUL TITLES

Carter, John. *ABC for Book Collectors.* 6th ed. Revised by Nicolas Barker. London and New York: Granada, 1980. A classic for book collecting; other titles by Carter are also good.

Gaskell, Philip. *A New Introduction to Bibliography.* Oxford: Clarendon Press; New York: Oxford University Press, 1972. Everything you might ever want to know in this field explained very clearly.

Magee, David Bickersteth. *Infinite Riches: The Adventures of a Rare Book Dealer.* New York: P. S. Eriksson, 1969.

Malkin, Sol. M. "ABC of the Book Trade." In *AB Bookman's Yearbook,* pp. 2–60. Clifton, N.J.: AB Bookman's Weekly, 1975.

Peters, Jean, ed. *Book Collecting: A Modern Guide.* New York: R. R. Bowker, 1977.

Randall, David Anton. *Dukedom Large Enough.* New York: Random House, 1969.

Rees-Mogg, William. *How to Buy Rare Books.* Oxford: Phaidon, 1985.

Rostenberg, Leona, and Madeleine B. Stern. *Old and Rare: Thirty Years in the Book Business.* New York: Abner Schram, 1974.

Stern, Madelaine Bettina. *Antiquarian Bookselling in the United States: A History from the Origins to the 1940s.* Westport, Conn.: Greenwood Press, 1985.

Acquisition of Books from Australia, with a Brief Reference to New Zealand and Oceania

Juliet Flesch

The book trades of Australia and the United States show more similarities than differences from the point of view of the acquisitions librarian, but the differences, though few, are substantial and may cause considerable problems.

THE PUBLISHING AND BOOKSELLING SCENE

Before examining the way in which North American librarians may best go about identifying and acquiring secondhand and out-of-print titles in Australia, it will be helpful to look briefly at the current publishing and bookselling scene.

In many ways, the current output of Australian publishers is readily accessible to the North American librarian. The most common language of publication and business communication is English and the structure of the book trade is not markedly different. Publishers are represented by the Sydney-based Australian Book Publishers' Association, and the retailers are represented by the Australian Booksellers' Association with its headquarters in Melbourne.

Australian books are well publicized. The most authoritative listing, which includes a substantial component of prepublication entries produced under a flourishing cataloging-in-publication scheme, is the *Australian National Bibliography,* published by the National Library of Australia. Other lists, of greater or lesser comprehensiveness, include *Australian Books in Print,* published in Melbourne by D. W. Thorpe; *Australian Books: A Select List of Recent Publications and Standard Works in Print,* published annually by the National Library of Australia; and another D. W. Thorpe publication, the monthly *Australian Bookseller & Publisher.*

Australian Book Scene is produced annually as a supplement to *Australian Bookseller & Publisher* and timed for release at the Frankfurt Book Fair. It provides a concise overview of the year's activities as well as a summary of the functions and activities of the various organizations concerned with the book trade. In addition to the organizations already mentioned, *Australian Book Scene* includes the National Book Council, the Christian Bookselling Association of Australia, the Literature Board, the Australian Society of Authors, the Fellowship of Australian Writers, the Association of Antiquarian Booksellers, the Australian Copyright Council and, of course, the Library Association of Australia. A listing of major prize winners is provided as is a select list of books published during the year.

IDENTIFYING AND ACQUIRING AUSTRALIAN BOOKS

A number of specialized listings and specialist reviewing media are produced in Australia. The most comprehensive, and most likely to be of interest to North American librarians seeking to build a collection of Australian material, is the *Australian Book Review,* published by the National Book Council. The major problem with this journal as with all review journals is timeliness of reviews—a problem common in any country.

Few difficulties occur for North American librarians who deal with Australian book suppliers. Publishers, library suppliers, and major bookshops are all accustomed to dealing with orders from overseas, as are the subscription agents. The types of material likely to cause trouble are those that do so in North America too: publications of federal or state governments not issued through the Australian Government Publishing Service, publications of university departments not published by the university press, publications of individuals or small local societies, and so on. Australian librarians have not yet found an easy way of procuring these materials; when we do, we will tell the world!

Another common factor in the Australian and North American book trades is that retail prices are not fixed. Unlike the situation in the United Kingdom, Australian books were not exempted from the 1971 law declaring all retail price maintenance illegal. The long-term effects of this law, foretold at the time by the Australian Book Publishers' Association, are generally agreed to have been detrimental to the book trade, both in terms of what is being published and, more importantly in the present context, in terms of how long books stay in print.

The differences in the Australian and North American book trade are principally ones of size. It is not surprising that with a population of between 15 and 16 million (spread over an area of 7,695,009 square kilometers, although mainly concentrated on the eastern coast) the publishing output is small in terms of the number of titles published and the number of copies printed. The February 1988 issue of the *Australian Bookseller and Publisher,* for example, reported "a massive jump in the number of new books published during 1987, and notes that 3,570 new titles (including new editions) were published that year, compared to 2,653 in 1984, 2,858 in 1983, and a mere 1,615 in 1974.[1] By 1987, the figure had grown to "an astonishing 4,219."[2]

A look at production statistics by subject provides an insight into the Australian book market. In 1987, for example, children's books totaled about 11 percent of all book production, while "readers" (that is, texts for gaining reading skills) took another 12 percent of the market. Other areas, including adult fiction, represented less than 10 percent of the market.[3]

Print runs of the works that North American libraries are likely to wish to acquire are also significantly smaller than the North American average, as might be expected given the small local market. It is hard to arrive at precise figures, but the Australian Book Publishers' Association estimates that 10,000 is a large print run for an Australian book; the average for an academic title or new novel is likely to be closer to 3,000 copies.

Adding to the North American librarian's problems is the fact that the books do not remain readily available for very long. The length of time for which a publisher may be expected to hold stock varies greatly from book to book. Some books may reasonably be expected to sell steadily over several years, while others are

1. "Record Output for Australian Publishers," *Australian Bookseller & Publisher* 67 (February 1988): 12.
2. John F. Baker, "Australia: A Visitor's View," *Publishers Weekly* 233 (May 6, 1988): 41.
3. "Record Output for Australian Publishers," p.12.

expected to have a fairly short selling life. In general, however, the Australian Booksellers' Association estimates that an Australian book can be expected to go out of print within two to five years of publication. This of course means that all librarians (not just those in North America) must work fast to secure titles in print as there may be considerable difficulties in tracking down publishers' stocks once the publishers have disposed of them.

Both *Australian Bookseller & Publisher and Australian National Bibliography* provide timely information on mainstream monographs, and many Australian publishers are represented in the United States. In addition, there are a number of Australian library suppliers and bookshops willing and able to supply books either title by title as ordered or within the context of tailored approval plans or blanket orders. A relatively recently established local source of supply of Australian books for North American libraries is the Australian Book Source, 1309 Redwood Lane, Davis, California 95616. Koala Books of Canada (14327-95A Avenue, Edmonton, T5N OB6, Canada) also provides a mail-order service. U.S. customers are billed and pay in U.S. funds.

Some of the major library suppliers are listed in the *Australian Book Scene*, and Australian Booksellers' Association members are listed in *Australian and New Zealand Booksellers*, and *Australian Books in Print*.

Identifying the dealer to whom stocks have been sold once a publisher decides to dispose of them is far from easy. Several remainder dealers buy up large stocks of Australiana; Academic Remainders of Canberra and Mary Martin of Adelaide are the most likely to hold academic titles. Other remainder dealers, although they hold considerable numbers of Australian titles, are more likely to concentrate on popular books.

Assuming that a North American librarian has been unsuccessful in attempts to acquire a title when it was published or to buy it new from a remainder merchant, the next step is likely to be to try to find a secondhand copy.

Unfortunately, finding even a comprehensive and informative listing of Australian secondhand and out-of-print booksellers is far from easy. *Australian and New Zealand Booksellers* does show some thirty booksellers who list secondhand and out-of-print material among their specialties. The most cursory investigation of the list reveals, however, many omissions as well as the fact that a number of secondhand book dealers listed fail to describe themselves as such.

Juliet Flesch

In addition, many of the secondhand dealers sell *rare* books rather than stocking *recently out-of-print* titles. American librarians seeking rare editions will probably be better advised to address their inquiries to an established specialist bookshop that covers the subject of the book rather than to a large generalist bookshop. For librarians seeking recently out-of-print titles, the outlook is not bright, although the larger antiquarian bookshops are probably the best bet. Paradoxically, it may prove easier for a library to obtain a copy of a work long out of print than one of which the publisher has only recently sold the stock.

There are a number of very out-of-date guides to Australian bookshops. Use of these is more likely to engender frustration than anything else; many of the shops have stopped trading since the publication of the guide and inquiries addressed to them are unlikely to produce a reference to an alternative supplier. The Victorian Committee of the National Book Council has prepared a detailed guide to Melbourne bookshops;[4] similar publications for other states would prove equally useful.

Several auctions of Australiana are held every year, both in Australia and overseas—most notably in Britain where so much of the nineteenth century material was published. Christie's and Sotheby's hold regular auctions in Australia and offer Australian titles in English sales; Kenneth Hince holds two auctions per year in Melbourne.

NEW ZEALAND

New Zealand's North Island covers an area of 114,688 square kilometers, and the South Island is 150,461 kilometers square. The country has a population of about 3 million. The principal language is English.

The New Zealand book trade is represented by two major organizations, the Book Publishers' Association of New Zealand and the Booksellers' Association of New Zealand. Other bodies connected with the book trade include the New Zealand Book Council and the New Zealand Book Trade Organization, which is a cooperative organization including representatives of the Booksellers' Association (British) and representatives of the various aspects of the New Zealand trade.

---

4. National Book Council, Victorian Committee, *Bookshops & Victoria: A Reader's Guide,* edited by Pat Miller. Sydney: Primavera Press, 1988.

Out-of-Print and Secondhand Markets

Information on newly published New Zealand books can be obtained from a variety of sources. *New Zealand National Bibliography,* the most comprehensive, suffers as a selection tool by being available only on microfiche. It is published by the National Library of New Zealand. D. W. Thorpe's annual *New Zealand Books in Print* provides a more convenient but selective listing. A more timely source is the National Library of New Zealand's *Books to Buy.*

The difficulties posed by a small population base and distance from major book publishing centers are no less notable in New Zealand than in Australia and are reflected in the small publishing output. In 1985, for example, commercial publishing output for the year was fewer than 650 titles.

Print runs are fairly small also and have declined markedly since 1980. In the twelve months ending March 1984, the average print run for a general title was 4,125, while for an educational title (encompassing both tertiary- and elementary school-level titles) the average was 3,349.[5] Given that school texts are likely to be produced in higher than average quantities, the print run for a New Zealand title likely to be of interest to American libraries may be expected to be under 3,000 copies.

No information is available on the length of time for which publishers usually hold stock, but it is unlikely to be longer than the Australian average of two to five years. The majority of titles are sold by the publisher in bulk to remainder dealers. The London Bookshop chain with fifteen stores throughout New Zealand is the second largest bookselling chain in the country. The business was founded primarily on remainder sales, but now it is turning steadily to a concentration on sales of new, full-price books.

New Zealand is a regular exhibitor at the Frankfurt Book Fair, and in 1986 about twenty publishers were represented at the collective stand. New Zealanders have found the return from representation at major North American gatherings such as the American Booksellers' Association and American Library Association conventions too small to justify continued participation. The New Zealand Book Publishers' Association also reports considerable difficulties in finding satisfactory U.S. distributors for New Zealand titles. All of this suggests that, failing employment of a blanket order or approval plan with a New Zealand agent, fast title-by-title ordering direct from a New

---

5. Figures provided by the Office of the Director of the Book Publishers' Association of New Zealand.

Juliet Flesch

Zealand bookseller or library supplier will be required in order to bring in a reasonable return for effort.

New Zealand booksellers of both new and secondhand titles are listed in *Australian and New Zealand Booksellers,* while *New Zealand Books in Print* provides an up-to-date listing of members of the Booksellers' Association of New Zealand. Some secondhand dealers (by no means all) will be found in the list of members of the Australian and New Zealand Association of Antiquarian Booksellers.

Reliable information on where a book may be found once its publisher has disposed of remaining stocks, however, is as difficult to obtain in New Zealand as it is in Australia. Libraries interested in building New Zealand collections, even at the most basic level, are well advised to place their orders with all due speed.

OCEANIA

Information about Oceania's book trade—new, out of print, secondhand, or antiquarian—is not particularly easy to come by. The structure of the book trade in the region is totally different from that of North America, Australia, or New Zealand. To begin with, depending on where the lines are drawn, there are about a dozen separate countries. Several hundred languages are spoken, ranging from ones that have about 4,000 speakers in all to others that are the first tongue of about 300,000. Although English is, in general, the lingua franca of the region, there are active publishing programs in about a dozen local languages. Pidgin (under various guises) is showing a steady growth; it is most obvious in periodical publications.

Historically, much of the publishing and dissemination of books in Oceania was undertaken by churches and church bookshops. Today, in some countries, these are still the best source of local publications. The influence of colonial administrators can still be seen in the relative importance of government printers, departments of education, and other government departments.

Relatively new developments include the Institute of Papua New Guinea Studies and the University of the South Pacific. The latter was set up by the ten Pacific Island nations of Solomon Islands, Vanuatu, Fiji, Nauru, Kiribati, Tuvalu, Tonga, Western Samoa, Cook Islands, and Tokelau. It maintains an active publishing program in English and several local languages and produces regular lists of its output.

Several national bibliographies are produced within the region, but these suffer as selection aids, much as the Australian and New Zealand ones do, from a lack of currency. Material may no longer be available by the time it is listed.

An interesting general picture of the book trade in Oceania was provided in the papers presented at the UNESCO Western Pacific Book Distribution Seminar in Melbourne in 1983, which was attended by participants from all over the region.[6] On the whole, it is clear that librarians wishing to acquire the output of the area should act quickly, since once the material goes out of print it will be virtually impossible to track down.

A list of major bookshops in the region is provided in the *UBD Business & Trade Directory: Pacific Islands,* which is published annually by Universal Business Directories. One of the best methods of acquiring publications is contacting directly the publisher or one of the major bookshops. Another source in the United States is a fairly new venture centered in Hawaii, Pan Pacifica (1511 Nuuanu Avenue, PT 194, Honolulu, Hawaii 98617).

There is little, if any, information on where newly out-of-print material might be found. Given the difficulties of obtaining current titles, the chances of getting older material are very low. Perhaps publishers and bookshops keep stocks longer, however, than those in Australia and New Zealand because of the overall small size of the output and market in Oceania.

Secondhand and antiquarian material from Oceania occasionally appears on the Australian and New Zealand market; sometimes this is the result of a scholar's disposing of a collection. Building a collection in the area of Oceania material, however, depends heavily on acquisition at the time of publication and in general directly through a publisher or local bookshop.

CONCLUSION

The problems of acquisition of material from Australia and New Zealand are quite different from those facing the North American librarian seeking material from Oceania. In Australia and New Zealand the book trade is highly developed, and librarians

---

6. Papers presented at this meeting were distributed to participants but never published. Regional UNESCO offices may be able to provide copies.

Juliet Flesch

should experience no difficulties in identifying or acquiring currently published titles. Because print runs are comparatively short, and because publishers do not hold stocks for many years, however, problems will be experienced in finding recently out-of-print titles. The antiquarian market, on the other hand, is vigorous, and the local antiquarian dealers are experienced in dealing with overseas clients. In Oceania, the problem lies principally in the state of development of the book trade. Distribution mechanisms for even currently published titles are not often developed to a point that makes dealing with American requirements easy, and once material goes out of print, it will be extremely difficult to trace.

B I B L I O G R A P H Y

Australian and New Zealand Booksellers 1983/84. Melbourne: D. W. Thorpe, 1983.

Australian Book Review. S. Melbourne: National Book Council, 1961–. Monthly.

Australian Books: A Select List. Canberra: National Library of Australia. 1933–.

Australian Book Scene. Port Melbourne: D. W. Thorpe, 19–.

Australian Bookseller & Publisher. Port Melbourne: D. W. Thorpe, 1925–. (Title varies.)

Australian Books in Print. Melbourne: D. W. Thorpe, 1956–.

Australian National Bibliography. Canberra: National Library of Australia, 1961–. Monthly.

Books to Buy. Wellington: National Library of New Zealand, 1984–. Semimonthly.

Fiji National Bibliography. Lautoka: National Library Service of Fiji, Ministry of Social Welfare, 1979–. Semiannual.

New Zealand Books in Print. Port Melbourne: D. W. Thorpe, 1957–.

New Zealand National Bibliography. Wellington, New Zealand: National Library of New Zealand, 1983–. Monthly.

Papua New Guinea National Bibliography. Waigani: National Library Service of Papua New Guinea, 1981–. Quarterly.

Robinson (H.E.C.) pty. ltd., Sydney. *UBD Business & Trade Directory: Pacific Islands.* Auckland: Universal Business Directories, 1978.

PART FOUR

Nonprint Publications

The Nonprint Trades

Charles Forrest

Radio and television, records and tapes, movies and slides—our homes as well as our libraries contain a sometimes bewildering variety of nonprint materials. We learn from these materials or are simply amused by them; we record important moments on tape or on film thereby making a permanent record for the future; we pass a spare hour or two in their pleasant and diverting company. Nonprint formats are becoming an integral part of our personal and professional lives.

Nonprint materials can be defined as library materials that require some form of media enhancement to be used.[1] This definition excludes items like still pictures, photographs, and maps but includes microforms and microcomputer software. A common characteristic of these media is their reliance upon equipment for access. Equipment is thus an integral part of a nonprint collection and central to issues of selection, acquisition, and use. Equipment innovation and the introduction of new technologies largely determine the character of the market for nonprint materials. This chapter will discuss audiorecordings (records, audiotapes, and compact discs), slide series and filmstrips, motion pictures (16-mm and 35-mm films), videorecordings (videotapes, videocassettes, and videodiscs), microcomputer-based software, and microforms.

---

1. J. Michael Pemberton, *Policies of Audiovisual Producers and Distributors: A Handbook for Acquisition Personnel* (Metuchen, N.J.: Scarecrow Press, 1984), p. x.

ACQUISITION IN A TIME OF CHANGE

The developments that brought most of the nonprint materials into existence occurred in the past hundred years, a period of rapid technological innovation that witnessed the introduction of the motion picture, radio, television, and the computer. Each medium thus embodies a certain technology that is the subject of continuous improvement and enhancement over time. Indeed, these technologies seem destined to demonstrate that the only constant is change. And each improvement, large or small, relegates previous versions to the back room of obsolescence. While this may not be so much the case for those media more or less fixed in a material object, such as motion picture films or records, it is especially true for media that employ some form of electronic storage and retrieval—audiotapes, videorecordings, and microcomputers.

Such media can entertain, educate, and train. Entertainment media include motion pictures, the broadcast media, the recorded music industry, and more recently consumer videocassettes. Nonentertainment media consist of documentary and educational materials, and materials produced for training and promotion in business and industry. Educational slides and filmstrips have been joined by motion pictures and more recently videorecordings.

These media also differ according to whether they contain sound or picture or both, whether they present motion sequences or still images, and the degree of user interactivity they provide. They can be further analyzed in their political and economic relationships according to a number of criteria: what is the sales product, how accessible is the medium, how much control does the consumer exercise over use, and which market component wields the most economic power.[2] These questions will be addressed in the following sections as each medium is considered.

Selection and acquisition of nonprint materials is generally considered to be more difficult and time-consuming than selecting and acquiring print materials. This is due in part to the scarcity of selection and acquisition aids and in part to market volatility.[3] Rapid advances in technology make obsolete what

---

2. James Monaco, *How to Read a Film,* rev. ed. (New York: Oxford University Press, 1981), p. 362.

3. Pemberton, *Policies of Audiovisual Producers and Distributors,* p. vii.

was state-of-the-art only a few years before. Further, the ease of copying many of these materials encourages demand publishing, particularly for videocassettes and microforms.

The fugitive nature of these media often presents unusual management problems for libraries and other institutions that undertake to collect them and make them accessible. Electronic recording and retrieval of the information these media contain— text, sound, still frames or motion pictures—and the widespread availability of equipment to duplicate the recorded signals, underscore the commercial nature of their content. The content is information that can be bought and sold and in fact stolen while remaining in the same place. There is, however, a mechanism whereby producers, distributors, and authors are guaranteed adequate compensation for the labor of creating such seemingly ephemeral works: the copyright law.

MEDIA AND COPYRIGHT

The basic aim of copyright is "to secure the general benefits derived by the public from the labors of authors."[4] Because everyone can be informed, educated, and entertained by an author's work, that author should be encouraged to continue producing such work. Copyright provides authors monopoly rights to their works in an attempt to guarantee them adequate personal gain as the best way to encourage their efforts. These rights do not automatically transfer to the owner of a *copy* of an original work. The mere "transfer of ownership of any material object does not of itself convey any rights (which inhere) in the copyrighted work."[5]

As replication technologies improve and become more convenient and readily available, it has become difficult to guarantee that every copy of a work is authorized or legitimate and to provide just remuneration to authors for their efforts. The fair use

---

4. *Audio and Video First Sale Doctrine: Hearings Before the Subcommittee on Courts, Civil Liberties and the Administration of Justice of the Committee on the Judiciary,* 98th Congress, 1st and 2d sessions on H.R. 1027, H.R. 1029, and S.32, October 6, 27, and December 13, 1983 and February 23 and April 12, 1984, Serial 101 (Washington, D.C.: U.S. Government Printing Office, 1985), p. 1.

5. *The Nuts and Bolts of Copyright* (Washington, D.C.; Copyright Office, Library of Congress, 1979), Circular R1; *Legal and Business Aspects of the Music Industry: Music, Videocassettes, and Records,* Course Handbook Series, No. 120, p. 75 (New York: Practicing Law Institute, 1980.

doctrine provides that it may not be an infringement of copyright if a work is used or reproduced for purposes of teaching, scholarship, or research. Factors that need to be considered when applying the doctrine include the intended use to which the copy will be put, the nature of the work, the amount copied, and the effect of copying on the market for the original work. The widespread practice of private copying of audiotapes and videorecordings is a matter of increasing concern to many in the affected industries; copyright issues related to particular formats will be discussed in the following sections.

AUDIO MEDIA

Broadcasting Industry

Many of the broadcast industries have seen a shift from vertical to horizontal integration. Radio and television began with a mass audience that was served by just a handful of stations and channels. Now audiences have been fragmented by proliferating broadcast channels, an explosive increase in the number of stations, and the availability of cable services and satellite television. Music, movies, and other program material are now produced in specialized packages for the individual consumer instead of for the mass audience.

In the first half of this century, American radio was a mass medium; it had a huge audience served by a few large networks. Network stations provided an amalgam of news, features, and mostly entertainment; often programs were broadcast live before a live audience and were paid for by sponsors eager for millions to hear their advertising messages. But with the success of commercial television in the years following the Korean War, radio found its revenues shrinking along with its audience. It responded to the challenge of television by breaking up its large networks and segmenting its mass audience. Programming was aimed at specifically targeted groups defined by demographic characteristics such as age, economic status, ethnicity, language, and geographical location.[6]

Recorded music became virtually the sole program content for

---

6. Erik Barnouw, *A History of Broadcasting in the United States: The Golden Web, Vol. II, 1933 to 1953* (New York: Oxford University Press, 1968), chap. 5.

many stations. This move from unitary programming to programming diversity led to the development of the "Top 40" radio format, which exerted an enormous influence on the recorded music industry; without radio, there would be no hits and no stars.[7] Broadcasting shaped the market for the products of the record industry.

Records and Audiocassettes

The international recorded music industry is dominated by the United States. Ten years ago the United States had 40 percent of the record market in western countries, a total of more than $3 billion. Of the ten leading record companies in the western world, seven are based in the United States: CBS, Warner Communications, RCA, MCA, K-tel, A&M, and Motown. EMI is based in the United Kingdom, Polygram in the German Democratic Republic (GDR) and the Netherlands, and Bertelsman in the GDR.

Sound recordings in the form of audiotapes and audiocassettes are also widely used for education and training. Audiocassette subscription services are available for many disciplines and subjects. Recorded lectures and interviews abound, and there are many motivational tapes available in the commercial market to help one stop smoking, lose weight, succeed in business, and achieve personal fulfillment. Along with recorded novels, these instructional and motivational programs are often promoted as an excellent way to maximize the utility of the inevitable driving time that so many commuters otherwise apparently waste.

Audiorecording offers one of the cheapest forms of production of educational and training materials. Planning an audiotape costs about $20 per minute of finished tape, production of a master tape costs about $30 per minute, and each duplicate costs about $4 per tape.

The main concentration of economic power lies in the production and distribution of the sales product—the actual record or tape. Records and tapes are readily available and are distributed around the world. The product is delivered in individual packages, which allows the consumer considerable control over the time and setting of use and makes access easy. It can be diffi-

7. Martti Soramaki and Jukka Haarma, *The International Music Industry* (Helsinki: The Finnish Broadcasting Company, Planning and Research Department, July 1981), pp. 4–5.

cult, however, for aspiring recording artists to break into the business, see their music distributed on records and tapes, and receive adequate compensation for their creative efforts guaranteed them under copyright law.

Private Copying and Copyright

Listening to records and prerecorded tapes is of interest to everyone, and it is with the recording of audiotapes that most people gain familiarity with the "production" of audiovisual materials. The widespread availability of high-quality recording equipment using electromagnetic tape makes it easy to produce original materials and reproduce records and prerecorded tapes. The introduction of compact discs, digital tape, and digital broadcasting encourages this practice by providing consumers with an excellent master for home duplication. The ready availability of audiotape recorders has thus had a far-ranging impact on the recorded music industry by encouraging private copying.

A report on private copying in the member states of the European Economic Community noted that "sales of legitimately produced copies of records and pre-recorded tapes have declined steadily since 1978...and...have been displaced by private copying on an enormous scale." In fact, it is estimated that "more minutes of music are privately copied per annum than are sold legitimately by producers of phonograms on records and pre-recorded tapes."[8] The authors conclude that "nearly all private copying substitutes for the copyright owners' protected product....Private copying will continue to injure the audio recording industry unless a solution is found."[9] Proposed solutions range from the technical (a spoiler system built into recording equipment which will render an unauthorized copy useless) to the political (government royalties on the sale of recording equipment and blank tape). Recently, the videocassette recorder has made the private copying of motion pictures on videocassette just as easy and nearly as widespread.

---

8. Gillian Davies, *Private Copying of Sound and Audio-visual Recordings* (Oxford: ESC Publishing, 1984), p. 138. Published for the Commission of the European Community Directorate—General Information Market and Innovation, Luxembourg.
9. Ibid., p. 145.

Charles Forrest

VISUAL MEDIA

Film Industry

The motion picture entertainment industry encompasses the three steps of production, distribution, and exhibition.[10] Production is the creation of a motion picture and can be thought of as the manufacturing aspect of the industry. Distribution is the placement of the finished motion picture in the marketplace; distributors serve the wholesale function. The last step is exhibition: the motion picture is shown for an admission price, with exhibitors serving as retailers of the finished product.

The main concentration of economic control in the motion picture industry lies in distribution of the sales product—entertainment. The film audience plays a relatively passive role as consumer of the product. The presentation of the product in individual packages does offer the consumer some control over selection of the movie, theater, and viewing time. Nearly every town has a movie theater, which insures good consumer access to the media. Entry into the movie industry itself, however, can be difficult.

Recent Distribution Developments How do films reach their intended audiences? A producer of movies, educational films, documentaries, or short subjects has available the following distribution channels: foreign television; domestic television (commercial or public); pay or cable television; theatrical release, foreign and domestic; nontheatrical release, including colleges and libraries; videocassette or videodisc; package rights (some combination of television, theatrical, nontheatrical, cassette, and disc); and miscellaneous channels such as the sale of stock footage.[11]

The distributor is responsible for getting the product to the marketplace, and that marketplace has undergone many changes in the course of the history of the industry. Theatrical exhibition is no longer the primary source of revenue for the entertainment film. In the United Kingdom, for example, it is estimated that theatrical exhibition accounts for only 25 percent of feature

---

10. Sheldon Tromberg, *Making Money Making Movies* (New York: New Viewpoints/Vision Books, 1980), p. 5.

11. Michael Wiese, *The Independent Filmmaker's Guide,* rev. ed. (Westport, Conn.: Michael Wiese Film Productions, 1981), p. 103.

film revenue, the home video market accounts for another 25 percent, and broadcast and cable television make up the remaining 50 percent.[12] In fact, the combined audience for only four films screened on television in the United Kingdom is greater than the number of admissions to all United Kingdom theaters in a year.[13]

The television industry itself is blurring the distinction between commercial and noncommercial public television. In the United States, for example, Exxon Corporation has underwritten public television programs. Conversely, the Children's Television Workshop (CTW), producer of "Sesame Street" and "The Electric Company," which started as a small venture with federal grant money, has in ten years grown to an annual budget of $18 million ($5 million in federal grants) largely financed with revenue from toys, books, records, magazines, and foreign broadcast rights. While still nonprofit, CTW has come to depend on profit-making subsidiaries.[14]

The attempt to realize the promise of additional revenues held out by alternative distribution mechanisms has led to developments such as pay-per-view cable television and premium cable subscription channels. Television broadcasting via satellite and the rapidly growing videocassette industry could lead to the formation of a two-class television audience: those who pay for what they want and those who take what they can get.[15]

Videorecordings

Videocassettes The wide availability of videocassettes and videocassette recorders has transformed movies and television. Here, the main concentration of economic control lies in manufacturing; the main sales products are equipment and the videocassettes themselves. The videocassette industry provides an increasingly open and accessible channel of distribution. As with theatrical exhibition of motion pictures, the audience's role is essentially passive. With the product bundled into individual units, the consumer is able to exercise considerable control over the choice of program, viewing setting, and viewing time. This

12. Graham Wade, *Film, Video and Television—Market Forces, Fragmentation and Technological Advance* (London: Comedia Publishing Group, 1985), p. 72.
13. Ibid., p. 1.
14. Marda Woodbury, *Selecting Materials for Instruction, Vol. 2, Media and the Curriculum* (Littleton, Colo.: Libraries Unlimited, 1980), p. 177.
15. Wade, *Film, Video and Television*, p. 1.

similarity with motion pictures is hardly surprising, since so many programs currently in distribution on videocassettes are feature length motion pictures.

There has been an absolute explosion in the purchase and use of the videocassette recorder (VCR) in the past ten years. In 1976, Sony sold an estimated 30,000 Betamax units. In 1977, the number had risen to 200,000, and in 1978, to 400,000. By 1984, 10 percent of American homes had one or more VCRs, a total of more than 7 million units. The trend is representative of a growing world market. By the end of 1986, it is estimated that the United Kingdom, for example, had a VCR market penetration of nearly 50 percent of homes, placing it sixth in the world after Kuwait, Japan, Iceland, Singapore and Hong Kong.[16] The VCR market in the United States topped 36 percent of all homes during that same year.[17]

Videodiscs A medium of interest to industry and educational institutions, but not as successful in the home market, is the videodisc. With several competing and incompatible systems already introduced, the many variations on the videodisc are reminiscent of the variety of videocassettes. While the videodisc can be recommended over the videocassette for durability and special program-access features, it has one major drawback which limits its consumer marketability: videodisc units play back only; they cannot record.

It has been estimated that compared with other media, planning costs associated with videodisc are high: in excess of $500 per minute of finished program.[18] However, the cost of producing a master disc has steadily declined to about $3,000 per disc from $20,000 and more just a few years ago. Duplication is quite inexpensive; it costs about $15 each for a disc, which can contain up to one hour of a motion picture program in addition to a stereophonic sound track.

The laser optical videodisc has captured a small but steadily growing share of the video market, and the promise of recordable and erasable videodiscs is being held out as a probable technological development in this field. Meanwhile, the videocassette

16. Ibid., p. 23

17. U.S. Bureau of the Census, *Statistical Abstract of the United States: 1987,* 107th ed. (Washington, D.C.: U.S. Government Printing Office, 1986), p. 531.

18. Jerrold E. Kempt and Deane K. Dayton, *Planning and Producing Instructional Media,* 5th ed. (New York: Harper & Row, 1985), p. 44. These and subsequent cost figures are provided for purposes of comparison only.

will command the major share of the home and entertainment market. The videodisc will be discussed later in this chapter as a nonentertainment educational and training medium with much to offer.

Video Distribution and Copyright With scores of television stations broadcasting on cable television and satellite and with nonbroadcast channels of distribution in the form of videocassettes, the motion picture and television industries currently confront a situation similar to that of radio earlier in its career, namely the move from large audiences and mass programming to special interest programming on a multitude of channels. Other characteristics that mass market video is beginning to share with the recorded music industry are the widespread availability of high-quality replication equipment and the familiar problem of private copying.

The film and television production industries have been relying increasingly for survival on subsidiary markets, including the video market itself. This trend will undoubtedly place additional pressure on those seeking remedies for economic damages caused by private copying. Government-administered royalties on the sale of recording equipment and tape have been suggested as a way to insure adequate remuneration for the producers of copyrighted works. Such legislation has been introduced in Austria, the Federal Republic of Germany, Hungary, and Sweden.[19] While it has long been possible to record music off the air, the much greater consumer demand to record video programs has prompted the drive for government intervention. Built-in timers that enable videocassette recorders to record programs for replay at a later time or for long-term retention are found on almost all videocassette recorders sold for home use.

The muting feature on a remote control device for a television enables a viewer to switch off the sound during commercial breaks in regularly scheduled programs. But recording a television program off the air for viewing at a later time (known as time-shifting) allows a viewer to press the fast-forward button and skip the commercial breaks altogether The practice of skipping commercials in time-shifted material undermined the case some broadcasters made when they suggested that the increased

---

19. Davies, *Private Copying of Sound and Audiovisual Recordings,* p. 139.

secondary market for broadcast advertisements (commercials seen again in recorded programs) justified raising per-minute advertising rates, which are based primarily on audience size.

It has also been suggested that time-shifting causes economic harm to the holders of copyrights of time-shifted programs. The copyright implications of time-shifting were assessed by the United States Supreme Court in 1984. The court ruled that private, in-home use of videocassette recorders to copy television programs did not cause harm to the entertainment industry and should not be prohibited. In what is sometimes referred to as the Betamax case, Sony Corporation (manufacturer of the Beta videocassette recorder) "demonstrated that substantial numbers of copyright holders who license their works for broadcast on free television would not object to having their broadcasts time-shifted by private viewers." Further, the respondents in the case, Universal Studios, Inc. and Walt Disney Productions, "failed to demonstrate that time-shifting would cause any likelihood of non-minimal harm to the potential market for, or the value of, their copyrighted works."[20]

A more serious concern is the time-shifting of programs into an open-ended future in what would amount to recording for permanent retention. The high-quality signal of broadcast channels such as cable and satellite television provides consumers with an electronic "bank" of material for copying. Much of this material is protected by copyright, and many of the copies made will be kept for a long time. The "permanent retention of privately copied video programmes—'librarying'—accounts for a significant and increasing amount of video recorder use."[21] While personal "librarying" of pirated videocassettes can be seen as an individual decision, libraries themselves should take care to purchase programs only from known or reputable distributors and should carefully examine any gifts. When doubt arises, it is useful to consider the effect of the library's action on the salability of the work in the legitimate market. A notice similar to that recommended for photocopying machines should be posted on videocassette players and recorders to educate and warn patrons about the existence of the copyright law.[22]

20. "The Betamax Ruling," *Consumers' Research Magazine* 67 (March 1984): 11–14. Highlights excerpted from the majority decision authored by Justice John Paul Stevens.

21. Davies, *Private Copying of Sound and Audiovisual Recordings,* p. 138.

22. Mary Hutchings Reed and Debra Stanek, "Library and Classroom Use of Copyrighted Videotapes and Computer Software," *American Libraries* 17 February 1986: A–D (special insert between pp. 120 and 121).

MATERIALS FOR EDUCATION AND INSTRUCTION

Sound Recordings

Audiotapes and audiocassettes are widely used for education and training and are inexpensive. Planning an audiotape costs about $20 per minute of finished tape, production of a master costs about $30 per minute, and duplicates cost about $4 per tape. Audiocassettes can serve as sound tracks for slides or filmstrips.

Slide-Tape Programs

Development of a synchronized slide-tape program more than doubles the estimated planning cost for an audiotape alone. Slides can be produced for about $3 a piece and duplicated for about sixty cents per slide. Since filmstrips resemble horizontal slides on a single strip of film, their production costs are roughly equivalent to those for slides. Development costs are about $25 per frame and the cost to produce is about $3.50 per frame. The duplication cost is only about thirty cents per foot since the individual frames do not have to be cut apart and mounted separately as is the case with slides.

So-called multi-image programs employ several slide projectors and other sophisticated equipment such as multiple screens and complicated sound tracks. Planning such a presentation for three screens, for example, might cost more than $50 per minute of program. While the actual cost of producing and duplicating the slides remains the same as that for less sophisticated applications, the equipment involved in multi-image presentations can cost $10,000 and up. Multi-image programs are more useful in promotion and motivation than in education and training.

Educational Films

Motion pictures and video programs are considerably more expensive to produce than slides and filmstrips. Planning for a 16-mm film can cost upward of $200 per minute, while production costs can easily amount to more than six times this amount. Duplication of a 16-mm film costs about $10 per minute.

The planning process for an educational film can be modeled on that for an entertainment film; relevant subjects include market identification and analysis of market needs along with an initial consideration of how the finished film will be distributed.[23] Most producers will wish to recover at least their production costs while hoping for something extra. The well-established market for educational films includes industry, schools, colleges and universities, churches, hospitals, social groups, and libraries. It is difficult to overrate the importance of the public library market. It offers not only an immediate sale, but through subsequent loan of its collection, a preview function that can promote further sales to other groups.[24]

A sizable portion of the profit from the sale of educational films goes to the distributor. Each year at least a thousand documentaries and short films are entered in the American Film Festival. Although organizations such as the National Endowment for the Arts and state arts councils fund production and exhibition of such films, they do not normally extend their support to distribution.[25] It can, therefore, be difficult and expensive to identify an appropriate commercial distributor.

Developments in lightweight, portable and less expensive equipment have enabled producers to reduce the costs of shooting and editing their films, while still guaranteeing a high-quality product. Such developments have also encouraged smaller, independent producers to enter the market. For a producer on a tight budget, self-distribution can be an attractive alternative to contracting distribution to a larger commercial firm. To reduce costs, independent producers don't maintain large catalogs and their materials go out of distribution quickly. The self-marketer relies heavily on brochures, pamphlets, broadcasts, conventions, and conferences as channels of promotion.

Videorecordings

Videotape costs are equivalent to film costs for planning and production, but duplication costs are only about one-third of what they are for 16-mm films. The lower cost and ease of duplicating videorecordings accounts in part for the increasing popularity of this medium for both production and distribution.

An enormous amount of material of interest to libraries of all

23. Wendy Lidell and Mary Guzzy, eds., *The AIVF Guide to Film and Video Distributors* (New York: Association of Independent Video and Filmmakers Inc., 1984), p. 1.

24. Ibid., p. 2.

25. Ibid., p. 7.

types is now available in videorecordings. Feature films, cartoons, vintage television programs, and dramatic productions all have educational as well as entertainment value. Documentaries and other instructional programs abound; entire for-credit courses are built around a series of video presentations. Videorecordings can serve as primary source material for sociological research. They also provide a medium for artistic expression; a wealth of program material explores the creative possibilities of the medium itself.

Broadcasting, cable television, and other channels of distribution make educational material widely available. More and more users of educational materials are coming to see these channels as an electronic source of material, which can be duplicated easily for immediate use and long-term retention. The Television Licensing Center administered by Films Incorporated attempts to insure economic return for producers by selling licenses to users for extended retention and use of video programs taped off the air.[26] Licensing can be an attractive alternative for libraries and educational institutions, since the license fee is often less expensive than the purchase price of the film.

Educational films and television, which were revolutionary when first introduced, have become mainstays of educational media. Their hold on the market, however, is now being challenged by a technology that has initiated a revolution which is sure to affect nearly everyone—the computer.

Microcomputer Software

Planning costs for microcomputer-based educational software are about $300 per minute—half again as expensive as costs for 16-mm film and videorecordings. Duplication costs are less expensive: about $5 per diskette for floppy diskette software packages. If an interactive video component is added to the instructional software package, costs go up considerably.

The microcomputer coupled with video display technology makes possible an instructional medium that can incorporate still pictures, motion sequences, sound, and graphics into a single, interactive workstation. Because of the flexibility and power that interactive video provides, it requires considerable planning and

---

26. Reed and Stanek, "Library Use of Copyrighted Videotapes and Computer Software," p. C. For additional information, contact the Television Licensing Center, 5547 N. Ravenswood Avenue, Chicago, Illinois 60640.

computer programming. Costs top the list at $1,000 per minute of program in planning costs, $2,000 per minute for production of the original, and $5 per minute to duplicate. Because of the high cost of individual workstations, interactive video has seen its biggest application in training in both the public and private sectors.

Many libraries are actively collecting software and making it available to their patrons. Since software is generally considered to be licensed rather than sold, it has been suggested that libraries add a phrase to their purchase orders indicating that the "purchase is ordered for library circulation and patron use. Then, if the order is filled, the library is in a good position to argue that its terms, rather than the standard license restrictions, apply."[27] It has also been suggested that libraries post a copyright notice similar to that for photocopiers and videocassette recorders on library microcomputers and circulating software, both to educate and warn patrons about the existence of the copyright law.

Micropublishing

Microforms fit the definition of nonprint library materials; that is, they require some form of media enhancement to be used. Microforms exist primarily to provide conventional textual materials in a different form. In libraries, microforms seem to be as widespread as complaints about them, which range from the inconvenience and marginal legibility of some microfiche and microfilm to the problem of getting a paper copy of the content. Microforms have, however, established a niche in the information environment by providing the means to store and retrieve large amounts of text and other data in a space-saving format. Because the silver halide film base meets national standards for permanent retention, microforms are important for preservation of fragile books and ephemeral library material.[28]

Microform publishing takes several forms: republishing or reprinting (also known as demand publishing); simultaneous publication of both a print copy and a microform copy of an item; and publication of original works first, and sometimes exclusively, in microform. Microforms are not predominantly an orig-

---

27. Lidell and Guzzy, *The AIVF Guide*, p. 7.
28. Francis Spreitzer, ed., *Microforms in Libraries: A Manual for Evaluation and Management* (Chicago: American Library Association, 1985), p. 4.

inal publication medium; the content of microforms is more often assembled than authored. Republication in microform usually doesn't add anything to the original, although large microform sets might include indexes or other finding aids.[29]

Simultaneous publication of both print and microform copies of a work can reduce the cost to libraries of additional copies while increasing an item's availability to patrons by providing a backup copy. In addition, simultaneous publication can result in an actual sale for the publisher (as opposed to supplying additional copies by library copying). Microform publishing could be extended to include publication of easily updatable supplementary material for a print publication. Microform publishers already make available a variety of original materials that might not otherwise enjoy such wide distribution, for example, doctoral dissertations from University Microfilms International (UMI) and documents from the Educational Resources Information Center (ERIC).

Microforms offer publishers certain economies over print publications. For example, 1,000 copies of a book don't cost much more to produce than the first 500. On the other hand, microforms are produced on demand, and 6, 21, or 51 copies represent break points in the manufacturing costs of microfiche duplicates.[30] Unlike the book publisher who has considerable capital invested in inventory and warehouse costs, the microform publisher can have a warehouse in a cupboard, although associated supplies such as boxes, labels, and accompanying printed materials do take up some space.[31]

On the basis of a needs survey or market analysis, a microform publisher will identify materials to be reproduced, purchase the rights to reproduce the materials, and examine and edit the materials before filming. A master film is made from which duplicates are struck and packaged with any additional user aids such as indexes. The negative is stored.[32] The product is then publicized and delivered to a market that consists almost exclusively

29. Ralph J. Folcarelli, Arthur C. Tannenbaum, and Ralph C. Gerragamo, *The Microform Connection: A Basic Guide for Libraries* (New York: R. R. Bowker, 1982), p. 60.

30. Peter Ashby and Robert Campbell, *Microform Publishing* (London: Butterworth & Co., Ltd., 1979), p. 26. By supplying material supplemental to *Microform Publishing* on a single microfiche in a pocket inside the back cover, the publishers estimate that they have reduced the purchase price by one-third.

31. Ibid., p. 88.

32. Folcanelli, Tannenbaum, and Gerragamo, *The Microform Connection,* p. 61.

of research libraries; there are virtually no microform readers
in homes and there are few in offices.[33]

But the market is growing. The proportion of microforms to
books in research libraries approaches 25 percent in page equivalents.[34] About 30 percent of the periodicals in *Ulrich's International Periodicals Directory* are available in microform: 40 percent
of the science and technical periodicals, 30 percent of law and
library and information science periodicals, and 15 percent of
art periodicals.[35]

Other factors have improved the market for microforms.
Developments in computerized storage and retrieval of information have increased the utility of microforms for many applications. Computer-assisted retrieval (CAR) provides indexing to
microfilm; after using a computerized indexing system to make
a selection, the operator simply inserts the correct cartridge and
the computer drives the microform to the desired frame.[36] In
addition, the recent increase in the importance of preservation
microfilming will result in more microfilm and more microfilm
readers in research libraries. Although preservation microfilming often involves only in-house production of microforms with
little or no commercial distribution of the final product, a secondary market is likely to develop as libraries buy each other's rare
materials and special collections.

THE FUTURE OF NONPRINT MATERIALS

We have considered many library materials that require some
form of media enhancement to be used. These nonprint materials
are produced both to entertain and to inform and are collectively
characterized by their reliance upon equipment for access. While
the technological developments that brought many of these nonprint materials into being began more than a hundred years ago,

---

33. Allen B. Veaner, ed., *Studies in Micropublishing—1853–1976: Documentary Sources*, Microform Review Series in Library Micrographics Management,
Vol. 2, p. 65 (Westport, Conn.: Microform Review, Inc., 1977).

34. Michael R. Gabriel and Dorothy P. Ladd, *The Microform Revolution in
Libraries*, Foundations in Library and Information Science, Vol. 3, p. 6 (Greenwich, Conn.: JAI Press, 1980).

35. Ashby and Campbell, *Microform Publishing*, p. 109.

36. Murray Astarita, "Micrographics Today and Tomorrow," *Plan and Print*
November 1982 55(11): 22–25; *Special Interest Package No. 3; Trends in the Micro-
graphics Market* (Silver Spring, Md: Association for Information and Image
Management, n.d.), pp. 3-33–3-36.

their rate of innovation has increased dramatically in recent years. Rapidly changing technologies pose special challenges to libraries that undertake to collect material in these nonprint formats and make accessible the information they contain.

Libraries have faced format incompatibilities within media, which has resulted in a market characterized by segmentation and fragmentation. Reluctance to invest in any particular new technology stems in part from the fear that rapid innovation will quickly relegate any equipment to the obscurity of obsolescence. For example, incompatibility among videorecordings is guaranteed by the existence of three different international television standards, videocassette formats that employ different tape widths, cassette sizes, and playback speeds, and the introduction of additional new formats. Microforms also exhibit this variety; they are distributed as both microfilm and microfiche in a variety of sizes and require an array of lenses for a range of magnifications. Microcomputers perhaps epitomize variability; they offer endless permutations of hardware and software with varying levels of incompatibility.

Most nonprint materials can be easily reproduced, which tests copyright laws based on the concept of proprietary ownership of information. The broadcast channels—radio, television, and cable and satellite television—are filled with program signals that can easily be recorded, stored, and played back at a later time. The more familiar magnetic storage media—audiocassettes and videocassettes—have been joined by the microcomputer's floppy diskette, an innovation in magnetic storage that makes it possible to copy large amounts of information quickly and easily and in fact steal it while leaving it in the same place.

The nonprint market is thus characterized by instability, innovation, and rapid change. Investment by both producers and consumers involves a certain amount of risk taking. What is state-of-the-art today is just one more incompatible format tomorrow. And now the computer facilitates the introduction of exciting new equipment and formats for electronic storage and retrieval of text, sound, and motion pictures, further accelerating the rate of dramatic change.

In fact, the microcomputer provides the means for integrating the functions of all media into a single-point-of-access workstation. The cathode-ray tube (CRT) is essentially the same video display system used in television sets and computer monitors. New storage and retrieval technologies such as improved magnetic media and optical discs support all the functions of records, tapes, motion pictures, videorecordings, and microforms. Text, data, graphs, pictures, sound, and movies can all be stored electronically and "played back" on the same screen.

Libraries will be challenged by new and costly alternatives as (1) recorded text, image, and sound converge on a single integrated technology; (2) online systems, local systems and single workstations become linked in integrated networks; (3) such devices and applications become more widespread and familiar; and (4) user demand for these materials and services increases. The electronic revolution is shaped by technological change and innovation; libraries are, and have a unique opportunity to remain, in the vanguard of that revolution.

Acquiring Special Formats

Joan Mancell Hayes

Acquisitions is one of the most dynamic areas of library work, and this is especially true in the case of acquiring special formats. Special formats have become increasingly important in the collections of all types of libraries. At the same time, they have always been the most difficult to acquire. They include the whole range of audiovisual materials: sound recordings, films, filmstrips, slides, videocassettes, videodiscs, and videotapes. Also included for discussion in this chapter are maps, microcomputer software, microforms, music in its written form, and pamphlets. The list could be expanded to include pictures, prints, reproductions of paintings, toys, games, puppets, regalia, even household tools—there seems to be no limit to what a creative library may choose to acquire and circulate. These more esoteric forms will not be covered in this chapter, but many of the general guidelines for acquisition can be applied to any special format.

Obviously one chapter is not going to present all information on such a complex and varied subject. The chapter is intended to be a starting point in the search for information about each format. The bibliography at the end of the chapter gathers the basic texts, sources of bibliographic verification, and sources of supply for each format. It is subdivided by format and then by texts and sources of verification or supply, since many of the latter contain both types of information. The relevant bibliographic tools are numerous; *Nonbook Media: Selection and Maintenance* is the only one that covers selection strategies for all formats.

The various special formats are discussed in the chapter in terms of bibliographic sources, essential order information, and other hints gleaned from interviews with many librarians currently working with special formats. The texts listed in the different sections of the bibliography are the most comprehensive sources of information about each format. They provide the basic facts about the formats summarized in this chapter and also contain extensive bibliographies and lists of suppliers.

GENERAL GUIDELINES

The general guidelines for ordering monographs and serials also apply to the ordering of special format materials. For some items, bibliographic verification is necessary to be sure that what is to be ordered actually exists. The second step is determination of the essential pieces of information necessary to order the item. The third and final step is selection of the best source of supply for the item.

Bibliographic verification of special format items, when the library chooses to engage in this activity, may require consultation of a variety of sources. As was mentioned before, there is no one comprehensive source like *Books in Print (BIP)* for all formats. Each format has its own sources as listed in the bibliography; however, not all of the possible sources could be included. The review media for each format are numerous and everchanging; they are useful for determining both bibliographic verification and sources of supply. Producer, distributor, and jobber catalogs are helpful in determining supply sources and in verification.

If access to one of the large bibliographic networks, such as OCLC, is available, records of special format materials may be found in the database. Of course, keep in mind that these are records of the acquisitions and cataloging of particular libraries. The item may or may not be currently available. Therefore, bibliographic utilities are a better source for determining essential order information than for verifying an item's availability for purchase.

Some of the details needed to order print materials are the same as those for ordering special format materials. They include purchase order (PO) number; date of order (which may become the order number if no PO number is used); bill-to and ship-to addresses; author, artist, or creator; title; publisher or produc-

Joan Mancell Hayes

ing company; publication date; price; and number of copies ordered. Depending on the format, other items of order information are essential, for example, the company or manufacturer's number for sound recordings or a specific format within a format, for example, Beta or VHS for videocassettes. Special instructions to the vendor can indicate necessary invoicing requirements. The acquisitions department may also become involved in the ordering of specialized storage units and equipment for using the different formats.

All of the guidelines for ordering regular print materials should be applied to special format materials. Because of the complexity involved in ordering such materials, however, some added care should be taken before an order is placed. The more information included to identify an item being ordered, the better. Inaccurate or incomplete order information may result in delays and in the wrong item being sent. One should also let the vendor know at the time of order if an itemized invoice is required. Often special format materials are identified on the invoice only by the company number and price or by the total number of items ordered and the total price.

Often there is only one source of supply when ordering special format materials. Direct orders are much more common for this type of material. Often, the selector handling searching and verification will do the preorder work as well as determining the source of supply. Depending upon the size of the library, the acquisitions librarian may only have to place the completed order, receive it, and pay the invoice. In medium- and smaller-size institutions, the acquisitions librarian is responsible for the whole order process. This may include dealing with calls and visits by company sales representatives. Walk-ins and telemarketing are an intrusion, and the advantage of meeting or speaking by appointment should be stressed.

Jobbers or discount vendors are less common in this field than they are for print materials. Some of the large book jobbers and library supply companies offer some special format materials, and it is necessary to check to see what each jobber supplies currently. In general, large companies supply what they stock and do not do special ordering for this type of material. The smaller book jobbers may try to get special format materials for a service charge.

Dealers, jobbers, and other good sources of supply for specific formats do exist. The trick is to find them. The library profession is unique in its willingness to share information. One need only tap into the information network. The best way to do that is through membership in state and national professional associations. The benefits of such memberships are many. The opportunity to attend conferences provides contact with colleagues in one's area and state and across the nation. Such informal contacts are especially useful for learning about local vendors in your area. Conference attendance also provides direct contact with many vendors; visiting the exhibits is an excellent way to do comparison shopping. Conference workshops, programs, and discussion groups provide a more formal medium for continuing education. One may learn what is new in the area of acquisitions and participate in creative problem solving. The journals that come as part of association membership are also a means of continuing education and are a good source of reviews and vendor advertisements.

The receipt of special format materials presents some unique problems. Often, this may not be the responsibility of the acquisitions department but of processing and technical services or the selection librarian. Errors may not be caught until much later, perhaps when a patron first uses the material. Therefore, it is important to check on the return policy of the vendor before ordering. That policy may determine whether the order is placed directly with the publisher, to a local dealer, or to a jobber. Several questions should be asked: Is permission for return required? Is the original packaging required for return? Is there a time limit for returns? Because of the complexity of the order and receipt and return procedures for this type of material, it is better not to prepay if it can be avoided.

The rest of this chapter will briefly describe each special format, noting the different forms within the format, the types of material most commonly found in the format, sources of bibliographic verification, essential order information for the particular format, and the best types of sources of supply.

SOUND RECORDINGS

Sound recordings are available in a variety of forms. The traditional and popular LP-, EP-, or 45-rpm records are the least expensive but are also the least durable recordings for library use. Tapes are more expensive and more durable; the eight-track tape cartridges have been phased out by four track cassettes. The newest form of sound recording is the compact disc (CD). Currently, this is the most expensive type of recording. However, CDs seem to be ideal for libraries because they are small and durable. It is predicted that the CD will replace the LP. This is a good example of how librarians dealing with special formats need to be aware of and ready to respond to trends created by new technology.

Sound recordings contain all types of music as well as the spoken word (plays, poetry, foreign language instruction, and entire books). Books on audiocassette are becoming very popular, as they fit well into our fast-paced, mobile lives. Book jobbers have begun to offer them to libraries at the trade discount rate. Books on audiocassette may be complete or in abridged versions, which one should be aware of when ordering. Three recent articles list sources of supply for books on audiocassette as well as more general information about the format.[1]

The *Schwann Record and Tape Guide* serves as the *BIP* for sound recordings along with the Library of Congress listing of its cataloging of this format.[2] The review media noted in the bibliography as items *American Record Guide, Billboard, High Fidelity, Rolling Stone,* and *Stereo Review* can also be used for bibliographic verification and to locate sources of supply. One of the articles in "Collecting Popular Music"[3] reviews the review media for sound recordings.

Essential order information to include when purchasing sound recordings is the manufacturer's number; the author, composer, or performer; title; and price. Magrill and Hickey suggest that it may be easier to keep the on-order file for sound recordings by manufacturer's number, since titles may vary because of translations into different foreign languages.[4]

Publishers and jobbers of sound recordings are specifically identified in the *Audio Video Market Place,* and advertisements

1. David Blairvas, "Books On Cassette: A Buyer's Guide," *Publishers' Weekly* 226 (September 28, 1984): 87–92; Blairvas, "Bookselling and Merchandising: Sidelines Update: Books On Cassette," *Publisher's Weekly* 225 (March 30, 1984): 36–40; Bryan Davis, "Books (On Cassette) Are Better Than Ever; *American Libraries* 15 (March 1984): 165–170.

2. *National Union Catalog. Audiovisual Materials (NUC.AV).* (Washington, D.C.: Cataloging Distributive Service, 1953–). *Music, Books on Music, and Sound Recordings* (Washington, D.C.: LC Cataloging Distributive Service, 1973–).

3. Issue title of *Drexel Library Quarterly* 19 (Winter 1983): 1–164; Tim LaBorie, editor.

4. Rose Mary Magrill and Doralyn J. Hickey, *Acquisition Management and Collection Development in Libraries* (Chicago: American Library Association), p. 142.

and listings for them can also be found in the review media and indexes listed in the audiovisual materials section of *Booklist, Choice, Educators Guides, Library Journal, Media Review Digest, NICEM Media Index, Publishers' Weekly, Guides to Educational Media,* and *School Library Journal.* A jobber who deals in sound recordings may offer a higher discount than that available when purchasing directly from the producer; however, it may take longer to receive the order. The advantage, as always, in ordering through a jobber is that there is only one source to deal with. Going directly to the various producing companies may result in quicker turnaround time, but the disadvantages are a lower discount and many sources to monitor. Some producing companies have standing order plans at a higher discount, but receipts need to be reviewed carefully to be sure the plan is worth the lower cost.

The quickest source of supply is the local record store. The advantages of dealing locally are that selections can be heard before purchase and savings can be realized on shipping costs and the ability to take advantage of sales. One disadvantage is that there is usually no discount; however, if the volume of business is high enough, a discount might be negotiated. Local vendors may not be able to deal with back orders or a large library's sometimes lengthy payment cycle.

VIDEORECORDINGS, FILMS, FILMSTRIPS, AND SLIDES

The subdivisions of this category—videorecordings, films, filmstrips, and slides—are numerous. In past years, 16-mm films have been the most popular in library film collections. The largest number of titles have been available in this format, but they are also the most expensive to purchase. In contrast, 8-mm films are less expensive. Some libraries carry both 16-mm and 8-mm films.

Recently, videocassettes have been replacing the film collections in many libraries. The cassettes are less expensive and more durable, and the selection broadens every year: first-run movies that may still be playing in theaters, classic oldies, and a wide variety of how-to-do-it topics. Videocassettes are available in Beta format, which has better sound quality, and VHS format. The VHS format is the most common, outselling Beta by four to one. Beta, and the even less popular videodiscs, may be going the way of the eight-track tape cartridges.

Joan Mancell Hayes

The many and varied sources of bibliographic verification for this format include the *NUC.AV* and the selection aids and the review media listed in the audiovisual materials and videorecordings sections of *Booklist, Choice, Educators Guides, Library Journal, Media Review Digest, NICEM Media Index, Publishers' Weekly, Guides to Educational Media,* and *School Library Journal.* Other useful sources are the catalogs of film producers and distributors and those of film loan and rental collections.

An essential item of order information to consider when purchasing films is that some companies often offer the same title on acetate and on Estar base film. Estar base is a polyester that gives longer wear and retains color better and is therefore preferable. Usually films may be previewed, and often companies sell the preview prints at a lower cost. These prints are usually on acetate film and may not be worth the dollar savings.

When ordering videocassettes, be sure to specify Beta or VHS format. Usually videos cannot be previewed before ordering, because they can be easily copied. Damaged tapes, or the wrong tape, is not uncommon, so be sure to check the vendor's return policies before ordering. Often, returns of new videos will not be accepted without the original packaging. If possible, all videos should be watched upon receipt—a real fringe benefit for staff with VCRs.

Specific suppliers for the different forms of this format are listed in the *Audio Video Market Place,* the *NICEM Index to Producers and Distributors,* and in the publications mentioned previously. Jobbers are becoming more common, especially for videos. Films have traditionally been ordered directly from producers and distributors, who tend to be either education- or entertainment-oriented. It is best to order at intervals that will allow a larger discount. Cooperative buying arrangements with other libraries in an area should continually be investigated, as the drawbacks of cooperative buying are usually outweighed by the time and money saved. Sources of verification and supply for filmstrips are *Educators Guides* and *NICEM Media Index;* information on slide libraries is found in Irvine and Fry's *Slide Libraries;* and an index to slides is in *NICEM Media Index.*

MAPS

Map libraries collect information in many different forms, including atlases, sheet maps, globes, charts, satellite photography, and remote sensing data. Sheet maps showing physical relief, called topographic sheets, are probably most commonly collected. In large institutions with a map department, the map librarian may select, verify, choose suppliers, and check the maps upon receipt; in smaller libraries, the whole job may fall to the acquisitions department.

Sources of verification include geographic and cartographic journals; *National Union Catalog. Cartographic Materials* and foreign national bibliographies; the *Monthly Catalog of United States Government Publications*; catalogs of publishers, manufacturers, and dealers; and the accessions lists from large map libraries. These libraries often offer items for duplicate exchange. Helpful lists of these sources are found in Larsgaard's *Map Librarianship.*

The most essential item of information to include when ordering maps is the scale. Maps should be checked carefully upon receipt because many maps of the same area are published at different scales.

Commonly, maps are ordered directly from their publishers. Larsgaard lists names and addresses under a sampling of commercial and association map publishers, sources of state highway maps and sources for state geological maps. County and city governmental agencies and the chambers of commerce of cities are good sources of local area and street maps. Many libraries make up form postcards requesting free maps and requesting, at the same time, to be placed on the mailing lists of these agencies. Some cities have a local map store which can be helpful in placing special orders.

Larger institutions may have depository arrangements with either the U.S. Geological Survey (USGS) or the Defense Mapping Agency (DMA). USGS provides topographic sheet maps. To become a depository, a library must provide adequate storage and allow public access to the maps. A library can be designated a partial depository and receive maps for only a given region or state. DMA provides selected topographic maps and nautical and aeronautical charts of areas of the world exclusive of the United States. The maps are on indefinite loan to the depositories and are subject to recall.

Beautiful maps of Europe and Africa are published by the Michelin Tire Company. Geo Center is another source of foreign maps. Foreign maps are hard to acquire because the mapping agencies are usually connected with the military and are sensitive to national defense. One can write to the travel and tourism bureaus of countries, but it is not advisable to prepay orders, because there may be little recourse in the event of an incorrect shipment.

MICROCOMPUTER SOFTWARE

Many programs and files are produced in microcomputer format, and increasingly libraries are providing public access to microcomputers and even circulating software. Dewey, as well as Lathrop and Goodson outline the range of programs available: computer literacy; programming in different programming languages; computer-assisted instruction; special interest programs, (for example, tax preparation programs); library skills; database management; word processing; electronic spreadsheets; software for children; and entertainment software.[5]

The sources of bibliographic verification for software include computer periodicals, such as *Classroom Computer Learning, Library Software Review,* and *Small Computers in Libraries*; indexes to software reviews; and directories of microcomputer software such as *Directory of Microcomputer Software; Online Micro-Software Guide & Directory, Software Encyclopedia,* and *Swift's Educational Software Directory.*

Software can be ordered directly from software companies. These companies produce their own catalogs, which are collected in *Software Publishers' Catalogs Annual.* Local computer stores are another source of supply; they may charge more for software than the catalog price, but they may allow previewing a program before purchasing it. Some of the larger library jobbers also deal in software, but their catalogs may only list the titles, prices, and system requirements without much description of what the programs do. Public domain software, often called shareware, can be obtained through clubs and user groups; caution is advised, however, as these programs often contain bugs and may not be worth adding to the collection.

One essential item of order information for software is system requirements. Software must be compatible with the machine it will run on (the hardware). Additionally, the version of the program purchased should be for the particular model of that brand

---

5. Patrick R. Dewey, *Public Access Microcomputers: A Handbook for Librarians* (White Plains, N.Y.: Knowledge Industry, 1984) Ann Lathrop and Bobby Gooden, *Courses are in the Classroom, Selecting, Organizing, and Using Software* (Menlo Park, Calif.: Addison-Wesley, 1983).

of machine. Software has two other important requirements of the machine it will run on: a certain amount of memory, measured in K (1024 bits, bytes, or words), and an operating system (such as CP/M or DOS, to name only two). A program may be issued in many versions, and one needs to be certain that the version of the software ordered is compatible with the hardware owned. All of these pieces of information must be checked before ordering, since most software cannot be returned. Most vendors will allow return only if the shrink-wrap packaging is unopened. If the software is returned because it is defective, it must be exchanged for exactly the same software.

MICROFORMS

There are a variety of microforms: microfilm (16-mm and 35-mm microfilm on open reels and cartridges), microfiche (which comes in a standard size of 4 inches by 6 inches and has a higher reduction ratio than microfilm—usually 24× and 48×), and microopaque. All of these forms require different types of readers and reader/printers.

Materials published in microform include reprints of out-of-print monographs and back files of journals; original publication of dissertations and research reports (for example, publications of the U.S. Government Printing Office); simultaneous paper and microform publication of serials; and large microform project sets. Microforms are usually hard-to-get materials that cover a period of time or a subject and are for sale as a set. They should come with a printed contents guide and index.

Sources of bibliographic verification and supply for microforms are fewer but more complete than for some other formats. The *Guide to Microforms in Print* and the *Subject Guide to Microforms in Print* serve as the *BIP* for microforms. Other sources are the *National Register of Microform Masters* and *Newspapers in Microform*. There are also the catalogs of the individual micropublishers, which are listed in the *Micropublishers' Trade List Annual* and the *Microform Market Place*, where micropublishers can be identified.

Usually there is no choice involved in choosing a source of supply for microforms—orders are placed directly to the microform publisher who carries the title one wishes to order. This is an area of publishing where libraries can have an effect on what is published. Libraries can communicate requests for a title to be published, and if the microform publisher gets enough requests, the title may be microfilmed and made available.

Another source of supply is from libraries that have a copying service and hold the title desired. The *Directory of Library Reprographic Services* identifies institutions that offer such a service. One librarian who works with this format advises that the best way to handle this type of order is to call a librarian who is directly connected with the collection that has the desired title. Ordering from the institution's acquisition department or the interlibrary loan department may only delay the order.

Essential order information for microforms centers around the silver halide-diazo-vesicular debate. Each of these is a method of manufacturing the actual film used in microfilming material. Silver halide film is of archival quality, and it is also the most expensive. But, as has been pointed out in the literature on the subject, archival permanence can only be achieved through a combination of archival-quality film, archival-quality processing, and archival-quality storage. If one of these elements is missing, the other two will not be enough to achieve permanence. This whole debate may be resolved soon by a new technology and yet another format, the optical disk.

Another choice that may have to be made in ordering microforms is between positive and negative microform prints. The positive film, which is dark print on light background, is easier to read; the negative film, which is light print on dark background, makes better copies. Which is ordered depends on the type of reader/printer the film will be used on; currently there is only one machine that is bimodal.

Microform publishing is a competitive business, and it may be best to order by phone and negotiate the best deal available. If a high enough dollar volume is ordered, the following items can be negotiated: discount, shipping costs, extra copies of printed guides and indexes, and additional discount for prepayment. As always, use caution with prepayments and ask for a guaranteed delivery date. Upon receipt, the labels on the boxes should be checked with the contents of the film. Ask for a long-term return policy, since rarely are microforms read immediately upon receipt.

MUSIC SCORES

Music in its written form can be purchased in sheet music and in bound books of music. Individual compositions, all types of scores, collected sets, and songbooks are available. As with many special formats, there is no one in-print list for music. The selection, verification, and choice of vendor is often done by music librarians. Sources of verification are the Library of Congress listing of its cataloging of music, *Music, Books on Music, and Sound Recordings,* and publishers' and dealers' catalogs. The Music Library Association's *A Basic Music Library* is primarily a selection tool, but the item numbers from this list can be used when ordering from some dealers.

Music is ordered directly from publishers. Local music stores can be a good source for some libraries. There are also general dealers or jobbers who specialize in music; these are listed by names and addresses in an appendix of *A Basic Music Library.* *Notes* also carries ads of dealers and their specialties. One librarian advises not to give up on out-of-print cancellations of orders for scores. Copyrights expire and another publisher may pick up the copyright so that what is wanted will then be back in print. A desiderata file is a helpful way to control the problem.

PAMPHLETS

The types of material published in pamphlets are seemingly endless. The sources for selection, bibliographic verification, and supply are the same tools: the *Educators Guides* published by the Educators' Progress Service, the *Public Affairs Information Service Bulletin,* and the *Vertical File Index.* Other sources are periodicals such as *Library Journal, Wilson Library Bulletin,* and *Booklist.* The *Encyclopedia of Associations* has the addresses of associations that publish pamphlet material.

Pamphlets are usually ordered directly from the publisher, distributor, or association. As with maps, libraries may want to develop a form postcard that simultaneously requests free pamphlet materials, a publications list, and placement on the mailing list. The basic texts on this format, Miller's *The Vertical File and Its Satellite* and Spencer's "Pamphlet Collection Development," suggest prepaying small amounts, as the cost of invoicing may be more than the price of the items ordered. Magrill and Hickey also suggest that the on-order file be kept by source rather than by title. Another useful hint is to test the quality of an organization's publications by making a subject request for materials.

Joan Mancell Hayes

CONCLUSION

Acquiring special formats is the true test of an acquisitions librarian. Fortunately, many experienced librarians who have worked extensively with particular formats and generally in acquisitions have shared their expertise through the texts listed in the bibliography. These texts should be the starting point of inquiry for anyone who chooses this challenging area of library work.

B   I   B   L   I   O   G   R   A   P   H   Y

AUDIOVISUAL MATERIALS

Texts

American Library Association, Audio-Visual Committee. *Guidelines for Audiovisual Materials and Services for Large Public Libraries.* Chicago: American Library Association, 1975.

Cabeceiras, James. *The Multimedia Library: Materials Selection & Use.* 2nd ed. New York: Academic Press, 1982.

Ellison, John W., ed. *Media Librarianship.* New York: Neal-Schuman, 1985.

Magrill, Rose Mary, and Doralyn J. Hickey. "Purchasing Nonbook Materials." In *Acquisitions Management and Collection Development in Libraries. Chicago: American Library Association, 1984.*

Nonbook Media: Collection Management and User Services. Edited by John W. Ellison and Patricia Ann Coty. Chicago: American Library Association, 1987.

Sive, Mary Robinson. *Media Selection Handbook.* Littleton, Colo.: Libraries Unlimited, 1983.

Weihs, Jean. *Accessible Storage of Nonbook Materials.* Phoenix, Ariz.: Oryx Press, 1984.

Sources of verification or supply

Audio Video Market Place. New York: R. R. Bowker, 1984–. Annual.

Booklist. Chicago: American Library Association, 1905–. Semimonthly.

Choice. Middletown, Conn.: Association of College and Research Libraries, 1964–. 11 issues per year.

Educators Guides. Randolph, Wisc.: Educators' Progress Service. Annual.

Educators Guide to Free Audio and Video Materials
Educators Guide to Free Films
Educators Guide to Free Filmstrips
Educators Guide to Free Tapes, Scripts and Transcriptions
Library Journal. New York: R. R. Bowker, 1876–. Semimonthly.
Media Review Digest. Ann Arbor, Mich.: Pierian Press, 1970–. Annual
with quarterly supplements.
National Union Catalog. Audiovisual Materials (NUC.AV.). Washington,
D.C.: Library of Congress, Cataloging Distribution Service, 1953–.
Quarterly on microfiche.
NICEM Media Index. Los Angeles: National Information Center for
Educational Media, University of California.
    Index to 8mm Motion Cartridges. New York: R. R. Bowker, 1969–.
    Index to 16mm Educational Films. New York: R. R. Bowker, 1967–.
    Index to 35mm Educational Filmstrips. New York: R. R. Bowker,
      1968–.
    Index to Educational Audio Tapes. Los Angeles: NICEM, 1971–.
    Index to Educational Videotapes. Los Angeles: NICEM, 1971–.
    Index to Educational Overhead Transparencies. Los Angeles:
      NICEM, 1969–.
    Index to Educational Records. Los Angeles: NICEM, 1971–.
    Index to Educational Slides. Los Angeles: NICEM, 1973.
    Index to Producers and Distributors. Los Angeles: NICEM,
      1971–.
    Update of Nonbook Media. Los Angeles: NICEM, 1973–.
Publishers' Weekly. New York: R. R. Bowker, 1872–. Weekly.
Rufsvold, Margaret I. *Guides to Educational Media.* 4th ed. Chicago:
American Library Journal, 1977.
School Library Journal. New York: R. R. Bowker, 1954–. Monthly,
September–May.
Sive, Mary Robinson. *Selecting Instructional Media: A Guide to Audio-
visual and Other Instructional Media Lists.* 3rd ed. Littleton, Colo.:
Libraries Unlimited, 1983.

SOUND RECORDINGS

Texts

Blaiwas, David. "Books On Cassette: A Buyer's Guide." *Publishers'
Weekly* 226 (September 28, 1984): 87–92.
Blaiwas, David. "Bookselling and Merchandising: Sidelines Update:
Books On Cassette." *Publishers' Weekly* 225 (March 30, 1984): 36–40.
"Collecting Popular Music." Issue editor, Tim LaBorie. *Drexel Library
Quarterly* 19 (Winter 1983): 1–164.
Davis, Bryan. "Books (On Cassette) Are Better Than Ever." *American
Libraries,* 15 (March 1984): 165–170.

Sources of verfication or supply

American Record Guide. Washington, D.C.: Heldref, 1984–. Bimonthly.
Billboard. New York: Billboard, 1894–. Weekly.
High Fidelity. New York: ABC Leisure Magazines, 1951–. Monthly.
Music, Books on Music, and Sound Recordings. Washington, D.C.: Library of Congress, Cataloging Distribution Service, 1973–. Semi-annual, with annual and quinquennial cumulations.
On Cassette: A Comprehensive Bibliography of Spoken Word Audio Cassettes. New York: R. R. Bowker, 1985–. Annual.
Rolling Stone. New York: Straight Arrow, 1967–. Bimonthly.
Schwann Record and Tape Guide. Boston: ABC Schwann, 1949–. Monthly.
Stereo Review. New York: Ziff-Davis, 1958–. Monthly.

VIDEORECORDINGS, FILMS, FILMSTRIPS, SLIDES

Texts

Irvine, Betty J., and P. Eileen Fry. *Slide Libraries: A Guide for Academic Institutions, Museums, and Special Collections.* 2nd ed. Littleton, Colo.: Libraries Unlimited, 1979.
Rehrauer, George. *The Film User's Handbook: A Basic Manual for Managing Library Film Services.* New York: R. R. Bowker, 1975.

Sources of verification or supply

Consortium of University Film Centers. *Educational Film Locator.* 2nd ed. New York: R. R. Bowker, 1980.
EFFLA Evaluation. New York: Educational Film Library Association, 1946–. 10 issues per year.
Feature Films: A Directory of Feature Films on 16mm and Videotape Available for Rental, Sale, and Lease. New York: R. R. Bowker, 1985–. Biennial.
Film & Video News. La Salle, Ill.: Gorez Goz, 1984–. Quarterly.
Landers Film Reviews. Los Angeles: Landers Associates, 1956–. 5 issues per year.
Science Books & Films. Washington, D.C.: American Association for the Advancement of Science, 1975–. Quarterly.
Sightlines. New York: Educational Film Library Association, 1967–. Quarterly.
Video Source Book. Syosset, N.Y.: National Video Clearinghouse; Detroit, Mich.: distributed by Gale Research Co., 1979–. Annual.

MAPS

Texts

Larsgaard, Mary. *Map Librarianship: An Introduction.* Littleton, Colo.: Libraries Unlimited, 1978.

"Map Librarianship and Map Collection." Issue editor, Mary L. Larsgaard. *Library Trends* 29 (Winter, 1981): 371–562.

Wise, Donald A. "Cartographic Sources and Procurement Problems." *Special Libraries* 68 (May–June 1977): 198-205.

Sources of verification or supply

Geo Center. *Geo-Katalog.* Stuttgart: Geo Center, Internationales Land-kartenhaus, 1974–.

National Union Catalog. Cartographic Materials (NUC.CM). Washington, D.C.: Library of Congress, Cataloging Distribution Service, 1983–. Quarterly on microfiche.

Special Libraries Association, Geography and Map Division. *Bulletin.* New York: Special Libraries Association, 1947–. Quarterly.

United States Superintendent of Documents. *Monthly Catalog of United States Government Publications.* Washington, D.C.: U.S. Government Printing Office, 1895–. Monthly.

Western Association of Map Libraries. *Information Bulletin.* Sacramento, Calif.: Western Association of Map Libraries, 1969–. Three times per year.

MICROCOMPUTER SOFTWARE

Texts

Costa, Betty, and Maria Costa. *A Micro Handbook for Small Libraries and Media Centers.* 2nd ed. Littleton, Colo.: Libraries Unlimited, 1986.

Dewey, Patrick R. *Public Access Microcomputers: A Handbook for Librarians.* White Plains, N.Y.: Knowledge Industry, 1984.

Lathrop, Ann, and Bobby Goodson. *Courseware in the Classroom: Selecting, Organizing and Using Software.* Menlo Park, Calif.: Addison-Wesley, 1983.

Source of verification or supply

Classroom Computer Learning. Belmont, Calif.: Pitman Learning, 1983–. 9 issues per year.

Directory of Microcomputer Software. Delran, N.J.: DataPro Research Corp., 1981–. Monthly.

Joan Mancell Hayes

Educational Software Directory: A Subject Guide to Microcomputer Software. Compiled by Marily J. Chartrand and Constance D. Williams. Littleton, Colo.: Libraries Unlimited, 1982.

Library Software Review. Westport, Conn.: Meckler, 1984–. Bimonthly.

Microcomputer Index. Santa Clara, Calif.: Microcomputer Information Services, 1980–. Bimonthly.

Online Micro-Software Guide & Directory. Weston, Conn.: Online, 1984–. Annual.

PC Clearinghouse Directory. Fairfax, Va.: PC Clearinghouse, 1983–. Two times per year.

Small Computers in Libraries. Westport, Conn.: Meckler, 1984–. Monthly.

Software Catalog. Microcomputers. New York: Elsevier, 1983–. Quarterly.

Software Encyclopedia. New York: R. R. Bowker, 1986–.

Software Publishers' Catalogs Annual. Westport, Conn.: Meckler, 1984–. Annual.

Swift's Educational Software Directory. Apple II ed. Austin, Tex.: S. Swift, 1982–. Annual.

MICROFORMS

Texts

American Library Association, Bookdealer-Library Relations Committee. *Guidelines for Handling Library Orders for Microforms.* Chicago: American Library Association, 1977.

Diaz, Albert James, ed. *Microforms in Libraries: A Reader.* Weston, Conn.: Microform Review, 1975.

Folcarelli, Ralph J., Arthur C. Tannenbaum, and Ralph C. Ferrangamo. *The Microform Connection: A Basic Guide for Libraries.* New York: R. R. Bowker, 1982.

Saffady, William. *Micrographics.* 2d ed. Littleton, Colo.: Libraries Unlimited, 1985.

Sources of verification or supply

Directory of Library Reprographic Services. 8th ed. Westport, Conn.: Meckler, 1982.

Guide to Microforms in Print. Westport, Conn.: Meckler, 1961–. Annual.

Microform Market Place. Weston, Conn.: Microform Review, 1975–. Biennial.

Microform Review. Westport, Conn.: Meckler, 1972–. Quarterly.

Micropublishers' Trade List Annual. Weston, Conn.: Microform Review, 1975–. Annual.

National Register of Microform Masters. Washington, D.C.: Library of Congress, Cataloging Distribution Service, 1965–83. (Now included in *NUC.BOOKS* and *New Serial Titles*).

Newspapers in Microform. Washington, D.C.: Library of Congress, Cataloging Distribution Service, 1948–83.

Subject Guide to Microforms in Print. Weston, Conn.: Microform Review, 1962–. Annual.

MUSIC

Texts

Brown, Peter Bennett. *Ordering and Claiming Music Materials: Tips from a Dealer.* Beverly Hills, Calif.: Theodore Front Musical Literature, 1981.

Bryant, E. T. *Music Librarianship: A Practical Guide.* 2nd ed. Metuchen, N.J.: Scarecrow Press, 1985.

Sources of verification or supply

Music Library Association, Committee on Basic Music Collection. *A Basic Music Library: Essential Scores and Books.* 2d ed. Edited by Robert Michael Fling. Chicago: American Library Association, 1983.

Notes. Ann Arbor, Mich.: Music Library Association, 1942–. Quarterly.

PAMPHLETS

Texts

Miller, Shirley. *The Vertical File and Its Satellites: A Handbook of Acquisition, Processing, and Organization.* 2nd ed. Littleton, Colo.: Libraries Unlimited, 1979.

Spencer, Michael D. "Pamphlet Collection Development." *Bookmark* 41 (Winter 1983): 91-98.

Sources of verification or supply

Educators Guides. Randolph, Wisc.: Educators' Progress Service. Annual.
   Educators Grade Guide to Free Teaching Aids
   Educators Guide to Free Guidance Materials
   Educators Guide to Free Health, Physical Education, and Recreation Materials
   Educators Guide to Free Home Economics Materials
   Educators Guide to Free Science Materials
   Educators Guide to Free Social Studies Materials

Joan Mancell Hayes

Educators Index of Free Materials
Elementary Teachers' Guide to Free Curriculum Materials
Guide to Free Computer Materials
Encyclopedia of Associations: A Guide to National and International Organizations. Detroit, Mich.: Gale Research Co., 1961–. Annual.
Public Affairs Information Service Bulletin. New York: Public Affairs Information Service, 1915–. Semimonthly, with quarterly and annual cumulations.
Vertical File Index. New York: Wilson, 1935–. Monthly.
Wilson Library Bulletin. New York: Wilson, 1914–. Monthly.

Methods
of Accounting
and Business
Practices

Basic Acquisitions Accounting

Betsy Kruger

An understanding of basic accounting theory and practice on the part of acquisitions librarians is essential for the effective management of any acquisitions department. Yet, the financial aspects of libraries and certainly the accounting aspects of acquisitions work are often neglected in graduate library education. As a result, some librarians come to acquisitions work unprepared for the nuts-and-bolts aspects of monitoring and expending a materials budget. This chapter provides a guide to acquisitions accounting by defining general accounting concepts and examining specific operations and records necessary for tracking expenditures for books, serials, and nonprint library materials. Other accounting concerns of libraries such as plant, salary, and equipment costs and expenditures are beyond the scope of this chapter.

Accounting operations, like size of materials budgets, vary widely among libraries. Depending on the accounting method used, libraries may have different year-end requirements. Many libraries have automated their accounting operations while others still use manual systems. The role of the acquisitions department in accounting operations also varies widely. Some acquisitions departments both contract for purchases and pay for them. Others issue purchase orders and approve invoices while payment is actually initiated by the library's business office. For example, one library department may initiate purchases and approve invoices after verifying receipt, and another department may prepare vouchers which are forwarded to various accounting departments. Some libraries must funnel all purchasing arrangements starting with the issuance of purchase orders through the central business office of a parent organization and have little autonomy in managing their fiscal affairs.

Despite these myriad differences, acquisitions accounting in *all* libraries is concerned with four basic questions: how much money is there to spend? (allocation); how much will a purchase probably cost? (encumbrance); how much is actually spent? (payment); and, how much money is left? (free balance). Good acquisitions accounting practices that carefully address these questions prevent overspending or underspending, aid in financial decision making and budget planning, and result in clear audit trails and good library-vendor relations.

THE IMPORTANCE
OF FISCAL ACCOUNTABILITY

As nonprofit organizations, libraries emphasize service rather than maximizing income. Nonprofit status does not, however, diminish or eliminate the necessity for fiscal accountability. All libraries are obligated to obtain and expend their money in an appropriate and legal fashion and to document revenues and expenditures for the organizational entities that fund them. Public libraries are accountable to local governments; academic libraries to their parent institutions; and corporate libraries to their parent corporations. Usually, the funding body, in turn, is accountable to state and federal governments. Any library that receives federal assistance or grants must account to the federal government directly for the expenditure of that money. Spending money appropriately means spending it for the purpose for which it was budgeted. Most libraries cannot use money allocated for books to replace a broken photocopying machine or pay an unexpectedly high utility bill.

Maintaining accurate accounting records makes it easier to monitor expenditures throughout the year, so that overspending and underspending are avoided. Overspending a materials budget is both sloppy financial management and illegal. Failing to keep track of outstanding purchase orders gives an inaccurate picture of the amount of money still available for purchasing materials and would no doubt result in a library being unable to meet its financial obligations to its vendors. Underspending budgeted funds is also risky. It may suggest to the funding entity that the library did not prepare its budget in an informed manner and may result in funding cuts the following fiscal year.

It is always important for a library to keep its own internal accounting records, even if all its purchasing is handled through the central purchasing and accounting departments of a parent organization. Even a simple ledger book for posting encumbrances and payments can help provide a clearer picture of current financial status than the less timely and often less specific reports of a large central accounting division.

Good accounting practices result in accurate financial data that form the basis for budgetary planning. A flexible accounting system can provide current and retrospective cost information that can aid in projecting future costs for various types of library materials and for materials in various subject areas.

Every library must be prepared for a financial audit—a systematic inspection of its financial records to confirm that accepted accounting principles are being used to track income and expenditures. Audits may be initiated by external regulatory agencies, by the central accounting office of a parent organization, or internally by the library itself to assure that the money it is responsible for is being spent appropriately. Good accounting practices include maintaining a clear audit trail, that is, a sequence of postings in an accounting system that are tied to original documents such as purchase orders, invoices, statements, and vouchers. An audit trail provides a clear picture of all financial transactions for a given purchase from the initial issuance of a purchase order through final payment.

Lastly, a library owes prompt and accurate payment to those vendors who, in good faith, ship materials promptly and in good condition prior to receiving payment. Vendors depend on a positive cash flow to maintain daily operations and may need to borrow money at high interest rates if customers do not pay their bills in a timely manner. Prompt and accurate payment makes for good library-vendor relations. The goodwill that accrues in such a relationship pays off in higher levels of service and a willingness on the part of the vendor to assist the library should special needs arise.

SOME BASIC CONCEPTS OF FUND ACCOUNTING

A library's operating fund is money used for day-to-day operations. The materials budget is derived from this fund and money is specifically earmarked for the purchase of books, serials, and various nonprint library materials.

While a very small library may maintain a single fund from which all materials are purchased, most libraries allocate money from the materials budget into a series of funds which may correspond to departments within the library, format of material, or subject. A public library may establish separate materials funds for the reference room, children's department, and branch libraries. If a library divides its materials budget by format, it may establish separate funds for monographs, serials, and nonprint materials. Serial funds may be subdivided into periodical and continuation or standing order funds. While a small public library may have only one or two funds, a large academic or research library may establish several hundred funds based on a combination of subject and format considerations. Libraries that collect core materials through one or more approval plans (for example, publisher based, subject based, university press, European blanket orders) may have separate approval plan funds in addition to subject area and format funds. Many libraries also establish a general fund from which replacements for lost or stolen monographs and serials are purchased.

An accounting system based on a collection of separate funds is known as a fund accounting system. Several accounts are maintained to track expenditures on each fund; these accounts include the allocation account, the encumbrance account, the payment account, and the free balance account. The accounts cumulate increases and decreases during the fiscal year. Bookkeeping involves careful analysis and recording of each transaction involving these accounts and requires access to financial information contained in purchase orders, invoices, statements, vouchers, credit memos, and all other fiscal documents related to a particular transaction.

Library accounting systems are based on the relationship between the money allocated in a particular fund and the expenditure of that money. This relationship is reflected in the classic bookkeeping equation:

$$\text{assets} = \text{liabilities} + \text{fund balance}$$

As the equal sign implies, the dollar amount of the assets must equal the sum of the dollar amounts of liabilities plus the fund balance for the fund to balance. Any change (addition or subtraction) in assets must be counterbalanced by an equivalent change in liabilities or the fund balance, or both.

Betsy Kruger

In a library, the money allocated to a particular fund is an asset because it provides the future means of purchasing materials or reducing the amount owed to a vendor. Liabilities are claims to a library's assets such as money earmarked, or encumbered, for a particular purchase or cash paid out to reconcile a debt. A fund balance is the difference between assets and liabilities. It represents free or unencumbered money still available to make future purchases of library materials.

For library materials funds, the bookkeeping equation is interpreted as follows:

$$\text{assets} = \text{liabilities} + \text{fund balance}$$
$$\text{fund allocation} = \text{encumbrances} + \text{payments} + \text{unencumbered balance}$$

Encumbrances are funds restricted for anticipated expenditures such as outstanding purchase orders. Even though a purchase order will not be paid until the library receives an invoice and the receipt of materials has been verified (except when prepayment is required), encumbrances are considered liabilities because the money has been committed and must be held in reserve until payment is made.

A fund's allocation account will probably remain fairly stable throughout the year. Most of the activity involving a fund will occur on the right (liability) side of the equation, resulting in increases and decreases in the encumbrance, payment, and unencumbered balance accounts where cost information from purchase orders, invoices, and other documents is entered.

Many libraries carry over encumbrances from one fiscal year to the next, but for simplicity's sake and for the purpose of illustration, let's assume that Library X paid for all of its encumbered purchases on a particular fund by the last day of its fiscal year. At the beginning of the new fiscal year, before any payments have been made or funds encumbered, the fund allocation will equal the unencumbered balance:

$$\text{fund allocation} = \text{encumbrances} + \text{payments} + \text{unencumbered balance}$$
$$\$12,000.00 = \$0.00 + \$0.00 + \$12,000.00$$

Throughout the year, as encumbrances and payments are posted, the unencumbered balance will decrease proportionately, so that the amount in the allocation account always equals the sum of the three accounts on the right side of the equation:

$$\text{fund allocation} = \text{encumbrances} + \text{payments} + \text{unencumbered balance}$$
$$\$12,000.00 = \$3,000.00 + \$4,000.00 + \$5,000.00$$

Accounting and Business Practices

If all the year's orders have been received and paid for by the last day of the fiscal year (again, an unlikely scenario in many libraries), the fund accounts would look like this:

fund allocation = encumbrances + payments + unencumbered balance
$12,000.00   = $0.00   + $12,000.00 + $0.00

A T account (shown in Figure 1) is a useful accounting form for visualizing the effects of various bookkeeping transactions which, whether performed manually or by a computer, affect a fund's accounts in the same manner. This form is shaped like the letter "T," with the name of the account noted above the horizontal line and increases or decreases to the account posted on the appropriate side of the vertical line. T accounts correspond to the columns for recording increases and decreases on a ledger sheet in a manual bookkeeping system. In a computerized system, a T account may correspond to a group of similarly coded items on a disk. The accounts in the library bookkeeping equation can be illustrated by T accounts (Figure 1).

The abbreviations dr and cr stand for debit and credit. Debiting and crediting are methods of recording transactions in an account in a way that maintains the balance of the bookkeeping equation. These terms can be confusing because of their associations in popular speech. *Debit* connotes negative and subtraction; *credit* connotes positive and addition. These meanings of the terms must be disregarded in accounting practice; instead, substitute in one's mind the terms *left* and *right*. Debit is a traditional accounting term meaning simply to record on the left side; credit traditionally means to record on the right side.

Debits and credits affect assets and liabilities differently. Debits increase assets and decrease liabilities. Credits decrease

	Allocation		−	Encumbrances		+	Payments		+	Unencumbered Balance	
	(dr)	(cr)		(dr)	(cr)		(dr)	(cr)		(dr)	(cr)
Balance											

FIGURE 1 Library Bookkeeping Equation Illustrated by T Accounts

Betsy Kruger

TABLE 1 Effects of Debits and Credits on Library Materials Accounts

	Fund Allocation	Encumbrances	Payments	Unencumbered Balance
Debits (entry on left)	Increase	Decrease	Decrease	Decrease
Credits (entry on right)	Decrease	Increase	Increase	Increase

assets and increase liabilities. They affect the accounts in a library materials fund as shown in Table 1.

T accounts are referred to throughout this chapter to illustrate how typical transactions involved in purchasing library materials affect the asset and liability accounts described and how transactions are recorded either manually or by a computer so that the accounts balance. These transactions include allocating money to a fund, encumbering funds to cover the expected cost of a purchase, posting payment for an invoice, and adjusting for differences between the amount encumbered and the amount actually paid.

FUND ALLOCATIONS: HOW MUCH IS THERE TO SPEND?

Establishing various funds for materials purchases enables a library to distribute available money equitably among different library units or subject areas. Among the many factors that may form the basis for allocation decisions are the average cost of monographs and serials in a subject area (for example, science versus humanities journals); the makeup and size of the population served (for example, the number of children versus adults in the community, or the number of undergraduate, graduate, and faculty members in a particular academic discipline); historic patterns of spending; the growth of new research areas; and fluctuations in publishing patterns. Dividing the materials budget into various funds aids in monitoring expenditures and coordinating collection development. An acquisitions librarian's role in budget allocation varies from library to library, but this person most certainly will be called upon to provide actual cost figures and projections of future costs garnered from a knowledge of the publishing industry and familiarity with the library's arrangements with its various vendors.

Accounting and Business Practices

At the beginning of the fiscal year, the amount allocated to each fund must be entered into the accounting system. Using T accounts, one can visualize the effect of this transaction. At the beginning of its fiscal year, Library X allocates $1,000 for its art monographs fund (Figure 2). No encumbrances have been carried over from the previous year.

	Allocation	−	Encumbrances	+	Payments	+	Unencumbered Balance	
	(dr) (cr)		(dr) (cr)		(dr) (cr)		(dr)	(cr)
Allocation	1,000							1,000
Balance	1,000							1,000

FIGURE 2 Allocating Money into a Fund

As noted earlier, debits increase assets and credits increase liabilities. Since the fund allocation (an asset account) has not been spent, the $1,000 is recorded as a debit and the balance of the account increases to $1,000. Any change in an account on the left side of the bookkeeping equation must be counter-balanced by an equivalent change to an account on the right side. The $1,000 debit to the allocation account is money available to be spent. Therefore, $1,000 is credited to the unencumbered balance account resulting in a balance of $1,000. In this double-entry transaction, a debit on the left is balanced by a credit on the right.

After the original allocation posting at the beginning of the fiscal year, most activity in a fund occurs on the left (debit) side of the ledger as funds are encumbered, invoices are paid, and adjustments are made. However, if the allocation is increased or decreased at any time during the fiscal year, this change will have to be counterbalanced by a credit or debit to the unencumbered balance. If the allocation is increased, the unencumbered balance also increases. If the allocation is decreased, the unencumbered balance also decreases.

ENCUMBERING FUNDS AND ISSUING PURCHASE ORDERS: HOW MUCH WILL IT PROBABLY COST?

The purchase of library materials poses some unique accounting problems that are not encountered with certain other expenses a library faces. Unlike predictable, regular expenses such as utility bills and payroll, the purchase of books and other library materials involves some uncertainty. The exact cost may be unknown at the time a purchase order is issued since discount, additional charges, and shipping fees are usually not known until the invoice arrives. The library also does not know when the vendor will actually deliver the item. The book may be out of stock or not yet published at the time it is ordered. If the book is out of print, the vendor may cancel the order altogether.

To keep track of how much money is tied up in outstanding orders, it is necessary to encumber funds to cover their estimated costs. The library would not know how much free (that is, available) money it had at any given moment if costs were only entered into the accounting system at the time payment was issued.

A purchase order usually is the first document in an audit trail. It serves as a legal contract between a library and a vendor for the purchase of materials that will be paid for at a later date. With its issuance, the library financially obligates itself for the timely payment of delivered goods. By accepting a library's purchase order, the vendor is obligated to the timely delivery of the ordered items in good condition.

In addition to providing needed information to the vendor, the purchase order is also used internally as an encumbering document. It provides the basic information needed for initially entering the purchase into the library's accounting system. A well-designed purchase order includes the following types of information:

1. reference information
    a. a purchase order number that ties an accounting entry to a specific purchased item
    b. the fund number or fund name, or both, to identify the specific library fund against which the cost of the item is to be charged
    c. the vendor name or vendor number, or both (either a standard address number or a number assigned by a library)
    d. date the material is ordered and received
2. financial information
    a. estimated and actual cost information (The estimated cost is the figure used for encumbering purposes. The actual cost can only be recorded once the library has received the material, verified that the material received was the material ordered, and approved the vendor's

Accounting and Business Practices

invoice, or if prepayment is made.)
    b. invoice number
3. descriptive information
    a. author or title of the item, or both.
    b. publisher's name and address
    c. date of publication
    d. quantity ordered
4. information for the vendor
    a. library's name and address
    b. specific billing and shipping requirements of the library
       (Many libraries request that the vendor invoice in tripli-
       cate and invoice each shipment separately.)
5. miscellaneous information for the library
    a. name of the person authorizing the expenditure
    b. specific location or cataloging instructions, or both

T accounts illustrate how an encumbrance transaction affects the accounts in a fund when a purchase order is issued against it. Suppose Library X issues a $50 purchase order against its art monograph fund (Figure 3).

The $50 is recorded as an encumbrance, rather than as a payment, because the book has been ordered but not yet paid for. Further, it is recorded as a credit to the encumbrance account. Because an encumbrance decreases the amount of money available to be spent, the unencumbered balance must be decreased by $50. A quick arithmetical check confirms that the accounts balance:

Allocation balance	=	encumbrances balance	+	payments balance	+	unencumbered balance
$1,000.00	=	$50.00	+	$0.00	+	$950.00

Monograph purchases are encumbered on a one-time basis. Funds are disencumbered once payment has been made. How-

	Allocation		=	Encumbrances		+	Payments		+	Unencumbered Balance	
	(dr)	(cr)		(dr)	(cr)		(dr)	(cr)		(dr)	(cr)
Allocation	1,000										1,000
P.O. 299					50.00					50.00	
Balance	1,000				50.00						950

FIGURE 3 Encumbering a $50 Purchase Order

ever, funds for periodicals must be reencumbered each year the subscription is renewed, and funds for continuations must be reencumbered early unless the order is canceled. Computerized accounting systems can automatically reencumber funds for the next year's serial payments. Once the books are closed at the end of a fiscal year, a special code (sometimes called a paytype) which was input at the time the purchase order was first entered into the system instructs the computer to reencumber the prior year's expenditures for the new fiscal year.

INVOICES, CREDIT MEMOS, STATEMENTS, AND VOUCHERS: HOW MUCH DID IT ACTUALLY COST?

Vendor and Publisher Invoices

An invoice is a document issued by a vendor or publisher that contains all the financial details of a purchase or transaction. Once an acquisitions department verifies that the material received was the material actually ordered, it can approve and pay the invoice or forward it, after approval, to the appropriate accounting department within the library or parent organization for payment.

It is well worth taking the time to become familiar with the invoice format of the library's larger vendors and publishers. Invoices can provide a wealth of information about both the vendor's business practices and the characteristics of the library account. Any arrangements made for discounts and handling and shipping fees should appear on the invoices. Inform the invoice processing staff of these arrangements so that invoices can be monitored to assure that the vendor is applying the correct discounts and fees.

Vendor invoices may provide the following types of information:

1. reference information
   a. library purchase order number and fund (It is useful to specify on the purchase order that this information should be included on the invoice. Large vendors and publishers with computerized billing systems can easily code the account so that purchase order numbers and funds are printed on the invoice.)
   b. invoice number and date
   c. customer name and number
   d. bill-to and ship-to information

Accounting and Business Practices

2. vendor information
   a. vendor name and address
   b. vendor's federal employee identification number (FEIN) (This number is assigned by the federal government and is usually required before a library can issue a check to a vendor.)
3. descriptive information
   a. author or title of the item, or both.
   b. quantity ordered
   c. information as to whether the item is coming on a standing order, approval plan, blanket order, or some other arrangement
   d. status codes indicating if an item is not yet published, out of stock, out of print, and so on
4. financial information
   a. list price (the publisher's stated price) and net price (the price charged to the library once discounts have been applied)
   b. the amount or percentage of discount
   c. postage, shipping, and handling charges
   d. total amount owed
   e. terms of payment (Invoices usually state the time limit on the vendor's receipt of payment before late charges begin accruing, for example, 30 days net. Many invoices also stipulate the conditions under which the vendor will accept a return.)
   f. currency and remit-to requirements.
5. shipping information
   a. how shipped, (for example, UPS, parcel post)
   b. date shipped

An invoice is often the expending document from which actual cost information is taken and charged against the appropriate library fund. It is also usually the second document in the audit trail for a particular purchase. For these reasons, careful verification of the accuracy of the financial and other information on the invoice is essential.

Although procedures and requirements vary from library to library, invoice approval usually includes the following steps:

1. date stamping the invoice upon receipt of the shipment
2. checking the items listed on the invoice against the material received and the original order record to verify that the items received were actually the items ordered

3. resolving any discrepancies
4. noting the purchase order number and fund by each item listed and checking the net price
5. noting the vendor number (if used) on the invoice
6. approving by initialing and dating

Invoices approved in this manner are properly prepared for entering the payment transaction in either a manual or automated accounting system. The payment record can be tied to the purchase order number that was entered into the system at the time the order was placed and funds were encumbered. When payment is posted, the originally encumbered funds are disencumbered and any adjustments to the free balance are made that result from additional charges or discounts not known at the time of encumbering.

Using T accounts, one can visualize how payment transactions affect a fund's accounts. Suppose Library X receives an invoice for the $50 purchase it has encumbered against its art monographs fund. The invoiced amount equals the amount originally encumbered, and the transaction is recorded as shown in Figure 4.

The $50 payment is posted as a credit or increase to the payment account and brings the balance of that account to $50. To balance the accounts, $50 must be debited to one of the other liability accounts. The payment does not effect the unencumbered balance since this balance was already reduced by the $50 encumbrance posted in the second line. Therefore, the $50 credit to the payment account is counterbalanced by a $50 debit to the encumbrance account. This posting, in effect, disencumbers the $50 originally reserved when the purchase order was issued, since this amount has now actually been paid to the vendor. A quick arithmetical check again confirms that the accounts balance:

$$\frac{\text{allocation}}{\text{balance}} = \frac{\text{encumbrances}}{\text{balance}} + \frac{\text{payments}}{\text{balance}} + \frac{\text{unencumbered}}{\text{balance}}$$

$$\$1,000.00 = \$0.00 + \$50.00 + \$950.00$$

	Allocation		− Encumbrances		+ Payments		+ Unencumbered Balance	
	(dr)	(cr)	(dr)	(cr)	(dr)	(cr)	(dr)	(cr)
Allocation	$1,000							$1,000
P.O. 299				$50.00			$50.00	
Invoice 114			$50.00			$50.00		
Balance	$1,000			$ 0.00		$50.00		$ 950

FIGURE 4 Posting a $50 Payment Equal to the Original Encumbrance

Accounting and Business Practices

More often than not, the amount encumbered for a purchase is not the exact amount the library actually pays the vendor. Most libraries encumber the amount of the list price since the discount passed on by the vendor (if any) is not always known at the time the purchase order is issued. At other times, an item may cost more than the original encumbrance. Posting payment in either of these situations effects the balances in all three liability accounts.

Let's assume that the book for which Library X encumbered $50 against its arts monographs fund was discounted 10 percent by the vendor, making the net price $45. The transaction is recorded as shown in Figure 5.

The $45 payment is credited to the payments account. Since the amount was $5 less than that originally encumbered, the $5 difference is credited to the unencumbered balance. The original $50 encumbrance is disencumbered since payment has now been made.

	Allocation		– Encumbrances		+ Payments		+ Unencumbered Balance	
	(dr)	(cr)	(dr)	(cr)	(dr)	(cr)	(dr)	(cr)
Allocation	$1,000							$1,000
P.O. 299				$50.00			$50.00	
Invoice 114			$50.00			$45.00		5
Balance	$1,000			$ 0.00		$45.00		$ 955

FIGURE 5 Posting Payment for Less Than the Amount Originally Encumbered

Shipping and Handling Charges

A library may have agreements with some of its vendors (and less frequently with publishers) whereby the vendor pays the cost of shipping. This is frequently the case with approval plans. Usually, however, the library pays for shipping and may also have to pay additional handling or service charges. Vendors make their money, in general, by keeping a portion of the discount they receive from the publisher for themselves. If the publisher does not give any discount to the vendor, which is frequently the case with nontrade presses, the vendor is apt to charge the library a handling fee. Periodical vendors almost always make their profit by assessing a service charge for each subscription they place for the library. The cost and time benefits of consolidating subscriptions and other orders with a vendor rather than ordering them all directly from the publisher are well worth the handling charges incurred when the number of subscriptions is large and the staff is small.

A library can handle payment of shipping and handling charges in one of two ways. By far the simplest is to pay them from one fund established specifically for this purpose. The other possibility is to charge back these costs to individual funds. On list invoices, these charges can be divided by the number of items on the invoice and charged in equal amounts to the funds involved. Some vendors are able to itemize these charges for each item on an invoice or to incorporate the charges in the net price for each item.

Credit Memos and Cancellations

Vendors and publishers may issue credit due a customer in the form of a refund or a credit memo. The form this credit takes frequently depends on the amount of business the library does with the particular vendor. Because a credit memo can only be used to offset all or a portion of an outstanding invoice from the same vendor, a vendor will usually issue credit memos to its regular customers. If a library is requesting credit from a vendor or publisher it uses infrequently, it may want to request a refund rather than a credit memo to avoid having unused credit memos in its files for extended periods of time. However, publisher and vendor credit policies vary; some vendors will only issue credit memos. In this case, the library may have to place another order with the vendor so that the credit memo can be reconciled. Before using a credit memo the library should verify that it did indeed pay the original invoice on which the vendor is issuing credit. Unless a library's internal policies dictate otherwise, credit memos and refunds should always be applied to the fund from which the original payment was made.

T accounts again illustrate how a fund's accounts are affected when a refund is posted. As an example, the $50 book that Library X purchased on its art monographs fund is found to be defective. Unfortunately, the library has already paid the invoice. To further complicate matters, the book has gone out of print, so a replacement cannot be sent. The vendor issues a refund.

The refund is posted as a debit to the art monographs payment account and a credit to its unencumbered balance. The encumbrance account is not affected since the original $50 encumbrance was disencumbered when the invoice was paid (Figure 6).

Accounting and Business Practices

	Allocation		–	Encumbrances		+	Payments		+	Unencumbered Balance	
	(dr)	(cr)		(dr)	(cr)		(dr)	(cr)		(dr)	(cr)
Allocation	$1,000										$1,000
P.O. 299					$50.00					$50.00	
Invoice 114				$50.00				$50.00			
Refund											
P.O. 299							$50.00				50
Balance	$1,000				$ 0.00		$0.00			$1,000	

FIGURE 6 Posting a Refund

Cancellations also affect a library's accounting system. A vendor may cancel an order because the item is out of stock indefinitely or out of print. Sometimes a library finds it necessary to cancel an order. In such cases, the original encumbrance should be disencumbered (increasing the balance in the encumbrance account) and the same amount should be credited to the unencumbered balance. Cancellations pose certain financial considerations. If the vendor or publisher ships the material before it receives the library's cancellation, the library is obligated to pay for the material unless the vendor agrees to accept a return. For this reason, it is wise to establish an internal procedure by which funds for cancelled orders are not disencumbered until a safety period has expired. This safety period assures that enough money is available to pay for the unexpected piece.

Vendor's Statements

Most vendors and publishers regularly issue statements that detail any outstanding invoices and credit memos on a library's account. In many cases the library has already processed the payment, but the vendor had not received it by the time the statement was generated. This frequently happens when checks are issued by a central business office of a parent institution or by the state, rather than by the library itself.

Statements from large vendors with computerized accounting systems frequently reference all the information necessary for the library to track down whether or not it has already processed payment. Such statements include invoice or credit memo number and date, library purchase order number, author or title (or both) of the ordered materials, and the amount. Many statements, however, are not nearly as descriptive; some may reference only the amount due and thus require quite a bit of hunting by the library staff to verify that the payment requested was already made.

A vendor may charge interest or late charges for any amounts not received by or received after the time period stated under terms of payment on its invoices. Libraries are obligated to pay late charges if they process an invoice after its due date. If a library initiates payment before the due date but the vendor receives it after that date, the vendor can still request payment of late charges. It is not unheard of for a library to receive a bill for late charges on payment past due by a few days. Most vendors and publishers expect payment within thirty days of receipt of material. It is useful in such situations to have the date of receipt stamped on each invoice.

Outstanding invoices listed on statements do not always reflect errors, failure to pay, or late payment on the part of the library. Vendors make errors, too. Outstanding charges on an invoice may actually be for items the library is withholding payment on because the items were missing from a shipment. Sometimes the charges are for items billed to the wrong library's account. If the library is current with its invoice processing and has a flexible accounting system, it will be able to determine with relative ease if the statement poses true discrepancies with the library's owns records or if there has just not been time for payment to reach the vendor.

Vouchers

When checks to cover payment for library purchases must be issued by the central business office of a parent organization, the library must prepare a voucher to forward with the approved invoice for payment. A voucher is an internal accounting document that authorizes the central business office to disburse cash from the library's account to pay the invoice. Like all other documents in an audit trail, vouchers must be carefully prepared. The voucher should provide the following information:

1. name and address to which the check is to be issued
2. invoice number, date, and exact amount in U.S. dollars or appropriate foreign currency
3. description of the purchased items
4. authorized signature

Accounting and Business Practices

TRACKING EXPENDITURES WITH MANAGEMENT REPORTS: HOW MUCH MONEY IS LEFT?

A flexible accounting system should be able to provide a current picture of a fund's free balance. The detail and frequency of management reports produced by the accounting system depend on its sophistication. Computerized systems with indexing capabilities can produce a variety of reports on a frequent basis. Such reports are more time-consuming to produce with a manual system. All systems should be able to produce some sort of summary report on at least a monthly basis. Overspending and underspending can be avoided only if the fund manager can closely monitor encumbrances, payments, and the free balance.

Figures 7, 8, and 9 are sample management reports produced by the computerized accounting system of a large academic library. Figure 7 is a printout of the outstanding orders, or encumbrances, on a monograph fund as of a specific date. The report provides the following information:

1. purchase order numbers—assigned by the library
2. vendor numbers—specific numbers assigned to vendors
3. current obligation—the amount encumbered on the referenced purchase order number
4. reobligation amount—does not apply to most monograph purchases (If the purchase order was for a serial purchase, this column would be used to indicate the next year's encumbrances.)
5. paytype—a code that determines if the encumbrance is dropped once payment is made or if the encumbrance is to be reencumbered for the following year's payment (This particular system uses the code "F" for one-time monograph encumbrances.)
6. order date—date the library issued the purchase order
7. date of last payment—not often used for monograph purchases since payment on a purchase order is usually only made once (For serials, this column would reflect the last date a payment was made.)
8. date of last update—the last date a correction or change was made to the record
9. author-title

The printout in Figure 8 shows payments made on a fund during a particular month. The printout provides all the information necessary to construct a complete audit trail for each item purchased: (1) purchase order number, (2) vendor number, (3) exact

Betsy Kruger

05-31-90   Outstanding Orders - Replacement Fund

Purchase Order	Vendor Number	Current Obligation	Reobligation Amount	Pay Type	Order Date	Date of Last Payment	Date of Last Update	Author-Title
A913306	60525005	32.50	0.00	F	05/07/90			Baudelaire, Charles. Mirror of Art. AMS Press. 1955.
A044502	60525005	6.95	0.00	F	03/18/90			Baumbeck, Jonathan. Moderns and Contemporaries.
A945250	60525005	21.00	0.00	F	03/04/90			Bierce, Ambrose. Stories of Soldiers and Civilians.
A872370	08720002	5.50	0.00	F	02/19/90			Blake, William. Poems. Routledge & Kegan
A945860	60525005	11.95	0.00	F	04/38/90			Bognad, Morris. The Manager's Style Book.
A044548	60525005	22.95	0.00	F	04/07/90			Bukowski, Charles. Women. Black Sparrow Press.
A945104	50962179	23.00	0.00	F	04/07/90			Carney, Thomas F. Content Analysis. Univ Manitoba Pr
A944694	60525005	16.95	0.00	F	04/29/90			Cather, Willa. My Antonia. Houghton Mifflin.
A946168	08725004	2.95	0.00	F	02/19/90			Chopin, Kate. The Awakening. Avon.
A941401	60525005	24.95	0.00	F	02/19/90			Coleman, Arthur. Drama Criticism, Vol. 2.
A943349	60525005	8.95	0.00	F	03/04/90			Cuddon, J.R. A Dictionary of Literary Terms. Penguin.
A911527	60525005	12.95	0.00	F	05/07/90			Didion, Joan. Salvador. Simon and Schuster.
A872377	50962179	23.00	0.00	F	04/29/90			Dunn, Delmer. Public Officials and the Press.
A945257	30336982	12.95	0.00	F	03/24/90			Esslin, Martin. Samuel Beckett: Critical Essays.
A936396	99950000	22.00	0.00	F	02/26/90			Fonda, Jane. Jane Fonda's Workout Book.
A946113	10282004	12.00	0.00	F	10/31/90		02/19/90	Furtado, Celso. Diagnosis of the Brazilian Crisis.
A945272	21995800	12.00	0.00	F	01/23/90			Gallery, Rob. Men in Erotic Art: A Catalog.
A941764	10282004	22.00	0.00	F	02/17/90			Hagler, Louise. The Farm Vegetarian Cookbook.
A908864	50962179	18.95	0.00	F	03/19/90			Heath, Stephen. Cinematic Apparatus. St. Martins.
A924094	60525005	34.95	0.00	F	09/11/90			Hinchcliffe, Mary K. The Melancholy Marriage. Wiley.
A907374	10282004	37.95	0.00	F	05/24/90			Hurty, Walter C. Dynamics of Structure. Prentice-Hall
A946124	10282004	8.95	0.00	F	04/29/90			Jaffe, Nora. The Evil Image. NAL.
A945278	42130000	8.95	0.00	F	04/25/90		04/07/90	Kaplan, E. Ann. Women in Film. U of I Press.
A944523	10282004	17.95	0.00	F	02/20/90			Keilor, Garrison. Lake Woebegon Days. Viking.
A944618	60525005	18.95	0.00	F	04/29/90			Lawrence, D. H. Lady Chatterley's Lover. Buccaneer.
A938427	08725004	14.95	0.00	F	01/23/90			Lee, Stan. Son of Origins of Marvel Comics. Fireside.
A928417	60525005	8.95	0.00	F	01/24/90			Lowe, David. Lost Chicago. Houghton Mifflin.
A938449	08725004	12.50	0.00	F	01/23/90			Martin, David. Wilderness of Mirrors. Harper & Row.
A041309	60525005	34.50	0.00	F	02/25/90			McGregor, Ronald. Exercises in Spoken Hindi. Cambridge.
A911571	60525005	6.95	0.00	F	02/26/90			Mendez, Pepe. Complete Course in Stained Glass.
A941756	10282004	24.95	0.00	F	02/21/90			Myers, Gustavus. History of the Great American Fortunes
A946107	60525005	7.95	0.00	F	04/29/90			Newhall, Beaumont. The Daguerreotype in America.
A936427	10282004	20.00	0.00	F	01/13/90			Okakura, Kakuzo. The Book of Tea. Richard West.
A936430	10282004	22.80	0.00	F	01/10/90			Porter, Gene. Her Father's Daughter.
A936460	60525005	16.95	0.00	F	02/25/90			Ray, Benjamin. African Religions. Prentice Hall.
TOTAL		611.70						

FIGURE 7 Outstanding Orders Report from an Automated Accounting System

Accounting and Business Practices

05-31-90

Payments – Replacement Fund

Purchase Order	Vendor Number	Payment Amount	Pay Type	Invoice Number	Voucher Number	University Account	Date of Order	Date of Payment	Author-Title
A941384	60525005	4.60	F	1729782	823331	12210246600	02/21/90	05/06/90	Alta, Momma. Times Change Press.
A941481	10282004	4.95	F	11.045282	823037	12210246600	03/18/90	05/06/90	Berry, Wendell. The Memory of Old Jack.
A937308	60525005	13.95	F	1729782	823331	12210246600	02/12/90	05/06/90	Borge, Tomas. Sandinistas Speak. Pathfinders Press
A944577	10282004	45.00	F	IL 045282	823037	12210246600	01/16/90	05/06/90	Borrow, George. Celtic Bards, Chiefs and Kings.
A941392	60525005	21.36	F	1729782	823331	12210246600	02/19/90	05/06/90	Bronte, Emily. Complete Poems of Jane Bronte.
A867579	18625008	2.50	F	117872	823755	12210246600	01/22/90	05/12/90	Canadian Architect, v.28 #1 Jan 1983
A937667	00475181	46.35	F	197610	822767	12210246600	03/17/90	05/04/90	Casey, H.C. Heterostructure Lasers. Academic Press
A941339	60525005	43.18	F	1729782	823331	12210246600	02/19/90	06/06/90	Cochran, William. Experimental Designs. Wiley.
A941267	60525005	30.15	F	1761993	823583	12210246600	01/08/90	05/11/90	Davis, M. Contributions of Black Women to America.
A939339	26668638	21.00	F	129168D	823777	12210246600	01/30/90	05/12/90	Depres, Josquin. Missa Pange Lingua.
A937677	60525005	46.45	F	1729782	823331	12210246600	02/19/90	05/06/90	Doremus, Robert. Glass Science. Wiley.
A945218	60525005	41.83	F	1761993	823583	12210246600	01/24/90	05/11/90	Dreiser, Theodore. Sister Carrie.
A940037	60525005	14.20	F	1729782	823331	12210246600	02/11/90	05/06/90	Eastman, Arthur. The Norton Reader. Norton.
A952989	60525005	14.69	F	1761993	823583	12210246600	01/08/90	05/11/90	Ekeh, Peter. Social Exchange Theory. Harvard Univ.
A927100	60525005	3.67	F	176993	823583	12210246600	10/11/90	05/11/90	Elgin, Suzette. Native Tongue. AW Books.
A860527	08720002	7.08	F	74014420	822786	12210246600	01/23/90	05/04/90	Encounter, v.62 #5 May 1984
A941352	60525005	11.17	F	1729782	823331	12210246600	01/23/90	05/06/90	Fadiman, Clifton. Lifetime Reading. Crowell.
A941317	60525005	11.35	F	1729782	823331	12210246600	02/25/90	05/06/90	Finegan, Edward. Attitudes Toward English Usage.
A943032	10282004	17.55	F	IL 045273	823036	12210246600	01/24/90	05/06/90	Harvey, Richard. Genealogy for Librarians.
A937679	60525005	106.95	F	1729782	823331	12210246600	02/19/90	05/06/90	Iler, Ralph. Chemistry of Silica. Wiley. 1979.
A860578	87889011	30.00	F	20499	823930	12210246600	03/21/90	05/12/90	Index to Book Reviews in the Humanities. v.24
A942722	10282004	5.35	F	IL 042178	823460	12210246600	03/04/90	05/04/90	Johnson, Curt. Civil War Battles. Outlet Book Co.
A932941	60525005	11.17	F	1761993	823583	12210246600	01/08/90	05/11/90	Katahn, Martin. The Rotation Diet. Norton.
A921053	72510038	71.50	F	547011	823906	12210246600	03/19/90	05/12/90	Klein, George. Advances in Viral Oncology, #1
A937643	60525005	43.70	F	1729782	823331	12210246600	02/19/90	05/06/90	Kuck, D. Structures of Computers and Computations.
A944552	08720002	4.45	F	49300032	823416	12210246600	03/04/90	05/11/90	Lear, Edward. Nonsense Songs.
A911612	10282004	31.50	F	IL 060947	823734	12210246600	01/09/90	05/11/90	Levi, Peter. Atlas of the Greek World.
A905454	10282004	18.95	F	IL 042178	823460	12210246600	01/25/90	05/11/90	Lister, Margot. Costume: An Illustrated Survey.
A941324	10282004	16.50	F	IL 042175	822853	12210246600	03/04/90	05/04/90	Luelsdorff. Segmental Phonology of Black English.
A941304	60525005	23.14	F	1729782	823331	12210246600	02/25/90	05/06/90	Miller, Roy. Japanese and Other Archaic Languages
A912120	08720002	23.62	F	74012142	822784	12210246600	01/16/90	05/04/90	Nutrition and Health, v.2 #2 1983
A931782	99950000	38.50	F	04-19-86	822973	12210246600	01/09/90	05/04/90	Ormsbee, T. Story of American Furniture.
A919021	90039652	43.00	F	3794822	822954	12210246600	09/26/90	05/04/90	Recreation Management, v.22, 23 Feb 1979-Jan 1981
A921100	48475108	6.50	F	Ch-327.5116	823547	12210246600	02/20/90	05/11/90	Studia Biophysica, v.93 #2
A896770	08720002	32.78	F	74011529	823015	12210246600	01/23/90	05/06/90	Theory, Culture and Society, v.2 #1 1984

TOTAL 908.64

FIGURE 8 Monthly Payment Report from an Automated Accounting System

amount paid, (4) paytype, (5) invoice number, (6) university account number, (7) order date, (8) payment date, and (9) author or title, or both.

Figure 9 is a summary report of year-to-date activity on all monograph funds in a large academic library. This kind of report is extremely helpful to acquisitions and collection development librarians who need to carefully monitor the status of a variety of funds. The report details the following information: (1) fund number, (2) fund name, (3) original allocation amount, (4) year-to-date payments, (5) outstanding orders, (6) unencumbered balance, (7) percent of the original allocation that has been spent, and (8) percent of the allocation that is still available for making more purchases, that is, neither spent nor encumbered. The report illustrates a balanced bookkeeping equation: the sum of the year-to-date payments, outstanding orders, and unencumbered balance equals the fund allocation. The percent spent and percent available columns are useful for monitoring expenditures at different times throughout the fiscal year.

As mentioned earlier, library materials expenditures have less predictable patterns during the year than expenditures for personnel and utilities. For example, at the end of the first quarter of the fiscal year, payroll and utility allocations are usually one-fourth spent. This is not necessarily the case with library materials. Delays in publication, erratic purchasing and publishing patterns, and other factors can prevent a predictable expenditure of funds throughout the year. It may be necessary to attempt to increase or decrease expenditures on a particular fund to prevent overspending or underspending. The monograph funds summary report in Figure 9 provides some examples.

The report is dated the last day of the second quarter of the fiscal year—December 31st in this library. Unlike most materials funds, expenditures on approval plan funds and blanket order funds may be fairly predictable and even throughout the year since the library is receiving regular shipments of these materials. The publisher approval plan fund (1) is right on target at the end of the second quarter with one-half of its allocation spent and one-half still available. (There are usually few if any individual encumbrances on an approval plan fund since shipments are automatic.) However, the European blanket order fund (2) is already three-fourths spent by the end of the second quarter. This fund should be monitored carefully over the next month or two, and the library should advise the vendor to reduce shipments or to stop them completely by a certain date to prevent overspending.

Accounting and Business Practices

MONOGRAPH FUNDS SUMMARY REPORT

12-31-90

FUND	FUND TITLE	ALLOCATION	YEAR-TO-DATE PAYMENTS	OUTSTANDING ORDERS	UNENCUMBERED BALANCE	% SPENT	% AVAIL
0001	Anthropology	2,516.00	612.98	1,280.41	622.61	24	25
0002	Architecture	5,203.00	1,275.42	2,422.85	1,504.73	25	29
0003	Art	7,810.00	781.29	858.81	6,169.90	10	79
0004	Biological Sciences	9,852.00	2,070.44	5,326.14	2,455.42	21	25
0005	Chemistry	10,391.00	3,040.66	5,180.71	2,169.63	29	21
0006	Chinese	1,743.00	512.58	890.40	340.02	29	20
0007	Commerce	16,734.00	4,083.70	9,817.64	2,832.66	24	17
0008 ③	Education	4,500.00	360.25	459.10	3,680.65	8	82
0009	Engineering	28,038.00	5,690.98	17,019.12	5,327.90	20	19
0010	English	6,788.00	1,512.14	3,594.26	1,681.60	22	28
0011 ②	European Blanket Order	36,000.00	25,821.45	.00	10,178.55	72	28
0012	French	2,215.00	412.72	1,407.28	395.00	19	18
0013	Geography	3,373.00	1,680.48	912.49	780.03	50	23
0014	Geology	3,433.00	768.43	1,821.17	843.40	22	25
0015	German	2,261.00	545.25	1,004.95	710.80	24	31
0016	History	11,686.00	2,826.85	5,784.29	3,074.86	24	26
0017	Italian	100.00	22.95	26.95	50.10	23	50
0018	Linguistics	2,075.00	103.75	1,556.24	415.01	5	20
0019	Mathematics	5,354.00	934.88	2,831.44	1,587.68	17	30
0020	Music	13,970.00	3,092.55	7,412.67	3,464.78	22	25
0021	Philosophy	1,977.00	394.95	964.88	617.17	20	31
0022	Physics	14,666.00	8,359.62	3,666.50	2,639.88	57	18
0023 ④	Political Science	3,241.00	863.44	2,012.43	365.13	27	11
0024 ①	Publisher Approval Plan	65,000.00	32,512.14	129.85	32,358.01	50	50
0025	Psychology	3,500.00	799.12	1,994.89	705.99	23	20
0026	Reference	7,460.00	1,612.45	4,416.85	1,430.70	22	19
0027	Religion	2,090.00	322.50	803.98	963.52	15	46
0028	Replacements	15,533.00	3,084.26	6,354.12	6,094.62	20	39
0029	Reserves	230.00	28.55	125.18	76.27	12	33
0030	Slavic	7,945.00	1,499.28	3,572.55	2,873.17	19	36
0031	Sociology	2,800.00	605.12	1,721.28	473.60	22	20
0032	Spanish	2,523.00	650.89	1,009.56	862.55	26	34
0033	Speech	495.00	128.55	205.49	160.96	26	33
0034	Theatre	566.00	180.18	299.45	86.37	32	15
0035	Women's Studies	3,648.00	568.84	1,429.95	1,649.21	15	45
	TOTALS	305,716.00	107,759.64	98,313.88	99,642.48	35	36

FIGURE 9 Monograph Funds Summary Report from Automated Accounting System

Underspent funds can also be detected. For example, the education fund (3) has spent only 8 percent of its allocation by the end of the second quarter. Only 10 percent of its funds are encumbered. With 82 percent of the allocation still unspent and unencumbered, purchases must be greatly increased to prevent underspending and a cut in allocation the following year.

Although the political science fund (4) is only 27 percent spent, 62 percent of its allocation is already tied up in encumbrances. Only 11 percent of the allocation represents a free balance. New purchases must be greatly slowed for the remainder of the year to prevent possible overspending.

A NOTE ON APPROVAL PLAN ACCOUNTING

Approval plans can provide a means for simplifying accounting procedures for a significant portion of a library's materials budget. They can eliminate the need to encumber hundreds and even thousands of firm orders each year, to disencumber funds once payment is made, and to process countless invoices. Instead, a single-sheet invoice can be processed for each shipment and the amount simply deducted from the approval plan allocation. This makes the approval plan fund one of the easiest to monitor. Some libraries charge back approval plan purchases to individual subject funds. This is usually done for political reasons—to make sure every fund gets its share of the approval plan pie. Unless this method is required by a central business office, it unnecessarily complicates what could be an efficient and streamlined approach to processing single payments for large shipments of materials. The approval plan vendor can always provide as a routine service detailed printouts by subject of approval plan expenditures.

ENDING THE FISCAL YEAR

The fiscal year is a period of twelve consecutive months selected by an organization as its accounting year. The fiscal year may or may not correspond to the calendar year. The fiscal year in many libraries runs from July 1st to June 30th, and generally it reflects the natural business year of the state legislature or other funding entity. The purpose of a fiscal year is to provide a means for measuring financial changes and tracking expenditure patterns from period to period. Data from several years can reveal trends not readily discernible from one year's data.

At the end of the fiscal year all fund accounts must be closed or zero balanced. Unspent money is added to the fund balance and excess expenditures are deducted from the fund balance. Depending upon the accounting method being used, libraries can either carry encumbrances over from year to year or they must clear all encumbrances at the end of the fiscal year. In the latter situation, all orders placed but not received from the end of the year may have to be cancelled and any money left in the fund forfeited.

It is important for libraries to understand the accounting method used by its parent organization or funding body and the specific year-end requirements under which it places the library. A good internal accounting system permits a library to closely monitor its funds so that at year end the library finds it is on target with its expenditures.

CONCLUSION

Monitoring and properly expending a materials budget is central to acquisitions work. From the issuance of purchase orders to the timely payment of bills, careful acquisitions accounting practices result in ready and accurate answers to the basic questions they should address: What is the allocation? How much has been encumbered? What was actually spent? What is the free balance? A library should design an accounting system that can monitor the peculiarities of its own budget and meet the fiscal requirements and policies of its parent institution or funding body. A good accounting system is simple enough to be flexible yet sophisticated enough to monitor properly current expenditures and provide data to reliably predict future spending.

B I B L I O G R A P H Y

Alley, Brian, and Jennifer Cargill. *Keeping Track of What You Spend: The Librarian's Guide to Simple Bookkeeping.* Phoenix, Ariz.: Oryx Press, 1982.

Betsy Kruger

Davidson, Sidney, and others. *Financial Accounting: An Introduction to Concepts, Methods and Uses.* 3rd ed. Chicago: Dryden Press, 1982.

Hoffman, Herbert H. *Simple Library Bookkeeping.* Newport Beach: Headway Publications, 1977.

Magrill, Rose Mary, and Doralyn Hickey. *Acquisitions Management and Collection Development in Libraries.* Chicago: American Library Association, 1984.

Smith, G. Stevenson. *Accounting for Librarians and Other Not-for-Profit Managers.* Chicago: American Library Association, 1983.

Trumpeter, Margo C., and Richard S. Rounds. *Basic Budgeting Practices for Librarians.* Chicago: American Library Association, 1985.

Accounting and Business Practices

William Z. Schenck

*"I say, let your affairs be as two or three, and not a hundred
or a thousand; instead of a million count half a dozen, and
keep your accounts on your thumbnail."*
Henry David Thoreau, *Walden*

This is the information age; it is also the age of record keeping
and accountability. In the past, most libraries kept accession
books. These books provided a handwritten record of each order,
including author, title, publisher, price, dealer, and date of receipt.
The accession book served as both the order file and as the
accounting record. It proved a simple yet effective way to keep
records. Today accession books, which are often kept in an institution's archives, seem anachronistic, although they provide valuable historical data on the development of a collection. As
acquiring library materials has become a much more sophisticated operation, so has the requirement for recording and storing information on the transactions.

Often it seems that the more we are supposed to be a paper-
less society, the more paper we actually generate and store. Perhaps future generations of librarians will work without paper,
but today paper records are still an integral part of any acquisitions operation. All libraries retain some records relating to the
ordering and receipt of materials and payment of invoices for
those materials. Specific requirements relating to the records to
be saved and the length of retention vary depending on the legal
requirements of each institution. Libraries that are part of a
governmental unit need to determine what the appropriate regulations are for their governing agency. Regulations may be based
on legal or procedural requirements of the organization; rare is
the library that can establish its own criteria.

Regulations differ widely depending on the size and complexity of the organizations. There are, however, certain basic accounting principles that should be followed regardless of the size and type of the library. Fortunately, most of these practices are not only basic to regular acquisitions work, but they can be done with a minimum of effort. They apply regardless of the type of acquisitions systems used, be it manual or automated. While automated systems make record keeping and retrieval of information much easier, they also raise their own sets of problems in ways records are stored and preserved.

Many earlier texts on acquisitions provided only rudimentary coverage of accounting and business practices, if they mentioned them at all. Articles that were published were often concerned with allocation of funds by subject or by formula. Perhaps at the time librarians thought it was unprofessional to be concerned with the business side of books. More likely, budgets were small and there was less emphasis on accountability. But as budgets have grown, so has the need for better accounting and monitoring of library expenditures. It is common for an acquisitions librarian to be responsible for a multimillion dollar purchasing operation. As Alley and Cargill state in their excellent work, *Keeping Track of What You Spend: The Librarian's Guide to Simple Bookkeeping*, "Budget planning and allocation formulas have been covered regularly in the literature, but the mechanics of managing the funds once the money has been allocated are often neglected."[1] The Alley and Cargill text provides a very good description of bookkeeping practices for librarians.

COMMUNICATION AND RECORD KEEPING

Managing an efficient acquisitions department depends on the application of accepted business practices. Librarians responsible for ordering materials should communicate on a regular basis with the business or purchasing officer of their parent institution in order to learn about new developments that affect record keeping. Academic librarians should establish a close working relationship with the professionals in their institution's business office. Public librarians involved in purchasing should work closely with their municipality's purchasing officer. Librarians in special libraries should be sure that their business practices

1. Brian Alley and Jennifer Cargill, *Keeping Track of What You Spend: The Librarian's Guide to Simple Bookkeeping* (Phoenix, Ariz.: Oryx Press, 1982), p. ix.

are compatible with the business office of their company or organization. Establishing close relationships promotes communication and understanding. This is especially important because the ordering, receiving, and payment procedures for books and periodicals differ from the majority of ordering and payment procedures for equipment and supplies. Communications early on may prevent serious misunderstandings later.

Efficiency in acquisitions requires accurate record keeping, the ability to retrieve appropriate records, and storage and retention of those records for a reasonable period of time. It involves a trade-off between access to the information and the time it takes to locate the information and make it available. Some procedures depend entirely on what is required by the parent institution or governmental unit. This is especially true in terms of the length of time records should be retained.

ACCOUNTING SYSTEMS

The primary purpose of an accounting system is to provide timely and accurate information on the status of the total allocation, encumbrances, and items received and paid for, and then to provide appropriate documentation of those transactions. An accounting system may be simple, with only one fund, or it may consist of multiple accounts for different types of items (books, serials, microforms, videos, and so on), for different subjects (history, science) and for various methods of receipt (approval plans, standing orders, and so on). The more complex the fund breakdown, the more difficult it is to keep accurate controls with a manual system. While the fundamentals of record keeping remain the same with manual and automated systems, the latter makes it much easier to have accurate and timely information with a larger number of funds.

Because of the many different ways of ordering materials and the various accounting regulations applied by different governing bodies, it is not practical to describe all practices. Some libraries can keep a minimum level of records, while others are required to keep duplicate or overlapping records. At minimum, the library should have a record of an order (be it for one, unique, title or several), a record of receipt (including the date of receipt and the name or initials of the receiver), and a copy of the invoice with a notation that the material was received and approved for payment, along with the date of that approval.

Accounting and Business Practices

Libraries with small allocations that are primarily used for purchasing materials that arrive quickly can keep the minimum of financial records. Some libraries do not encumber (that is, create a financial record showing an item has been ordered) at the time of ordering. Other libraries find it useful to begin creating a financial record from the time an order is placed. If a library using the encumbrance method orders a book costing $50, that library would, at the time of ordering, encumber that amount, indicating that there is an outstanding order for $50. The rationale for *not* keeping a record of the encumbrance is that some books ordered will not be received (some will be out of stock or out of print). In other instances, the price the library actually pays will be significantly different than the encumbered price would have been.

But the practice of not encumbering outstanding orders can be dangerous, for encumbrances represent commitments to pay for items ordered and such commitments should be recorded. Encumbering outstanding orders can save libraries from either overspending or underspending and can help to make ordering and spending patterns more orderly throughout the year. Any library that orders more than $1,000 of books per year should encumber all orders.

Most libraries encumber at the time the item is ordered, using either the known list price (with the knowledge that the price may change by the time the item arrives) or an estimated price. Estimates can be done simply by using the overall average cost of a book for the current year or by using the average cost of a book in that subject. An alternative practice is to use the average book price when ordering in those areas in which books are more expensive (for example, art or science) and the general average price for all other titles. These figures are available from the price indexes produced annually by the Library Materials Price Index Committee of the Association of Library Collections and Technical Services (ALCTS). The indexes are published annually in *Library Journal* and reprinted in the *Bowker Annual of Library and Information Science*.

Unless there is some reason to suspect that the desired item will be very expensive (for example, a limited, signed edition), an estimated price should suffice if it would take additional staff time to locate the actual price. The decision on whether to encumber with an estimated price or the actual listed price depends on the library's selection and preorder search process. If selection is done from a source that includes prices or if selected items are searched to determine availability (for example, a search of *Books in Print*), then the actual price can be located without additional work. Estimates using average prices should suffice *if* all other bibliographical information necessary to order and acquire the book is available. If an estimate is used, the price listed on the order should state that it is estimated. This can be most easily done by indicating "est" after the price.

Encumbrances should be based on the list price of the item, not the expected discounted price, as that price will usually not be known at the time of ordering. However, a library that receives books on a prenegotiated discount from a publisher or a vendor might consider encumbering at that expected discounted price if there is a significant difference.

AUDIT TRAILS

The point at which the item is ordered is the beginning of the audit trail. An audit trail is a record of what happens to an order from its initiation through receipt and payment. *Audit* is one of those words with a negative connotation. However, unless a library has reason to believe that there is evidence of possible fraud or theft, an audit can, and should, be considered a positive activity. An auditor not only examines existing financial records, but also considers how information is kept and in what form. Because the ordering and receipt of books and periodicals differs in many ways from procedures the auditors will likely be more familiar with, it is important to spend time with the auditors in advance of the actual audit to provide background and explanations of library procedures. A library that orders materials and spends money has an obligation to its funders (be they private donors or government agencies) to demonstrate that the funds are spent carefully and wisely.

Alley and Cargill define the audit trail as "a logical sequence of filed purchasing and accounting documents with which you have identified the steps from purchase to payment."[2] To keep an audit trail does not mean keeping *every* document generated as part of the acquisitions process, but it does require keeping the basic documents relating to the order process described earlier in this chapter.

---

2. Ibid., p. 82.

It is not necessary to keep other information about an order. For example, claiming records do not need to be kept. General correspondence with dealers should be kept in a separate dealer file. Not only will such a file serve as a historical record, it also will serve to preserve important agreements between dealers and the library. Such agreements can be especially important in an audit if the auditor questions the discount that the library is receiving.

An important item in any audit is proof that the material was actually received. In many businesses, ordering and receiving are two departments, administratively separate. This, however, is not feasible or even desirable in libraries where staffing levels do not permit this level of specialization. With the complexity of the world book trade, there are, in fact, advantages in having these operations in the same department. Even in large libraries, ordering and receiving frequently are done in the same department, although often by different sections. Checking-in ordered materials should be done by staff other than those directly involved in the ordering.

In an audit, a library may be asked to prove that an item that was paid for was actually received. This can be difficult, especially if the item is older, popular (and therefore may be missing), or was never cataloged but instead was kept as a desk copy. Some ways to prove receipt are to locate the actual book in the collection (or, failing that, to use circulation records to show the existence of the book in the library); to locate the invoice noting the date and approval for payment (signifying receipt); or, on occasion, to use a catalog card or bibliographical record in an online catalog. Most auditors will understand the isolated volume that cannot be located; they are looking for evidence of trends—evidence of specific categories of missing materials (such as art books) or books that may have been received in ways outside normal ordering patterns (such as repeat purchases from a person not involved in the book trade on a regular basis).

Records of the various parts of the acquisitions process can be kept in various formats: paper, microform, or machine-readable data. If the last is used, some type of offline storage of the records will be necessary to avoid using valuable online space needed for current information. Microform can be an effective method of storage as it is easy to store and relatively easy to use. A further advantage of microform is that the equipment needed for retrieval changes very little. It is not necessary to microfilm paper records; microfilm is practical only if it can be produced directly from computer-generated records. Data in machine-readable format may not be usable after several years unless the programs are updated or older equipment is kept in working order.

Records should be kept for an appropriate period of time. The exact time will depend on the regulations of the library or its parent unit. Records do not need to be kept in the regular work area when they are no longer needed for daily operations. Those consulted less than monthly are candidates for storage. Records should be kept in a secure area, but no special preservation facilities are needed because records are not meant to last forever.

The best audit trails are those in which the amount of work involved in locating the various elements is minimized. It should be possible to locate easily a record of the original order and the invoice from which that item was paid. Vendors usually invoice many items on one invoice, making it impossible to match a unique invoice with a unique order. By keeping copies of the invoices, filed by payee in chronological order, it should be possible to locate a needed invoice.

Begg's article, "Internal Control Systems in the Library Environment," points out the irony of librarians spending large amounts of money for security against book thefts while not carefully controlling other areas within the library, such as the ordering process, where there is the possibility of major financial loss.[3] Fortunately, the number of cases of actual embezzlement of library funds has been small.

CONDUCTING AUDITS

Audits should be done to insure that the department is adhering to all appropriate regulations. An audit should be done at least every five years; a person newly appointed to head an order-acquisitions unit should determine when the last audit was done (if ever) and request a new audit if one has not been done within the past five years *or* if procedures have dramatically changed since the last audit. An audit does not necessarily mean that there is a problem. In fact, an audit can be beneficial as it can point out operational problems and duplicative procedures. As Alley and Cargill point out, "there are considerable benefits to

3. Robert T. Begg, "Internal Control Systems in the Library Environment," *Journal of Academic Librarianship* 10 (January 1985): 337.

be realized from a thorough audit."[4]

There are various types of audits. Recommendations for improving procedures as well as record keeping can come from an audit. An audit can point out delays in payment of invoices, for example. Invoices should be paid within thirty days if at all possible. Suppliers often operate on small margins, and quick payment can mean the difference between profit and loss. This is especially true for out-of-print dealers, who prefer doing business with institutions that have a tradition of rapid payment. Thus quick payment may well bring offers of other important titles for the library. The library may also receive a better discount from its regular vendors through faster payment.

Audits may be done by the staff of the library's parent organization, an outside organization, or by an auditing division of the governmental unit to which the library belongs. Outside auditing is less common in governmental agencies, as these agencies often have internal auditing departments.

As with any review, an audit will go more smoothly if there is full cooperation of all staff and if records are clear and readily available. Cooperation of staff can be encouraged by including appropriate staff members in the planning for the audit. Secrecy breeds concern and worry. The purpose of the audit should be made clear, and, unless actual theft is suspected, staff should be reassured and told there has not been any indication of financial irregularities.

Two areas may create problems in an audit: petty cash and prepayments. Petty-cash accounts can be helpful to an acquisitions department in obtaining materials that are difficult to acquire through normal processes. Such a fund can also save the library significant money. A petty-cash fund should be small and probably contain no more than $25. Many organizations, for example, will supply materials if a small cash donation is sent. Issuing a purchase order and check is a slow and expensive process, while just sending a dollar in the mail can expedite delivery and save paperwork. Unless carefully monitored, however, a petty-cash fund will cause problems in an audit for, as Begg writes, "cash control is an almost universal problem in libraries."[5] Cash accounts, no matter how small, always attract an auditor's attention. Begg provides a checklist of seven steps

---

4. Alley and Cargill, *Keeping Track of What You Spend,* p. 82.
5. Begg, "Internal Control Systems in the Library Environment," p. 341.

to follow in using such a fund.[6] Included here is the advice that one person should be responsible for the fund and that access to the money should be limited as much as possible. The petty-cash fund should be kept in a secure place. If the fund is large, employees should be bonded, although this probably will not be necessary for a small fund in acquisitions. Monitoring should be done by a person other than the one responsible for expenditures. Following these guidelines should allow successful operation of the fund. Procedures for a cash account in an order unit should parallel procedures used with such cash accounts in other areas of the library.

The other problem area for an audit is prepayments. Advance payments are common in libraries; serial subscriptions, for example, are always paid in advance. Advance payment for other materials such as books and microform sets can be a problem, especially if a large amount of money is involved. If done with care and proper safeguards, prepayment can be an effective way to acquire materials. In fact, prepayment can often be used to obtain higher discounts on approval plans or lower prices on major microform or reprint sets. Done without care or safeguards, however, prepayment can mean a loss of money. Acquisitions librarians should be familiar with the guidelines for prepayment issued by the ALCTS's Bookdealer Library Relations Committee (now the Publishers/Vendor-Library Relations Committee).[7] Prepayments should be made only to a reputable firm that has a history of actually publishing and delivering titles. The firm should list a telephone number in its advertisements, and there should be a street address, not just a post office box number. Prepayment should never be a requirement, only an option. Librarians should be especially wary of publishers who offer extremely large discounts for prepayment. Appropriate safeguards should be built into the prepayment process. This can be done by being sure that the department head approves all prepayments or all prepayments above $100. If you are unsure of the reputation of a publisher, your regular library vendor is a good source of information. If unsure, don't make a prepayment. Records should be kept on all prepaid orders and careful claiming should be done to insure receipt or refund for undelivered materials.

---

6. Ibid.
7. "The Prepayment Dilemma: A Consumer's Guide," *American Libraries* (November 1977): 571–572.

Accounting and Business Practices

AUTOMATED SYSTEMS

Obviously an audit trail can be easier to follow in an automated acquisitions system. As Boss and Marcum reported in 1981, "there are several reasons that librarians are considering automated acquisitions systems. Acquisitions consumes a large part of every library's budget and the pressures to account for expenditures are greater than ever."[8] However, few of the acquisitions systems on the market have a good financial management package. Boss and Marcum note the dilemma that the systems which do not include a component that will keep records of encumbrances and expenditures are seen as unacceptable, while those that do are considered unsatisfactory because the accounting package does not match the requirement of the institution.[9]

Laughrey and Murray, in their article "Evaluating and Selecting an Automated Acquisitions System," provide a checklist of twenty-three questions on fund accounting to consider when evaluating an automated system.[10] Because each library's requirements are different, no one system can be expected to meet every need. In this respect, flexibility is probably the most important component of an accounting system.

While accounting can be a problem for automated systems, automation can also provide specific management information. For example, an automated system should be able to prorate postage and handling charges—a labor-intensive operation with a manual system. The best automated system is that which can merge the financial and management needs of the organization and provide the information necessary to both areas.

CONCLUSION

An order department, whether it is manual or automated, should follow accepted business practices. While teaching such practices is rarely part of the library school curriculum, the practices can be learned by talking with colleagues in other libraries and in the business unit of the library's parent organization, by read-

8. Richard W. Boss and Deanna Marcum, "On-line Acquisitions Systems for Libraries," *Library Technology Reports* 17 (March-April 1981): 117.

9. Ibid., p. 165.

10. Edna Laughrey and Mary Kay Murray, "Evaluating and Selecting an Automated Acquisitions System," in *Issues in Acquisitions: Programs and Evaluations,* edited by Sul Lee (Ann Arbor, Mich.: Pierian Press, 1984), pp. 81–83.

ing, and by attending state, regional, and national library association meetings. Fortunately, good business practices not only help to create a fiscally sound department, but also help to acquire materials in the quickest and most economical manner.

B I B L I O G R A P H Y

Alley, Brian, and Jennifer Cargill. *Keeping Track of What You Spend: The Librarian's Guide to Simple Bookkeeping.* Phoenix, Ariz.: Oryx Press, 1982.

Begg, Robert T. "Internal Control Systems in the Library Environment." *Journal of Academic Librarianship.* 10 (January 1985): 337–342.

Bloomberg, Marty, and Edward G. Evans. *Introduction to Technical Services for Library Technicians.* 5th ed. Littleton, Colo.: Libraries Unlimited, 1985.

Boss, Richard W., and Deanne Marcum. "On-line Acquisitions Systems for Libraries." *Library Technology Reports* 17 (March-April 1981).

Laughrey, Edna, and Mary Kay Murray. "Evaluating and Selecting an Automated Acquisitions System." In *Issues in Acquisition: Programs and Evaluation,* pp. 69–90. Edited by Sul H. Lee. Ann Arbor, Mich.: Pierian Press, 1984.

Magrill, Rose Mary, and Doralyn J. Hickey. *Acquisitions Management and Collection Development in Libraries.* Chicago: American Library Association, 1984.

"The Prepayment Dilemma: A Consumer's Guide." *American Libraries,* (November 1977): 571–572.

Schenck, William Z. "To Pay Or Not To Pay: Guidelines for Prepayment," *North Carolina Libraries,* (Spring 1980): 39–42.

Payment Ethics:
Librarians as Consumers

Corrie Marsh

Acquisitions librarians and staffs should be aware that the business arrangement involved in ordering, receiving, and purchasing of library materials is a contract for goods and services. For the most part, this chapter will address the concerns of a library's acquisitions operations in dealing with specific types of problems and possible recourses when the need arises for consumer protection. However, it is also necessary for those involved in the acquisitions process to know the terms outlined in service contracts and to conduct the business of acquisitions using professional business negotiation techniques and ethics.

EXAMPLES OF SPECIFIC PAYMENT PROBLEMS

Whether the library is purchasing one or many books, maps, sound recordings, computer software, or an electronic database, it is contracting for service with a vendor or supplier.[1] The contractual arrangement may be in the form of a purchase order, letter, telephone call, or electronic transmission. Whatever the means of contact, it is important to communicate exactly what is desired and any special instructions or expectations. The ser-

---

1. Rose Mary Magrill and Doralyn J. Hickey, *Acquisitions Management and Collection Development in Libraries* (Chicago: American Library Association, 1984), pp. 75–94; see also: Stephen Ford, *The Acquisition of Library Materials* (Chicago: ALA, 1973).

vice contract should specify length of service, price, quality and format of materials, special handling and shipping requirements, and payment schedules. Communication between both parties should be clear and specific in order to avoid payment problems and to avoid misunderstandings in the future.

Receipt of Damaged or Poor-Quality Materials

The quality of the product received has often been a source of contention. In the past decade, librarians and publishers have developed standards of quality for printed materials.[2] Acquisitions librarians should be aware of minimum standards and recognize any products received that do not meet them. Librarians should not hesitate to complain if there is a problem with the quality of paper, printing, or binding of books and journals. With the increasing acquisition of microforms, audiovisuals, facsimiles, and electronic formats, libraries have experienced increased problems with the quality of materials. The production standards for these nonprint formats are still in the development stages. Just as with printed materials, nonprint items should be examined during the receipt verification process to assure that the product supplied meets the library's quality standards.

Libraries need to establish a returns policy with dealers so they can return materials that do not meet quality standards for durability and readability in library use. Several American Library Association committees such as the Micropublishing Committee and Audio-Visual Committee monitor problems with the quality of products. Further information concerning the standards for library materials may be obtained by contacting the National Information Standards Organization (NISO-Z39).

Methods of shipping and packaging materials can contribute to product damage. For example, a shipment from overseas may be sent in large or small crates and supplied by sea or air. Cargo shipped by sea will be supplied more slowly as well as handled

2. American National Standards Institute, Z39 Committee, various materials standards in *Z39 ANSI Standards,* ANSI, 1430 Broadway, New York, NY 10018; see also various reports of the National Information Standards Organization (NISO-Z39, previously ANSI), U.S. Department of Commerce, National Bureau of Standards, Administration Building 101, Library E106, Washington, D.C. 20234, and the Book Industry Study Group, Inc., Book Industry Systems Advisory Committe (BISAC), and Serials Industry Systems Advisory Committees (SISAC), 160 Fifth Ave., New York, NY 10010.

more roughly, thus allowing for a higher possibility of damage. Packaging must be satisfactory to protect all materials, including individual items, in shipping.

Suppliers and publishers offer a variety of types of packaging. Methods of wrapping individual volumes include plastic vacuum-wrapped coverings, paper or newspaper wrapping with strapping or postage tape, or no covering of individual volumes. In this last case, items are shipped loosely in cartons and boxes, packaged in reinforced mailers, or packed in Styrofoam cushioning materials. Each method requires the careful attention of library staff when unpacking the materials. Tightly packing and taping a carton of individual volumes that is to be cut open with a knife will quite often result in damage to a volume packed too closely to the top. Plastic vacuum-wrapped volumes require time-consuming unwrapping and, unfortunately, the plastic offers no apparent protection. Librarians must decide if their receiving areas can accommodate streams of Styrofoam peanuts and packing paper.

Librarians need to assess the best means of shipping and packaging and to analyze the variety of packaging techniques in order to identify those best suited to their library's receiving procedures. *Both the library and supplier should agree to the methods of shipping and packaging materials in consideration of timely delivery and condition of the product.* Where single-title or one-time contracts are entered into with a publisher or agent, packaging agreements may not be possible or cost-effective. If repeated use of a publisher or agent is planned, then agreements should be reached.

Fulfillment Schedules

Librarians involved in the acquisition of serials, continuation sets, and databases are familiar with contracting for length of service when they arrange for extended open orders and subscriptions. Many disputes have resulted from simple misunderstanding of order fulfillment time schedules. Librarians should communicate special requirements for timely service and allow for problems that may be beyond the control of the supplier. The reverse is also true: suppliers should promptly notify their customers of delays or special problems. Often vendors supply status reports to libraries.

Many acquisitions departments specify the time period for fulfillment of their purchase orders; commonly this is a 90-day cancellation period for domestic orders and a 180-day cancellation period for foreign orders. These preestablished periods allow libraries some control in their internal fund accounting for outstanding orders. Clarification of the order period to the supplier specifies the time in which the supplier must act. If the supplier is unable to fill the order within the granted time, the library may unencumber the funds and reorder elsewhere. In contracting for service with a dealer, it is advisable to document restrictions and set an automatic cancellation period if necessary, so that both the library and the supplier agree to feasible terms.

Understanding Additional Charges

Special service requirements such as rush service and shipping quite often incur extra handling charges which are passed on to the customer. Most suppliers offer a price guide to their standard extra charges for special handling and shipping. Charges for shipping and postage differ according to the method of supply. Many suppliers offer free postage for domestic shipments; the cost of foreign shipments varies greatly with shipping requirements. Direct foreign shipments are further complicated by customs regulations. Foreign purchases through a North American distributor usually are handled by the distributor for the library. While library materials are for educational use and do not incur U.S. customs charges, the shipments still require a customs broker to arrange for removal of the shipment from customs and to supply delivery to the library. The services of a customs broker are not free. A library should contact a customs broker in advance to determine charges and make sure the broker can meet the library's shipping requirements.

Often it is difficult to identify additional charges in an invoice. For many items shipped together, some suppliers may include postage and handling fees in the cost of each item or combine the fees at the end of an invoice. In such cases, the library has to calculate the separate charges. Compare each item's cost to that of the original order, and compare the total postage and handling charge in relation to the total item charges. Most domestic suppliers charge a standard postage percentage rate to an invoice total. The postage, handling, and service costs are usually outlined in the supplier's service contract. Librarians should be aware of additional costs and how to identify them on each invoice.

The terms for additional charges should be understood before entering into a business arrangement. Individual libraries vary

Corrie Marsh

in the way they process extra charges: some are able to absorb the additional costs for postage or handling in the costs of materials, while others need to provide itemized details of cost charges to their accounting agencies.

In recent times, libraries have had to face the cost dilemmas of monetary conversion rates and pricing differentials, especially those involving overseas service arrangements. Regularly monitoring foreign exchange rates as a means of estimating encumbrances at the time of ordering as well as comparing the costs to actual invoices will enable the librarian to keep track of unusual fluctuations. Fluctuating values of the U.S. dollar have forced many publishers to pass on extra costs to their customers to compensate for price increases. However, U.S. libraries rarely receive a credit for overpayment due to a sudden rise in dollar value. The legitimacy of imposing such extra costs without issuing equivalent credits may be debatable depending on the terms of the original order; it is wise to check extra costs and communicate concerns to the supplier as soon as possible.

Payment Schedules

The payment process for materials is perhaps the most diverse of all library procedures. In general, the library controls its own payment processing system or it supplies documentation verifying receipt of items to a unit within its governing organization which processes payments. In either case, the issue of expeditious payment is important to producers and suppliers. Libraries with the ability to process payments and produce their own payment checks have greater control over the paying activity than do those who rely on accounts payable departments outside the library. These departments can further complicate the payment process when item-by-item invoice costs and elaborate voucher systems are required.

The acquisitions staff must be thoroughly familiar with their organization's payment system, not only for assessing their department's processing of debits and ability to spend, but also for anticipating the need to negotiate terms of payment with suppliers. Typical business operations supply invoices requiring thirty-day payment. Libraries need to be concerned with their organization's capacity to meet this requirement—one of the quickest ways to upset the profitability of a small publisher or local bookstore is to fail to meet their payment time schedules. Knowledge of the library's accounts payable system will help

Accounting and Business Practices

determine if there is a problem in meeting a supplier's payment schedule. If necessary, terms can be renegotiated to guarantee a convenient and realistic system for both the library and its suppliers.

If a supplier's terms for payment are not met, the library may face the accrual of late charges as a penalty for its neglect in processing timely payment. The penalty is a justified action on the part of the supplier, but fortunately it is rarely used. Libraries have an extremely difficult time in processing additional invoices for penalties and in justifying the additional costs to auditing agencies. It is important to examine whether the penalty is justified as a fair business practice and to investigate the cause(s) in order to avoid future occurrences. The library must also determine how to absorb the extra charge in its materials budget and must be prepared to justify the cost to administrators if necessary. Many publishers and suppliers offer inducements toward faster payments in the form of volume discounts for payments received within specific time periods. If the library is able to process payments quickly, it can receive a substantial cost savings.

Prepayment Requirements

Many suppliers, especially serial subscription agents, require prepayment of orders or offer discounted prices for prepayment of orders. The library in turn must analyze (1) its ability to pay for products not yet received, (2) the suppliers' need and justification, and (3) the risks involved in prepayment ventures.

An excellent set of guidelines for prepayments is provided in the appendix to *Guide to Performance Evaluation of Library Materials Vendors*.[3] These guidelines are applicable to all types of libraries and dealers. They suggest various aspects to consider in ordering materials, for example, order forms, claiming, returns, and payments. The special section about prepayment decisions explains the reasons why publishers may require prepayment, how the library can "investigate" the publisher, and precautions in processing prepayments.

As with all other aspects of payments, restrictions imposed by the library's governing organization must be considered. Many

---

3. Publisher/Vendor-Library Relations Committee (formerly Bookdealer-Library Relations Committee). American Library Association, *Guide to Performance Evaluation of Library Materials Vendors* (Chicago: ALA, 1977), appendix; see also: *Guidelines for Handling Library Serial Orders* and *Guidelines for Handling Library Orders for Microforms* (Chicago: ALA, 1977).

organizations are simply unable to process prepayments due to state or local restrictions. In such cases the library may pursue other arrangements with the publisher or vendor or consider borrowing the publication from other libraries. If the library is able to prepay for materials, it should consider how it will process the order and payments simultaneously.

Unsolicited Receipts with Invoices

Libraries often receive unordered and unsolicited materials accompanied by invoices, which are discovered in the verification process. It is advisable to have a library policy for handling unordered materials and their invoices. The library is under *no obligation to pay* for such materials. Unsolicited receipts may be regarded as gifts according to U.S. Postal Service regulations:

a) . . .the mailing of unordered merchandise or of communications prohibited by subsection (c) of this section constitutes an unfair method of competition and an unfair trade practice. . . .

b) Any merchandise mailed in violation of subsection (a) of this section, or within the exceptions contained therein, may be treated as a gift by the recipient, who shall have the right to retain, use, discard, or dispose of it in any manner he sees fit without any obligation whatsoever to the sender. All such merchandise shall have attached to it a clear and conspicuous statement informing the recipient that he may treat the merchandise as a gift to him and has the right to retain, use, discard, or dispose of it in any manner he sees fit without any obligation whatsoever to the sender.

c) No mailer of any merchandise mailed in violation of subsection (a) of this section, or within the exceptions contained therein, shall mail to any recipient of such merchandise a bill for such merchandise or any dunning communications.

d) For the purposes of this section, "unordered merchandise" means merchandise mailed without the prior expressed request or consent of the recipient."[4]

Further, it does not matter if the publications are foreign or domestic since all materials mailed to the United States fall under the jurisdiction of the U.S. Postal Service.[5]

The acceptance of unordered materials as gifts would appear

---

4. 39 U.S. Code, sec. 3009.
5. 18 U.S. Code, sec. 1692.

to be a simple solution to the matter; in fact, the situation is very complicated. Problems may occur in several ways: telephone or written inquiries may be misunderstood as orders and result in shipped materials; foreign distributors may not be familiar with U.S. laws concerning unsolicited mail; and, more recently, publishers may have used "creative" marketing techniques to anticipate acquiring new customers.[6] In spite of legal protections, libraries cannot afford to avoid taking action in the event they receive unsolicited items. For example, a library may receive unsolicited materials from a supplier whom the library uses for other business, and the supplier may consider the invoiced item as an outstanding payment until the matter is settled.

The library should choose its actions in accordance with its own procedures. Acquisitions librarians should establish a policy of action and responsibility in order to clarify who will be responsible for handling unsolicited orders and what actions will be taken. Whether the library decides to accept the materials as a gift, pay for them, or mail them back, follow-up communication that educates the supplier is recommended.

CONSUMER PROTECTION

When payment problems occur and the library has made repeated attempts to solve them, its only recourse may be to pursue consumer protection. The library can contact local, state, or federal agencies for advice and assistance. In addition, various sections in regional library organizations and in the American Library Association serve as consumer advocates for libraries.

Federal Trade Regulations

A responsibility of librarians as consumers is to develop a practical knowledge of U.S. trade regulations. The *United States Code* provides explanations of the regulations required for sellers of merchandise. In addition to the postal regulations already cited, the following U.S. Code regulations may be consulted for clarification on various issues:

6. Bookdealer-Library Relations Committee, American Library Association Midwinter Conference, January 1986, committee meeting discussion.

U.S.C., Title 15, Section 41—Consumer Credit Protection
  Subchapter I—Consumer Credit Cost Disclosure
    Section 1607—Administrative Enforcement
    Part A, Section 1612—General Provisions
        (These sections designate enforcing agencies and review
        procedures for enforcing regulations.)
    Part B, Section 1638—Credit Transactions
        (This section outlines forms and timing of transaction
        disclosure.)
    Part C, Section 1661—Credit Advertising
        (This section describes regulations about catalogs and
        advertisements.)
    Part D, Section 1666—Correction of Billing Errors
        (This section provides regulations concerning procedures
        for correcting billing errors.)[7]

Although the acquisitions staff need not be legal authorities,
they should be familiar in general with federal regulations in order
to establish policies and procedures about payment problems.

Federal agencies are responsible for the enforcement of the
regulations. Specifically, the Federal Trade Commission (FTC)
and U.S. Postal Service are the primary agencies that a library
may turn to for assistance as a consumer.

Federal Trade Commission

The FTC is charged with maintaining free and fair competition.
The Federal Trade Commission Act prohibits "unfair methods
of competition" and "unfair or deceptive acts or practices." In
addition, one of the main functions of the FTC is to provide consumer protection. Libraries requiring information about consumer protection or registering a complaint should contact their
nearest FTC regional office.[8]

U.S. Postal Service

The U.S. Postal Service is responsible for more than mail processing and delivery services for individuals and businesses within

---

7. 15 U.S. Code, sec. 41; sec. 1607, 1612a, 1638b, 1661c, and 1666d.
8. Office of the Federal Register, National Archives and Records Service,
General Services Administration, *United States Government Manual 1984/85*
(Washington, D.C.: U.S. Government Printing Office, May 1984), pp. 522–529.

the United States. It also protects the mails and apprehends those who violate postal laws. Libraries in need of information or with complaints to register should contact their regional postal inspector.[9]

Local and State Agencies

Libraries that have problems with or questions about a supplier may contact their local Better Business Bureau or state consumer protection agencies for advice. They may also inquire about the supplier through these same agencies in the supplier's state of residence. If formal complaints or legal actions are deemed necessary, the library may pursue these actions through the state attorney general's office for clarification in regard to interstate trade. An understanding of one's state agencies can help when information is needed on how to obtain consumer protection.

Library Organizations

Local library consortia and state library organizations may be of assistance with consumer protection. Inquiries about a specific publisher or vendor may be forwarded to the Publisher/Vendor-Library Relations (PVLR) Committee (previously Bookdealer-Library Relations Committee). This is a committee of the Association for Library Collections and Technical Services (ALCTS). The charge of the committee is:

> To serve as the review and advisory committee on all matters of vendors of library materials—library relationships; to investigate these relationships; and to prepare recommendations and develop guidelines of acceptable performance for libraries and vendors for ordering and supplying of library materials.[10]

In the past, the PVLR Committee has issued lists of publishers who have engaged in fraudulent practices. Librarians can monitor current consumer relations by keeping up-to-date with PVLR Committee activities. A library that wishes to file a complaint after all reasonable efforts have failed may send a letter detailing

---

9. Ibid., pp. 641–643.
10. American Library Association, *ALA Handbook of the Organization 1989/1990* (Chicago: ALA, 1989), p. 44.

the problem and a copy of all documentation to the Publisher/Vendor-Library Relations Committee at ALCTS, American Library Association, 50 E. Huron St., Chicago, IL 60611.

A MODEL FOR CONSUMER PROTECTION

The postal laws and U.S. Code of federal regulations provide protection from unfair trade and business practices. Most citizens, however, are familiar with the red tape involved in pursuing official government action. As a result, librarians have often relied on library consumer groups to intervene with suppliers when problems arise. Although positive actions results from these groups' activities on a library's behalf, consumer groups are usually not in a position to take legal recourse.

One model for consumer legal action has been established: *Guides for the Law Book Industry*, developed by the FTC in cooperation with the American Association of Law Libraries (AALL). The development of the guidelines began in the late sixties with an article that outlined eleven offensive practices in the law book industry and called for consumer action on the federal level if necessary.[11] In late 1969, the FTC announced it would conduct an investigation of the law book industry. In 1970, the American Bar Association (ABA) displayed its support of these efforts by creating a Special Committee on Lawbook Publishing Practices to investigate problems and recommend means for protection. In a related action, the AALL created a Committee on Relations with Publishers and Dealers. The AALL also established standards for advertising new law publications.[12] In 1973, the FTC proposed guides that were meant to encourage voluntary compliance in fair trade practices and to "afford interested or affected parties an opportunity to present to the Commission their views, suggestions, objections or other information...."[13] By August 8, 1975, the FTC established the *Guides for the Law Book Industry*.[14]

The definitions in FTC's guides precisely describe all formats of legal publications, including nonprint materials, and establish the scope of the materials as those "designed primarily for use

11. Raymond M. Taylor, "Lawbook Consumers Need Protection," *ABA Journal* 55 (1969): 553.
12. *Law Library Journal* 64 (1971): 440.
13. 38 CFR, sec. 5351 (February 28, 1973).
14. 16 CFR, Chap.1, p.256 (January 1, 1986).

by members of the law profession and by law schools. . . ." The guides present a statement of the FTC's interpretation of the laws for fair practice between law book publishers and customers. The guides specify seventeen areas of fair trade; included are revisions, supplementation, titles of texts and treatises, subscription renewal notices, and billing practices.

Since the establishment of the guides, law book customers may present their complaints directly to the FTC or may choose to go through the ABA or state bar associations. The majority of law libraries have elected to channel problems through the AALL's Committee on Relations with Publishers and Dealers. Complaints are publicized in the committee's periodical publication, the *Publications Clearing House Bulletin*.

Recently law librarians have reassessed the effectiveness of the FTC's guides and have determined:

> The FTC Guides for the Law Book Industry have resulted in improved consumer protection and better relations with publishers. Now is not the time, however, to be satisfied with our accomplishments. It is instead the time for us to become such effective consumers that the lawbook industry will be proclaimed as a model in fair dealing and cooperation.[15]

Further analysis by law librarians suggests that the definition of the industry product, or law books, as materials is intended *only* for members of the legal profession and law schools. As publishers have recently broadened their markets to schools and consumers outside of the legal profession, it is unclear if these new materials fall beyond the scope of the guides.[16]

The success of law consumers in obtaining the FTC's guides was due to the support contributed by the strong lobby of the ABA and its members in Congress and the FTC itself—both of which are consumers of law publications. Many of the same issues dealt with in the guides for the law book industry exist in other areas of publishing: fair practice, advertising, and payment problems. The guidelines presented for bibliographic information and content revisions are also directly related to similar problems libraries have with the general publishing industry. Obviously, librarians are reexamining the scope of the law book guides; a

---

15. Reynold Kosek (Appendix 1 by Sue Welch), "Law Librarians as Consumer Advocates—Some Thoughts and Recommendations Based on the FTC Guides for the Lawbook Industry," *Publications Clearing House Bulletin* 9 (Feb. 1986): 2.
    16. Ibid.

Corrie Marsh

broader application is needed. Perhaps the guides can serve as a model of consumer action for all libraries. As noted earlier, numerous organizations are addressing standards for quality and format (National Information Standards Organization, Book Industry Systems Advisory Committee, Serials Industry Advisory Committee, and so on), and various consumer groups and government organizations exist to assist with business problems. Such groups should take note of the precedent set by the *Guides for the Law Book Industry.* If they can join together and document industrywide problems, the FTC may act on a broader interpretation.

CONCLUSION

This chapter has outlined examples of specific payment problems faced by libraries and has suggested procedures for dealing with them using business techniques. If the library is confronted with a problem, it may resort to its own policies or turn to the wide variety of consumer protection services available on local and national levels. The following summary suggests professional ethics to be applied when dealing with payment problems:

1. Educate library staff about the business practices and policies of the library and its governing organization. Provide clear documentation that explains how to handle specific problems as they arise. Send a library fact sheet with orders to new vendors. It is also useful to educate the suppliers with whom the library does frequent business so that they are aware of the library's policies.
2. Provide friendly and courteous communication at all times with the library's business partners. There is no excuse for rudeness; often problems are solved through an agreeable exchange of information that allows differences to be negotiated.
3. Document all business transactions. An audit trail of orders and payments is a necessity in providing proof of actual transactions. Many suppliers require copies of purchase orders, payment checks, and all correspondence before they will settle a payment problem.
4. Take consumer action. Do not procrastinate when a problem arises. None of the resources for consumer protection can be of assistance if the library is not willing to right

Accounting and Business Practices

a wrong. As a general precaution, do not pay for materials until you are satisfied with delivery, price, and quality of service. The acquisitions operation represents the library as the consumer; for this reason, acquisitions has an obligation to negotiate and solve any violations in service contracts. Furthermore, if a problem is brought to public attention, other libraries may be spared a similar situation. Professional cooperation is important to the entire library community and may result in public recognition of unfair trade practices.

CONTRIBUTORS

Gary Brown is Manager of Marketing Support for the F.W. Faxon Company. Prior to joining Faxon in 1984, Dr. Brown held editorial and marketing positions with Scott, Foresman; Addison-Wesley; and the Scholarly Book Center.

James Campbell is the North Europe Bibliographer at the University of Virginia. Formerly, he was the humanities bibliographer at Rutgers University's Alexander Library.

Mae Clark is Head of the Acquisitions Pre-Order Search Unit at the University of Florida Libraries in Gainesville. Formerly, Ms. Clark was the gifts and exchange librarian at the University of Florida.

Gay Dannelly is the Collection Development Officer at The Ohio State University Libraries in Columbus. Previously, Ms. Dannelly was the head of library acquisitions at OSU.

Kathy Flanagan is Director of Marketing and Sales for the Little, Brown Publishing Group. She previously served as director of sales at Elsevier Science Publishing, Inc.

Juliet Flesch is Principal Librarian (Collections) at the University of Melbourne Library, Melbourne, Australia.

Charles Forrest is Director of Instructional Support Services at Emory University's Candler Library. Mr. Forrest formerly was media coordinator at the undergraduate library, University of Illinois at Urbana-Champaign.

Donna Goehner is Director of Libraries at Western Illinois University. Previously, Dr. Goehner was the associate librarian for technical services at Illinois State University Library and acquisitions librarian at WIU.

Joan Grant is Director of Collection Management at New York University's Bobst Library.

Joan Mancell Hayes is Head of Technical Services at the Huron Valley Library System, Ann Arbor, Michigan.

Betsy Kruger is Assistant Acquisitions Librarian and Head of the Binding Unit at the University of Illinois at Urbana-Champaign.

Margaret Landesman is Head of Acquisitions at the University of Utah Library.

Contributors

Corrie Marsh is the Head of Acquisitions at George Washington University Library in Washington, D.C. She previously held positions as head of acquisitions at Brown University Library and Georgetown University Law Library.

Audrey Melkin is Library Sales Manager at John Wiley and Sons in New York City.

Marion Reid is the University Librarian at California State University at San Marcos. She has served as the acquisitions librarian and the associate director of technical services at Louisiana State University Library.

William Schenck is Collections Program Officer at the Library of Congress. Mr. Schenck formerly served as the collection development librarian at the University of Oregon library.

Karen Schmidt is the Head of Acquisitions at the University of Illinois at Urbana-Champaign. Dr. Schmidt is the author of several articles on acquisitions-related topics.

Scott Smith is Regional Sales Manager for B. H. Blackwell, Blackwell North America and Boley International Subscription Agency, Inc. Currently, Mr. Smith is based in Portland, Oregon.

Jana Stevens is Acquisitions Librarian at Adelphi University, Long Island, New York.

INDEX

Index

Index